Bootstrap Yourself with Linux-USB Stack: Design, Develop, Debug, and Validate Embedded USB

Rajaram Regupathy

Course Technology PTR

A part of Cengage Learning

SO-AAZ-857

COURSE TECHNOLOGY
CENGAGE Learning

Australia • Brazil • Japan • Korea • Mexico • Singapore • Spain • United Kingdom • United States

COURSE TECHNOLOGY
CENGAGE Learning™

Bootstrap Yourself with Linux-USB Stack: Design, Develop, Debug, and Validate Embedded USB
Rajaram Regupathy

Publisher and General Manager, Course Technology PTR: Stacy L. Hiquet

Associate Director of Marketing: Sarah Panella

Manager of Editorial Services: Heather Talbot

Marketing Manager: Mark Hughes

Senior Acquisitions Editor: Mitzi Koontz

Project/Copy Editor: Karen A. Gill

Technical Reviewers: R. SelvaMuthuKumar and Vishnu Vardhan

Interior Layout Tech: MPS Limited, a Macmillan Company

Cover Designer: Mike Tanamachi

CD-ROM Producer: Brandon Penticuff

Indexer: Larry Sweazy

Proofreader: Gene Redding

For product information and technology assistance, contact us at **Cengage Learning Customer & Sales Support, 1-800-354-9706.**

For permission to use material from this text or product, submit all requests online at **www.cengage.com/permissions.** Further permissions questions can be e-mailed to **permissionrequest@cengage.com.**

QT is a trademark of Nokia Corporation. STN8815 and ISP1362 are trademarks of ST-Ericsson. STUSB02E is a trademark of ST Microelectronics. OMAP is a trademark of Texas Instruments Incorporated. R8a66597 is a trademark of Renesas Electronics Corporation in Japan, the United States, and other countries. Linux is a registered trademark of Linus Torvalds. Ubuntu is a registered trademark of Canonical Ltd.

All other trademarks are the property of their respective owners.

All images © Cengage Learning unless otherwise noted.

Library of Congress Control Number: 2011920276

ISBN-13: 978-1-4354-5786-7

ISBN-10: 1-4354-5786-2

Course Technology, a part of Cengage Learning
20 Channel Center Street
Boston, MA 02210
USA

Cengage Learning is a leading provider of customized learning solutions with office locations around the globe, including Singapore, the United Kingdom, Australia, Mexico, Brazil, and Japan. Locate your local office at: **international.cengage.com/region.**

Cengage Learning products are represented in Canada by Nelson Education, Ltd.

For your lifelong learning solutions, visit **courseptr.com.**

Visit our corporate Web site at **cengage.com.**

Printed in the United States of America
1 2 3 4 5 6 7 13 12 11

To my father.

ACKNOWLEDGMENTS

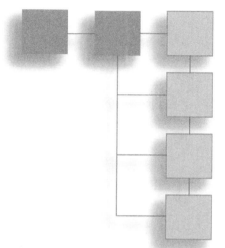

I look at this book as a product that I have taken through various stages, from conceptualizing the idea, to designing it, and finally realizing it. This book would not have been possible without collaboration and support by many at various stages. I take this opportunity to thank them all.

Over the years, I have been fortunate to have had good mentors and colleagues who have supported and inspired me personally and professionally. I am thankful to every one of them. I am especially grateful to Mr. R. Raghavan, who has supported me both personally and professionally.

I would also like to thank Cengage Learning and senior acquisitions editor Mitzi Koontz for providing me this opportunity. I also thank Mitzi and Karen Gill, my project and copy editor, for continuously supporting me throughout this process.

I would also like to thank Kumar and Vishnu for their valuable time and effective feedback that allowed me to maintain a certain amount of consistency.

Last but not least, I thank my wife, mother, and other family members for their support in making this book journey a smooth one.

About the Author

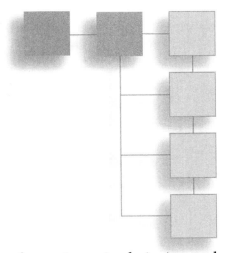

Rajaram Regupathy has more than a decade of experience in designing and managing embedded and programming tool products. He loves to design and program new and emerging technology products and has successfully engineered products based on universal serial bus (USB) from scratch. A Linux and open source enthusiast, Rajaram has published open source articles for *Linux for You* and Embedded.com, among others. In his free time, he enjoys watching *National Geographic* and playing with his daughter. Rajaram's Web site (http://www.kernelkahani.com) is a good place to obtain additional resources and get in touch with him.

Contents

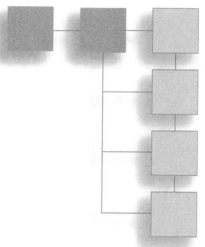

INTRODUCTION

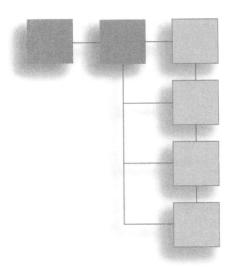

Before starting a new task, you generally do research so you can avoid mistakes. In the computer realm, bootstrap sessions provide a head start and help you minimize mistakes and surprises. As an example, to design a protocol stack, build a bootstrap session so you can understand the protocol specification and the system on which it is to be developed.

This book discusses how the Linux USB host and device stacks are designed and how different Linux USB modules export interfaces to pass on information. Understanding the pains of test development, this book provides comprehensive coverage of the necessary frameworks available on Linux for USB systems to effectively debug, test, and interface with USB devices.

WHAT YOU'LL FIND IN THIS BOOK

This book discusses the internal interface application programming interfaces (APIs) and data structures of the USB stack and offers practical examples of how Linux USB modules interface within the Linux system.

- Linux is becoming the de facto standard for students to train and explore. This book is a practical guide book to exploring Linux USB.

- This book explains a platform developer's perspective of Linux USB drivers: the gadget driver for a USB device and the host controller driver development for a host.

- You will find topics that enhance your understanding of user mode programming of the Linux USB framework and easy methods to use it with USB devices.

- This book also explores methods to test and debug USB devices using Linux USB. The CD accompanying the book contains an exclusive tool for USB testing.

WHO THIS BOOK IS FOR

This book is for students interested in exploring the emerging embedded Linux market and Linux internals. The book teaches them Linux USB internals and enables them to complete a project based on the Linux USB subsystem. The book also furthers their understanding of software stack design by exposing the blocks, interfaces, and data structures of the Linux USB system.

This book is also for engineers who take up Linux-USB development. In the industry, the trend while assigning jobs is creating module owners and module experts. It is common to move them to different modules.

Finally, this book is for managers of the Linux platform who want to know the features or analyze the complexity of the Linux USB. This book's visual representations act as a definite bootstrap session.

HOW THIS BOOK IS ORGANIZED

The book is organized into four major parts: USB Host, USB Device, USB OTG, and Miscellaneous Linux USB Subsystems. Before getting into parts, the initial three chapters provide a quick overview of USB in general and how to manage the Linux USB framework. Part I explores the Linux USB host framework that implements USB host requirements. The USB device implementation referred to as USB gadget is explored in Part II. Dual role On-the-Go (OTG) devices are covered in Part III. Part IV covers various frameworks available on Linux that you can effectively use for USB development. The book narrates the Linux USB system using the Linux 2.6.34 kernel.

Following is a more detailed breakdown of the content in each chapter.

Chapter 1, "USB and Linux: Introduction," introduces the history and path of USB and Linux and how both technologies are placed in the embedded space.

Chapter 2, "USB: An Overview," is a snapshot of the USB specification, covering only parts that are essential from a software perspective.

Chapter 3, "Overview of the Linux USB Subsystem," explores the various configuration options available in the Linux USB subsystem so that you can configure features you're interested in.

Chapter 4, "Linux USB Host Driver," provides an overview of the various blocks of the Linux USB host subsystem and sets the tone for the subsequent chapters that explore the Linux USB host framework.

Chapter 5, "USB Device Notification," discusses how the device connection and disconnection information is passed on to other modules and within the Linux USB framework and how to use it.

Chapter 6, "Device File System," explores the essential framework required to create Virtual File System (VFS) files along with the Linux USB host framework that creates them. The Linux driver model represents devices as VFS files, and the Linux USB host subsystem creates VFS files for the devices connected to it.

Chapter 7, "Power Management," looks at the power management framework of the Linux USB host subsystem. Power management is an essential framework for embedded systems running on battery. The Linux kernel has implemented different power management techniques as part of it.

Chapter 8, "Hub," discusses the Linux USB hub design requirement and offers a practical example. A USB hub lies between a USB device and a host providing electrical, connection/disconnection, and transaction translation.

Chapter 9, "Generic Driver," explains the core data structures and interfaces of the Linux USB host framework.

Chapter 10, "Host Driver for Embedded Controller," explores the USB host controller driver requirements and the design requirements to implement them. The USB specification, such as the Enhanced Host Controller Interface (EHCI), the Universal Host Controller Interface (UHCI), or the Open Host Controller Interface (OHCI), defines the host controller requirements.

Chapter 11, "Linux USB Gadget Driver," provides an overview of the Linux USB gadget design and the generic USB stack design and sets the tone for the subsequent chapters of the gadget driver.

Chapter 12, "Peripheral Device Controller Driver," delves into the peripheral device controller driver design requirements and demonstrates a sample driver implementation.

Chapter 13, "Gadget Driver," discusses the gadget driver design and the internal sequence of activities. In addition, it includes a sample implementation.

Chapter 14, "Class Driver," details the design requirements of the class driver. It also shows the composite driver framework and a class driver implementation.

Chapter 15, "Linux USB OTG Driver," explores the OTG framework design requirements and a sample implementation. The Linux USB OTG driver is necessary to enable devices to support OTG functionality.

Chapter 16, "USB Virtual File Systems," looks at the different files exported by the Linux USB subsystem along with the format of the USB files. The Linux USB subsystem exports devices as files, which user space applications employ to interface with the device.

Chapter 17, "User Space USB Drivers," covers the various USB user space drivers available and practical examples of using them. The Linux USB subsystem provides a complete abstraction of devices, thus facilitating driver development at the user space.

Chapter 18, "Debugging Using Linux USB," discusses different debugging frameworks that the Linux USB subsystem provides and how to debug USB systems using the Linux USB subsystem.

Chapter 19, "Test Using Linux USB," explores the Linux USB test framework and the various options available on Linux to test USB systems.

The book ends with an appendix that explains the various features of the USB regression tool and how to write test cases for it.

The companion CD contains the complete Linux 2.6.34 source, documents referenced in the book, sample logs, and sources that were used in the book. The CD also has an alpha version of the regression test tool.

CD-ROM DOWNLOADS

If you purchased an ebook version of this book, and the book had a companion CD-ROM, you may download the contents from http://www.courseptr.com/downloads.

If your book has a CD-ROM, please check our Web site for any updates or errata files. You may download files from http://www.courseptr.com/downloads.

CHAPTER 1

USB AND LINUX: INTRODUCTION

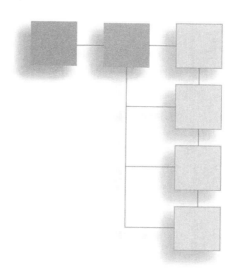

In This Chapter

- USB: The Path and the Market
- Linux USB

Universal serial bus (USB) is one of the leading components in PC/user and device connectivity. More than six billion devices (http://www.intel.com/technology/usb/) use USB to connect to a host machine, varying from consumer devices such as cameras and mobile phones to networking devices such as routers, medical devices, and car navigation systems. Thus, USB has become an integral part of most embedded devices, as illustrated in Figure 1.1.

Platforms based on Linux (such as Android and MeeGo) will emerge and penetrate into this embedded device market in an exponential way. This means that most of the devices with USB as an interconnect will start adopting Linux-based platforms. That's why USB on Linux is an unavoidable key component in most of the embedded systems.

This chapter provides a brief overview of where USB started, how the market is placed in terms of hardware availability, and which companies work on USB technology so you understand USB's reach. The section that follows explores how Linux USB started and which markets Linux may make its way into.

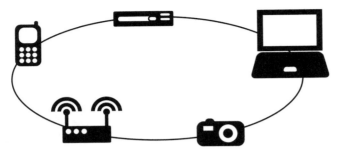

Figure 1.1
An imaginative representation of embedded devices that use Linux USB.

USB: THE PATH AND THE MARKET

USB came into the market in 1996 and has become a leading peripheral interface. The USB standard was formulated by industry leaders such as Intel, Microsoft, HP, and IBM. The objective of the USB standard is to provide an open architecture that enables vendors to design and build systems and peripherals that operate with each other. Over the years, the USB specification has matured and improved as an interface protocol. Now more than six billion devices use the USB interface.

One factor for the USB's heavy use is that with interfaces like serial ports or parallel ports, expansion of the ports in a personal computer (PC) is impossible. In contrast, USB is flexible and allows port expansion, enabling multiple peripheral devices to connect to a PC. The USB interface and peripherals such as keyboards and mice provide an easy plug-and-play capability, allowing end users to avoid hard restarts to detect a newly attached peripheral.

Over the years, the capability of PCs also has increased, thereby increasing the need for higher data transfer rates between its peripherals. Newer peripherals such as digital cameras and media players have emerged with larger memory capacities and better performance, raising the bar for USB because it is the leading PC-peripheral interface. The USB specification evolved to meet these needs by providing different data rates such as 1.5Mbps (low speed), 12Mbps (full speed), and 480Mbps (high speed). The following is a brief outline of these speeds taken from the USB specification.

N o t e

Low speed. Devices that do not transfer large amount of data fall into this category. These include interactive devices such as keyboards and joysticks. The typical transfer rate for these devices is 10–100kbps.

Full speed. Applications such as microphones and broadband fall into this category, which requires a transfer rate of 500kbps–10Mbps. One of the important attributes is guaranteed bandwidth and latency.

High speed. High-bandwidth devices such as imaging and storage that require higher and sometimes guaranteed bandwidth fall into this category. A typical transfer rate is 25–400Mbps.

The year 2001 introduced a new generation of device supplement that provides a minimal host facility, enabling the devices to act as host and connect to other USB devices. These are called On-the-Go (OTG) devices. OTG mainly evolved to support handheld devices such as mobile phones directly connecting to devices such as printers.

The USB specification has a complex low-level protocol implementation with strict timing requirements. Most of the complexity is implemented as hardware. Although this book concentrates on the software aspect of USB, it is important to know the different hardware configurations available in the market. This information helps you when you write drivers for these controllers. The following section captures in broad terms various USB hardware configurations available in the market.

USB Hardware

A USB system implements the most complicated portion of the USB specification as part of USB hardware, which includes a physical layer, a link layer, and some part of the USB protocol. The physical portion includes electrical characteristics that are necessary for data transmission, speed detection, timing, and power. The hardware protocol management includes bandwidth management, error handling, and packet management.

In the market, you may find USB hardware in different configurations and casings, providing flexibility to a platform when adopting a USB solution. These USB solutions extend the functionality of a platform in a shorter time to integrate,

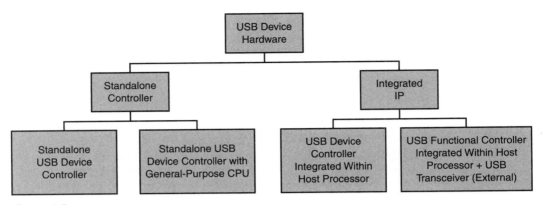

Figure 1.2
USB hardware configuration at a broad level.

which enables faster time to market. Figure 1.2 illustrates different configurations of USB controllers available in the industry.

The USB controllers can be standalone or integrated with an application processor. A standalone controller provides easy integration using simple interfaces available in the host processor. It provides an easy solution for fixing hardware errors by replacing the USB controller with the new corrected one. However, in an integrated solution, fixing any bug involves a high cost. On the other hand, USB in an integrated Internet Protocol (IP) means a single-point powerful solution that helps build complex systems.

In general, USB controller chips available on the market can be USB transceivers, standalone USB controllers, or application processors with USB controllers as part of them. The following section offers a brief overview of these hardware configurations and can help you when you implement a low-level driver.

USB Transceiver

A *transceiver* is a simple mechanism that sends and receives signals from the same circuitry. A USB transceiver enables processors to have a digital USB core integrated on-chip, without the analog circuitry. The USB transceiver thus supports connection detection functionality and provides the analog electrical signalling requirement defined by the USB specification. Figure 1.3 illustrates a USB system block diagram, demonstrating how a USB transceiver fits in a USB system.

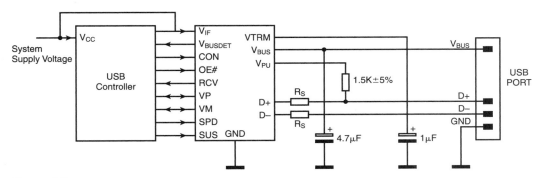

Figure 1.3
A USB transceiver and a USB controller interface. (REF: STUSB02E datasheet)

There are many reasons for platform developers to use a USB transceiver as part of their development efforts. Adding a transceiver to a platform allows you to keep the digital portion of the USB separate from the analog signals. This reduces the cost and risks involved in mixing analog and digital design in a single chip.

A standalone USB transceiver takes care of the compliance and signal quality and any problem in the differential signals on the USB cable. Thus, the transceiver helps stop adverse signals on the cable passing to the application processor and saves the application processor from damages.

A typical transceiver converts USB differential voltages to digital logic signal levels and converts logic levels to different USB signals. Figure 1.4 provides a cross-sectional overview of a USB transceiver to illustrate its internal components.

A typical transceiver chip has common pin-outs for D+, D−, receive data, and voltage. Internally, the transceiver converts the D+ and the D− lines from single-ended logic output to the output pin.

Standalone USB Controller

A standalone or general-purpose USB controller is an integrated circuit that is complete USB hardware (transceiver + digital portion) in a single package that implements USB hardware requirements. Again, the advantage of having a

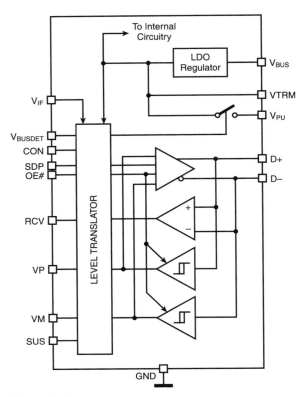

Figure 1.4
A cross-sectional view of a USB transceiver. (REF: STUSB02E datasheet)

separate USB controller is that it's easy to extend an application processor's capability, and a defect in the USB controller can be easily fixed by replacing the USB portion without damaging the application processor.

A typical standalone USB controller extends interfaces to glue the USB controller with a master or an application processor. Figure 1.5 illustrates a typical standalone USB device controller interfacing with a general-purpose central processing unit (CPU).

Some of the common interface lines include read/write enable, address, data, and chip select. The application processor can access the necessary USB data directly using data lines, or the USB controllers can provide DMA support to access the USB data, as illustrated in Figure 1.6.

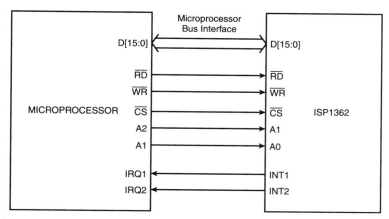

Figure 1.5
General-purpose interface of a standalone USB controller with a processor. (REF: ISP1362 datasheet)

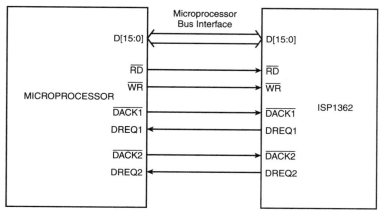

Figure 1.6
DMA interface of a standalone interface. (REF: ISP1362 datasheet)

These standalone USB controllers sometimes integrate a general-purpose micro-controller within the package. This supports the application processor by doing some of the work of the application processor within the controller. This processing allows the application processor to do other important tasks. When a USB controller contains a general-purpose controller, it provides mechanisms to download firmware onto it.

Integrated USB Controller

An integrated USB controller solution comes as part of high-end application processors. These processors have multiple features with different interconnects. A USB functionality will be added to the application processor along with other interconnect facilities, as illustrated in Figure 1.7.

An application processor is a single-chip solution for platform developers, which is a nice advantage.

These USB hardware components are available as part of embedded platforms or as USB evaluation boards in the market. The USB evaluation boards are generally PCI based, whereby you can evaluate USB features on an x86 PC. One popular PCI-based USB evaluation board is NET 2280 PCI to Hi-Speed USB,

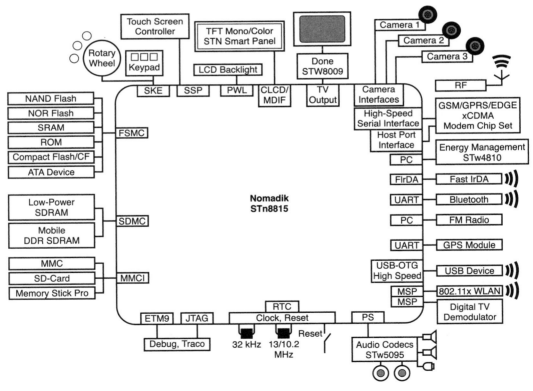

Figure 1.7
USB feature as part of an application processor. (REF: STN8815 datasheet)

which was used to develop and demonstrate the USB gadget driver. Many popular embedded Linux platforms are available, where you can evaluate USB features. Beagle board, a low-cost evaluation board with an open design, is one such popular embedded Linux platform that enables you to evaluate Linux USB.

USB Market

Some companies focus only on USB technology for their business. USB serves as their exclusive product in their product portfolio. The products vary from small footprint-embedded USB stacks to USB hardware with custom designs to meet the device's functional requirements to PC side drivers that enable end users to interact with a device in a host PC.

Some companies that provide embedded USB solutions are MCCI, Jungo, Green Hills, IAR, and Express Logic, to name a few. These and similar companies offer USB solutions as a key product. The USB stack solutions can be deployed in mobile phones, set top boxes, and PC peripherals.

Companies such as ST Ericsson, TI, Renesas, Atmel, Cypress Semiconductor, and FTDI provide USB chips with custom solutions for the functional requirement. For example, some USB device controllers provide Advanced Technology Attachment with Packet Interface (ATAPI) or similar interfaces, whose controllers are targeted for USB-based memory devices.

USB technology is in more than six billion devices, and that number is increasing at a rate of 2 billion a year (REF: http://www.intel.com/technology/usb/).

This exponential growth is highly influenced by other technological advances such as cheaper flash memory, leading USB-based flash drives, mobile phones, and other handheld devices.

LINUX USB

The Linux initiative was started somewhere in the early 1990s. From there, it has grown exponentially, penetrating into PC and server markets, through collaborative development. Linux has a stable USB host stack and device drivers for most of the USB devices, enabling end users to connect their USB devices to a Linux-based PC. Later, when Linux got into embedded devices, the USB device (gadget) stack was added to the Linux kernel. Over time, with many products adopting Linux, the USB stack was stabilized and came up with different support tools.

The Linux USB community is an active one. Companies such as IBM, Google, Samsung, Texas Instruments, and Nokia play important roles. The Linux USB mailing list typically gets 1,000 e-mails or more per month (http://marc.info/?l=linux-usb).

The official Web site of the Linux USB subsystem is http://www.linux-usb.org/. Refer to the Web site if you want to better understand the transformation of the Linux USB stack from Linux kernel 2.2.7 to where it is now. The Linux-USB community's current goals for the Linux 2.6 kernel are correctness, reliability, performance, functionality, portability, power management, and driver coverage.

In a recent development, big players such as Google have adopted Linux as part of their embedded platform Android, the first free, open source, and fully customizable mobile platform. Other mobile phone vendors have joined the bandwagon of open-source platforms. Nokia now offers MeeGo, an open-source mobile platform based on Linux and Samsung with Linux-based platform bada. Some of these platforms are also being deployed in set top boxes, in IVI systems (in vehicle infotainment), and in navigation systems. Their market potential is growing fast, and the trend is positive toward embedded Linux platforms.

Figure 1.8 provides a market share of various operating systems. Android, based on Linux and other Linux-based products, represents approximately 20 percent of the total and is approximately three times the share in 2009.

Company	2Q10 Units	2Q10 Market Share (%)	2Q09 Units	2Q09 Market Share (%)
Symbian	25,386.8	41.2	20,880.8	51.0
Research in Motion	11,228.8	18.2	7,782.2	19.0
Android	10,606.1	17.2	755.9	1.8
iOS	8,743.0	14.2	5,325.0	13.0
Microsoft Windows Mobile	3,096.4	5.0	3,829.7	9.3
Linux	1,503.1	2.4	1,901.1	4.6
Other OSs	1,084.8	1.8	497.1	1.2
Total	**61,649.1**	**100.0**	**40,971.8**	**100.0**

Figure 1.8
Market share of various mobile operating systems.

Figure 1.8 shows how fast the open-source Linux platform is penetrating the market. This growth makes it essential to study a successful interconnect such as USB's subsystem on Linux. The subsequent chapters of this book detail each component of the Linux USB stack.

SUMMARY

Originally, Linux was used predominantly as a host operating system in PCs or servers. Now the Linux market is expanding exponentially in the embedded arena with the introduction of open platforms conquering different products. USB functionality is an essential part of these products, which makes Linux USB an interesting topic to explore. Both USB and Linux USB have taken a long path to reach this successful stage. The Linux USB stack is mature and being used in most of the embedded Linux products. The chapters of this book dissect the Linux USB stack to enable enthusiasts to have an understanding before jumping in to any activity on Linux USB.

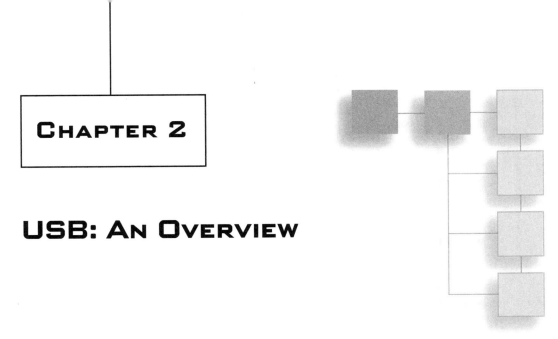

CHAPTER 2

USB: AN OVERVIEW

In This Chapter

- USB System Architecture
- Enumeration
- USB Transfers
- Terms to Remember

The universal serial bus (USB) technology works in the master-slave communication model. The USB host controls complete communication (playing the master's role), and the USB device responds to the USB host's request (playing the slave role). The devices are connected to the USB host in a tiered-star fashion, with a maximum of 127 devices connected to the host. Figure 2.1 from the USB 2.0 specification illustrates the star-tier topology of a USB setup.

To an end user working on a USB host or a device, these topological layers are invisible. The USB device looks as if it's connected directly to the USB host, as shown in Figure 2.2. This is done through the host's system software, which hides all these topological information and presents direct access to a device.

Because this book focuses mainly on the software aspect of a USB system, this chapter explores some key points from software development's perspective, extracted from the USB specification. This chapter begins with the system architecture of USB, which gives you an idea of the functional blocks of a USB system and how information

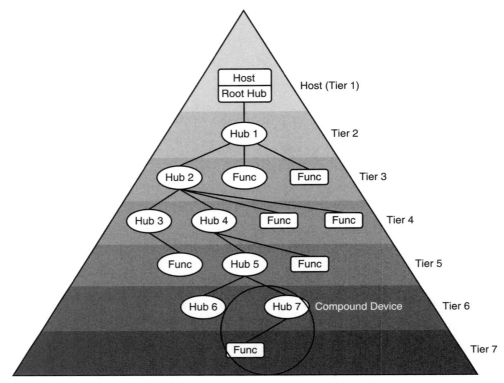

Figure 2.1
USB bus topology. (Ref: USB 2.0 Specification)

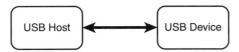

Figure 2.2
USB host/device view.

flows across these blocks. The information flow can be divided into the device enumeration and the data flow. The enumeration process helps the USB host identify devices through the descriptors that the device sends. The subsequent sections of the chapter explore the enumeration process along with the various descriptors that expose the device to the host. The USB specification defines four transfer types catering to the needs of the device classes supported. Note that the former enumeration activity contains USB-specific information, and the transfers contain information that is class specific. This chapter explores these transfer types.

USB SYSTEM ARCHITECTURE

A USB system can be divided into three major areas: the USB device, the USB host, and the USB interconnect. The *USB device* refers to the physical entity that performs the required function. The *USB host system* refers to the system that installs the host controller to interface with the devices. Finally, the *USB interconnect* refers to the manner in which USB devices are connected to and communicate with the host.

Figure 2.3 from the USB specification (Figure 5-9: USB Host/Device Detailed View) illustrates in detail the relationship between a USB host and a USB device. If you closely watch the blocks, you'll notice that three layers make up the USB system.

The three layers—the functional layer, the USB device layer, and the USB bus interface layer as represented in the figure—are common for both the USB host

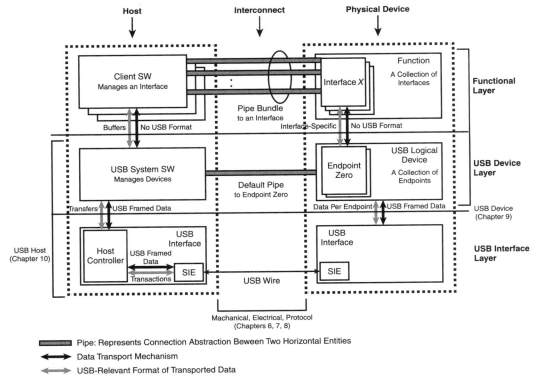

Figure 2.3
The internals of a USB host and USB device in detail.

and the USB device. These layers establish a logical connection between these layers across the host and the device through the pipes at the functional level and the endpoint at the lower layers. Also, notice that the device and bus interface layers work on USB-specific data, and the upper functional layer is specific to the class that the device implements. The following sections go into more detail about these layers for the host and the device, followed by the enumeration process and the USB transfer types.

USB Host

The USB protocol is host driven. The host is made up of three major layers: client software, USB system software, and USB host controller, which is the USB bus interface of the USB host. These layers are responsible for the complete USB system operation as a host, which includes detection and removal of device attachment, control and data flow management with the device, and collection of status and control of the electrical interface. Figure 2.4, taken from the USB specification, is a simplified version of Figure 2.3, illustrating the blocks of the USB host.

Client Software

The *client software layer* refers to the software applications that interact with the USB devices using their functional aspect. For example, perhaps you connect a USB Web camera to your personal computer. The application that streams video is the client software for the USB Web camera. Thus, this layer interacts with the USB peripheral via the USB system software's exposed interfaces in a level above the USB protocol. Generally, these software layers are unaware of USB activity other than identifying and opening required USB devices.

USB System Software

The *USB system software* is the core of the USB host system, performing most of the USB host activities. The USB system software is implemented above the host controller hardware and acts as an interface between the client software and the host controller. The system software consists of two major blocks: the host controller driver (HCD) and the USB driver (USBD). The HCD acts like a hardware abstraction layer, extending the USB host controller's feature in a transparent way. Thus, the HCD layer allows the USBD to support different host

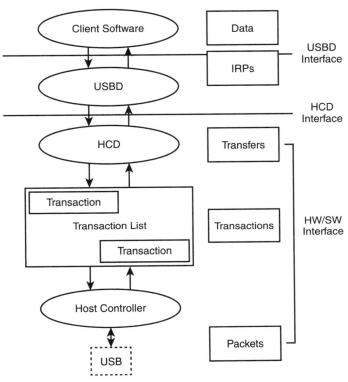

Figure 2.4
USB host layers and information flow.

controllers without having specific knowledge of the host controller implementation. The USBD acts as an interface between the USB system software and the client software. The driver module handles the USB device enumeration and manages the input/output request packets (IRPs) to and from the host. The system software sits on host software and uses the host software's infrastructure to perform its operations, including device and data management.

Host Controller

The *host controller* is typically a hardware implementation and the one that adds USB interface support to the host computer. The host controller hardware translates the USB bus activities to transactions and vice versa. The host controller also provides a mechanism reporting the status of a transaction, such as done, pending, or halted, to the USB system software. This status report allows the system software to take appropriate action. The host controller ensures USB protocol rules for bus management, such as interpacket timings and timeouts.

Now that you've read a brief overview of the USB host system's internal blocks, the following sections focus on the internal details of a USB device system.

USB Device

A USB device to an end user provides additional capability, such as Web camera or printer, to a host computer through a USB interface. In fact, a USB hub is referred to as a USB device that provides additional USB attachment points to a host computer. A USB device is generally self-powered or bus powered (powered by the USB host). Figure 2.5, taken from the USB specification, is a simplified version of Figure 2.3 illustrating the blocks of USB device. The subsequent section provides an overview of these USB device layers.

Function

The function layer implements the functional characteristic of the USB device. This layer implements the USB class specifications such as mass storage, HID, and communication defined by USB.org. In Figure 2.3, notice that the USB

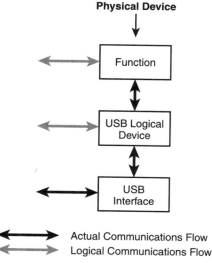

Figure 2.5
USB device layers and information flow.

function layer's data is not USB specific. The data is mostly specific to the functionality that the layer implements. The function layer decides the configuration of the USB device that is passed on to the USB host through the layers below. The functional layer appears to a host system as an interface collection that exposes the implemented functionality.

USB Logical Device

The logical device layer implements the USB-related portion of the USB device activity. This layer appears to the USB host system as a collection of endpoints that includes the default Endpoint Zero and other endpoints as required by the function layer. The logical layer is also responsible for maintaining the state machine defined by the USB specification. The logical device layer performs almost the same functionality in all USB devices, and the host communicates with the logical device as if it is directly connected.

USB Bus Interface

The bus interface layer is a hardware implementation for a USB device; it is commonly referred to as the USB device controller. The USB bus interface layer implements the physical layer, link layer, and protocol layer. The bus interface layer is common for the USB device and the USB host, but the device implementation is simpler than the host. A typical USB device controller facilitates above logical and function layers to transfer data and provide status information on the data transfer and USB-related information.

Communication Flow

Having seen the USB host and the USB device internal details, you need to know how both systems are logically connected, because communication at the software level is logical. The two key interconnects of the USB communication flow are the USB device endpoint and the pipe. The following section discusses these two logical interconnects.

Endpoints

An *endpoint* is a uniquely identifiable location of a USB device, which is the source or sink point for the communication flow between the USB host and the USB device. A device is made up of a number of endpoints based on its function.

As you connect a device to a host, the host assigns it a unique address, referred to as a *device address*. Each endpoint on a device has a unique device-assigned number called an *endpoint number*. The endpoint can be referenced uniquely with a combination of the device address, endpoint address, and endpoint direction. An endpoint operates simply, supporting data flow in one direction, either from the device to the host or vice versa.

Endpoint Zero is a special endpoint that all devices must implement. The USB host uses it to initialize and gather information about the device. An endpoint has a characteristic that determines the type of transfer it provides. As per USB specification, an endpoint describes itself by the following.

- The bus access frequency/latency requirement
- The bandwidth requirement
- The endpoint number
- The error-handling behavior requirements
- The maximum packet size that the endpoint is capable of sending or receiving
- The transfer type for the endpoint
- The direction in which data is transferred between the endpoint and the host

The following section provides an overview of how the USB system software maps these endpoints as pipes.

Pipes

A *pipe* is a logical representation of the association between a device endpoint and the host software. There are two types of pipes: stream pipe and message pipe. The former moves data with no USB-defined format, and the latter moves data with some USB-defined structure.

Figure 2.6 from the USB specification neatly illustrates the relationship between the endpoints, pipes, and client software running in the USB host.

A pipe adopts the characteristics such as the transfer type and payload size of the endpoint it associates and claims the necessary bus bandwidth required from the USB

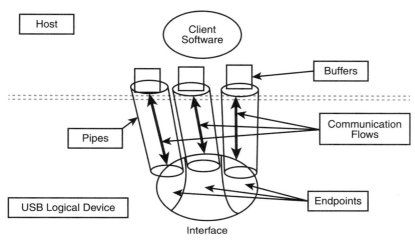

Figure 2.6
USB communication flow illustrating the endpoint, pipe, and client software relationship.

bus. One of the important pipes is the default control pipe, which is associated with Endpoint Zero and is available once the device is powered and has been reset. The host system software uses the default control pipe to identify and configure the device.

ENUMERATION

The process of identifying the device and setting a unique address is referred as *bus enumeration*. The enumeration process is handled by the system software on the host and the USB logical layer on the device side. The enumeration process starts when a device is attached to the host and the device gets the power. The USB specification includes simple steps for enumeration.

1. The USB device is attached to the host, which receives an event indicating a change in the pipe's status. The USB device is in the powered state, and the port it is attached to is disabled.

2. The host queries about the change in the bus.

3. Once the host determines that a new device is attached, it waits for at least 100ms for the device to become stable after power, after which it enables and resets the port.

4. After a successful reset, the USB device is in a default state and can draw power to a range of 100 mA from VBUS pin.

5. Once the device is in a default state, the host assigns a unique address to the USB device, which moves the device to an address state.

6. The host starts communicating with the USB device in the default control pipe and reads the device descriptor.

7. Subsequently, the host reads the device configuration information.

8. The host selects the configuration, which moves the device to a configured state and makes it ready for use.

This state transition in the enumeration is an important portion of the USB logical layer. Figure 2.7 captures an ideal state transition during the enumeration process.

This state machine is part of the USB logical layer software implementation of the USB device. The state transition forms descriptor requests and replies to the host. The following section offers a brief overview of the various descriptors and how they are arranged.

Descriptors

A *descriptor* as per USB specification is structured data that describes the attributes and provides information about a USB device to the USB host. The

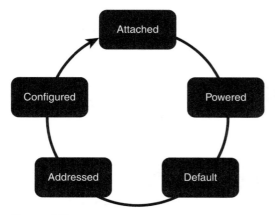

Figure 2.7
A simplified state transition of a USB device during perfect enumeration.

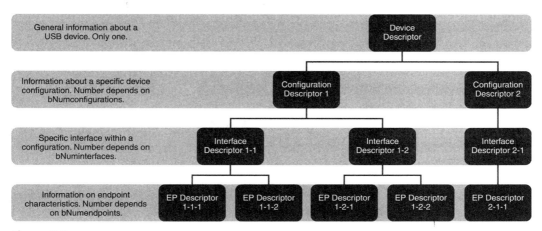

Figure 2.8
Illustrates relationship between the descriptors in a hierachial fashion.

USB specification defines a standard set of descriptors: device, configuration, interface, endpoint, and string.

Figure 2.8 provides a hierarchical relationship between the descriptors. Descriptors are passed top down from the device descriptor to the endpoint descriptor.

A device descriptor contains information about the USB device to host. The information includes the device speed, USB version, vendor details, and number of configurations available.

A configuration descriptor contains information about a particular configuration and a device support, which includes powering mechanism, power requirements, and interface requirements.

An interface descriptor contains information on a configuration's particular interface, which includes the class of the device and protocol details.

An endpoint descriptor contains information about a particular endpoint, which includes characteristics of endpoints such as the transfer type supported, timing details, and address.

Chapter 9 of the USB specification contains more details about the USB descriptor.

USB TRANSFERS

The USB specification defines four transfer types. The transfer type determines various characteristics of the communication flow. As per the USB specification, a transfer type determines the following characteristics of a USB communication flow.

- Direction of communication flow
- Constraint in the packet size
- Bus access constraints
- Latency constraints
- Required data sequences
- Error handling

An application chooses any of the following four transfer types based on the application's requirement.

Control Transfer

The system software uses a control transfer with a maximum size of 64 bytes to retrieve information and configure the device as part of the enumeration process. A control transfer, which is nonperiodic, is generally used for command/status operations initiated by the host software. The USB system makes a best effort to deliver the control packet from the host to the device.

A control transfer occurs in three stages: setup transaction, which is a request from host to device; optional data transaction, depending on the type of request; and status transaction, which provides status information of the request from device to host. These control transfers are performed in message pipes.

A control transfer's setup request is defined by Chapter 9 of the USB specification. It supports vendor-specific transfers that help retrieve vendor-specific information.

Bulk Transfer

A bulk transfer is used by applications that transfer large amounts of data to and from the USB host to the device with no strict time requirements. A USB printer or a digital camera is a typical user of bulk transfers. A USB bulk transfer has a maximum transfer size of 512 bytes, is nonperiodic, and uses any available bus bandwidth. Because bulk transfers occur only on the basis of the bandwidth available, the transfers are faster when there are large amounts of free bandwidth.

A bulk pipe happens on a stream pipe, and the communication flow is either into or out of the host for a given pipe. A bulk transfer provides guaranteed data transfer with no guaranteed delivery time. A bulk transfer does retry a transfer to ensure a guaranteed delivery of data in the case of occasional delivery failure due to errors on the bus.

The data in the bulk transfer is specific to the functional driver. It is not defined by a USB format.

Interrupt Transfer

An interrupt transfer is used for nonperiodic, small data and supports a maximum packet size of 1,024 bytes. It is generally used to report status information (such as a cursor point) or a small amount of data (such as characters from a keyboard). This data is delivered in a limited latency; most of the application lacks explicit timing requirements.

An interrupt transfer is transferred in a stream pipe, and the data transferred is not USB specific. An interrupt transfer provides guaranteed delivery of data, in which the protocol does retry in case of any errors on the bus.

Isochronous Transfer

An isochronous transfer is used for applications such as Web camera or audio transfers, which require periodic transfer of data from the device to the host. Because isochronous data is continuous and real time, on-time delivery is important. The isochronous transfer supports a maximum packet size of 1,024 bytes, and the on-time delivery is ensured by allocating a dedicated portion of USB bandwidth. However, the timely delivery comes at the expense of potential losses in the data stream on the bus.

An isochronous transfer is transferred in a stream pipe, and the data transferred is not USB specific. Because isochronous data is bound by time, no retrying attempt to deliver the data is made for bus errors.

For a complete understanding of the transfer types defined by USB specification, read Chapters 5 and 8 of the USB specification.

TERMS TO REMEMBER

Besides the terms already introduced in this chapter, here are some others you will come across when you study or implement USB software.

Short packet. A *short packet* can be defined as a packet whose payload is shorter than the maximum size or zero length packet (ZLP). A short packet could indicate the end of a transfer.

Zero length packet (ZLP). A zero length data packet transfer does not contain data as part of the transfer. When the data to be sent is an exact multiple of wMaxPacketSize, a ZLP has to be sent after the data transfer is complete to indicate the end of the transfer. Sometimes a ZLP feature is implemented as part of the hardware or has to be taken care when designing Chapter 9/USB.

STALL. A STALL indicates that a function is unable to transmit or receive data or that even a control pipe request is not supported. The state of a function after returning a STALL is undefined.

SUMMARY

The USB specification is huge and detailed, so it is difficult to summarize in a small chapter. However, this chapter captures some important topics that are essential for an understanding of the USB software system. The device identification, management, and data flow constitute the major portion of the USB software system, and most of the complex protocols in the physical and link are implemented as part of USB hardware. As a USB software developer, generally if you read Chapters 4, 5, and 9 of the specification, you can understand most of the software implementations. The functional details referred to as USB class are defined in separate USB class specifications, which you must read based on the USB function you are planning to study or implement. The "More Reading" section that follows provides details on the USB specifications.

More Reading

This chapter provided a basic overview of the USB specification that is necessary for a USB software engineer. You can read more about the USB protocol and other developer topics at the USB specification available at http://www.usb.org/developers/docs/. The specification defines the implementation details of the USB bus interface layer and the USB logical layer. The function layer implementation is out of the scope of USB specification and is defined as the USB class specification available at http://www.usb.org/developers/devclass/.

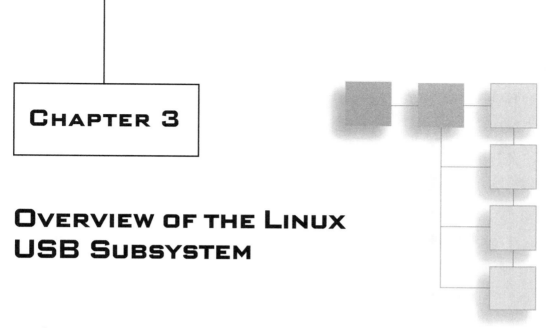

CHAPTER 3

OVERVIEW OF THE LINUX USB SUBSYSTEM

In This Chapter

- Linux USB Host Subsystem
- Linux USB Gadget Subsystem

The Linux kernel source tree is a complex set of source codes, which the kernel organizes in separate folder hierarchies based on their functionalities. Each functional framework folder contains a makefile of its own and can be independently built. The kernel configuration utilities manage these sources and help create required kernel configuration for a kernel user. You can manage the kernel configuration using any one of the following commands.

- `make config`
- `make menuconfig`
- `make xconfig`

Over and above understanding the kernel source code, it is essential to know how to configure the kernel, which enables you to build the required features as part of the kernel. This chapter provides a brief overview of the Linux universal serial bus (USB) subsystem and explores the various configuration options available in the kernel to configure the Linux USB subsystem, which helps you build the necessary USB modules.

Table 3.1 Linux USB Framework Directory Structure

Folder Name	Description
Core	Part of the Linux USB host framework that contains sources implementing the USB system software, including the hub, the USB file system, and the USB protocol implementation of the host.
Host	Part of the Linux USB host framework that contains the host controller drivers. This source code includes EHCI[1], UHCI[2], and OHCI[3] drivers for embedded USB host controllers.
Gadget	Contains source code that implements USB peripheral framework and drivers for the USB peripheral controller. The USB device part of the class implementation and the related framework are also available in this folder.
Otg	Contains source code that implements OTG[4] driver framework and drivers for OTG controllers.
Class	Contains source code that implements a USB class protocol such as ACM[5] for the USB host and others that don't fall under any of the categories that follow.
Storage	Contains source code that implements a USB storage class driver for a USB host, which includes support to different memory types.
Image	Contains source code that implements drivers for imaging devices such as cameras or scanners for the USB host.
Atm	Contains sources that implement drivers for modem devices for the USB host.
Serial	Contains source code that implements drivers for serial devices such as serial consoles or adapters for the USB host.
Misc	Contains source code that implements drivers for the USB host that do not fall into this category, such as the USB test drivers.
Mon	Contains source code that implements the USB monitor framework, a debug utility that supports Linux USB development work by dumping USB transactions.

[1]EHCI = Enhanced Host Controller Interface
[2]UHCI = Universal Host Controller Interface
[3]OHCI = Open Host Controller Interface
[4]OTG = On-the-Go
[5]ACM = Abstract Control Model

You can download the Linux kernel source 2.6.34 from http://www.kernel.org/. The Linux USB framework is organized under the drivers/usb folder of the Linux kernel source package. The drivers/usb folder contains source of the USB framework, which can handle both USB device and host functionalities. Table 3.1 is an overview of the directory structure of the Linux USB framework.

Having gathered a basic understanding of how the source code of the Linux USB subsystem is placed in the kernel tree, the following sections provide a brief overview of the Linux USB subsystem, along with various configuration options available in those subsystems that can help you add specific USB functionalities to the platform.

LINUX USB HOST SUBSYSTEM

The Linux USB host subsystem, or the system software, as referred to by the USB specification, consists of drivers for the host controller, driver modules that implement the USB protocol, and functional drivers. There are additional driver modules, such as the file system and debugging functionalities available as part of the host subsystem. Figure 3.1 illustrates an architectural view of the Linux USB host subsystem.

The lowermost layer of the USB host software is the driver layer of the USB host controller hardware. This driver acts as an abstraction layer to the hardware and exposes generic interfaces to the above USB host system software layer. On the

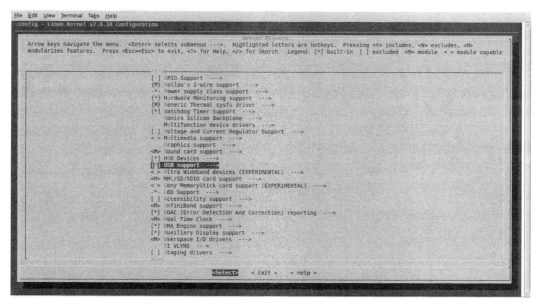

Figure 3.1
A block-level representation of the Linux USB host system.

Linux USB subsystem, the usbcore module implements the debug infrastructure, power management, USB file systems, and USB host protocol. Some of the USB class specifications and debug monitoring tools are implemented as part of the USB host subsystem.

The configuration and selection of the kernel modules are based on the Kconfig files. The root configuration file for the USB subsystem is drivers/usb/Kconfig. To enable USB support in the kernel, the configuration option is available in Device Drivers, USB Support. The following snap of the drivers/usb/Kconfig file provides the menu for USB support. The USB support depends on the IOMEM (Input/Output memory part of lib/Kconfig) option, which should be enabled for USB to be supported.

The following configuration from drivers/usb/Kconfig shows the dependency of USB on the IOMEM module.

```
menuconfig USB_SUPPORT
            bool "USB support"
            depends on HAS_IOMEM
            default y
```

Figure 3.2 illustrates the USB Support option when you use make menuconfig to configure the kernel.

The USB support menu is enabled by default, as are the EHCI and OHCI menus. Subsequent menu entries depend on these flags.

The following configuration from drivers/usb/Kconfig shows that host-side USB depends on having a host controller support.

```
config USB_ARCH_HAS_HCD
        boolean
        default y if USB_ARCH_HAS_OHCI
        default y if USB_ARCH_HAS_EHCI
```

The following sections explain key configuration options that are part of the USB host functionality in the Linux USB subsystem.

USB HCD Driver Menu

A USB host controller implementation is based on specifications ECHI, UHCI, or OHCI, or sometimes it's customized for certain embedded controllers that are

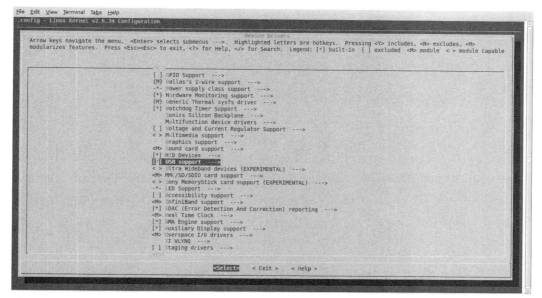

Figure 3.2
Menuconfig option displaying USB Support option.

not fully complaint with these specifications. The `drivers/usb/host` folder contains drivers for all USB host controllers.

The `drivers/usb/host/Kconfig` file contains the host controller driver configuration menu options, which allow you to choose the necessary host controller interface (HCI) drivers. The host controller driver configuration depends on USB support, which you enabled earlier.

The following configuration from `drivers/usb/host/Kconfig` shows that host-controller drivers depend on USB configuration.

```
#
# USB Host Controller Drivers
#
comment "USB Host Controller Drivers"
        depends on USB
```

Enable EHCI HCD Support

An EHCI allows you to connect to USB 2.0 high-speed devices. When you configure the USB EHCI option, it generates the `ehci-hcd.ko` kernel module.

```
<M>     EHCI HCD (USB 2.0) support
[*]       Root Hub Transaction Translators
[*]       Improved Transaction Translator scheduling (EXPERIMENTAL)
< >     OXU210HP HCD support
<M>     ISP116X HCD support
< >     ISP 1760 HCD support
```

Figure 3.3
Menuconfig option displaying EHCI option.

Figure 3.3 illustrates the menuconfig option available as part of the EHCI menu configuration.

The EHCI HCD support is provided by USB_EHCI_HCD. There are other EHCI-specific menu options that you might need to choose if the support for transaction translators or big endian mode is required for certain controllers.

The following configuration from drivers/usb/host/Kconfig shows the EHCI driver configuration and its dependency.

```
config USB_EHCI_HCD
        tristate "EHCI HCD (USB 2.0) support"
        depends on USB && USB_ARCH_HAS_EHCI
```

The configuration (drivers/usb/host/Kconfig) also provides an option to selectively enable the transaction translator feature, which enables the HCI driver to support full- and low-speed devices.

```
config USB_EHCI_ROOT_HUB_TT
        bool "Root Hub Transaction Translators"
        depends on USB_EHCI_HCD
config USB_EHCI_TT_NEWSCHED
        bool "Improved Transaction Translator scheduling (EXPERIMENTAL)"
        depends on USB_EHCI_HCD && EXPERIMENTAL
```

Enable OHCI HCD Support

The Open Host Controller controllers allow you to connect to USB 2.0 low- and full-speed devices. When you configure the USB OHCI option, it generates the ohci-hcd.ko kernel module.

The following configuration from drivers/usb/host/Kconfig shows the OHCI driver configuration and its dependency.

```
config USB_OHCI_HCD
        tristate "OHCI HCD support"
        depends on USB && USB_ARCH_HAS_OHCI
        select ISP1301_OMAP if MACH_OMAP_H2 || MACH_OMAP_H3
        select USB_OTG_UTILS if ARCH_OMAP
```

Figure 3.4 illustrates the menuconfig option available as part of the OHCI menu.

```
<M>     OHCI HCD support
[ ]       OHCI support for Broadcom SSB OHCI core
```

Figure 3.4
Menuconfig option displaying OHCI option.

Enable UHCI HCD Support

The Universal Host Controller is a proprietary interface specific to Intel for full- and low-speed devices. When you configure the USB UHCI option, it generates the `uhci-hcd.ko` kernel module.

The following configuration from `drivers/usb/host/Kconfig` shows the UHCI driver configuration and its dependency.

```
config USB_UHCI_HCD
        tristate "UHCI HCD (most Intel and VIA) support"
        depends on USB && PCI
```

Figure 3.5 illustrates the menuconfig option available as part of the UHCI menu.

```
<M>     UHCI HCD (most Intel and VIA) support
```

Figure 3.5
Menuconfig option displaying UHCI option.

USB Class Driver Menu

Another important requirement of the Linux USB host subsystem is supporting USB classes such as Mass Storage Class devices (thumb drive) or HID devices (USB mouse). Support of these functionalities makes the USB system complete and useful to a user. The following section covers the major class driver support available in the Linux USB host subsystem.

```
<M>    USB Mass Storage support
[ ]      USB Mass Storage verbose debug
<M>      Datafab Compact Flash Reader support
<M>      Freecom USB/ATAPI Bridge support
<M>      ISD-200 USB/ATA Bridge support
<M>      USBAT/USBAT02-based storage support
<M>      SanDisk SDDR-09 (and other SmartMedia, including DPCM) support
<M>      SanDisk SDDR-55 SmartMedia support
<M>      Lexar Jumpshot Compact Flash Reader
<M>      Olympus MAUSB-10/Fuji DPC-R1 support
< >      Support OneTouch Button on Maxtor Hard Drives
<M>      Support for Rio Karma music player
< >      SAT emulation on Cypress USB/ATA Bridge with ATACB
[*]      The shared table of common (or usual) storage devices
```

Figure 3.6
Menuconfig option displaying Host Mass Storage options.

Mass Storage Class

The USB Device Working Group defines the class specification for storage devices such as flash drives and hard drives, referred to as Mass Storage Class. To enable the USB host to enumerate such devices successfully, you need to add drivers to the kernel, along with additional drivers such as Small Computer System Interface (SCSI).

Figure 3.6 illustrates the USB Mass Storage Class menu when you run a make menuconfig.

The following configuration from the drivers/usb/storage/Kconfig file shows menu options to configure a USB host to support storage devices.

```
#
# USB Storage driver configuration
#

comment "NOTE: USB_STORAGE depends on SCSI but BLK_DEV_SD may"
comment "also be needed; see USB_STORAGE Help for more info"
        depends on USB

config USB_STORAGE
        tristate "USB Mass Storage support"
        depends on USB && SCSI
```

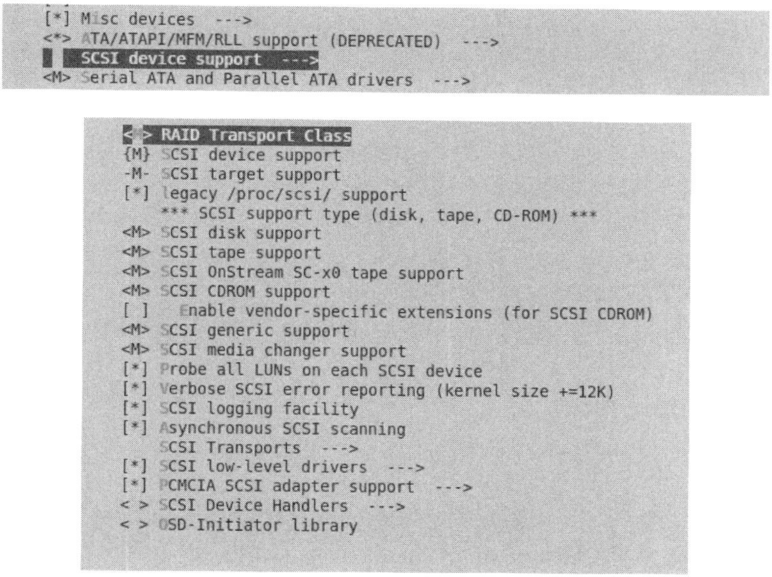

```
[*] Misc devices  --->
<*> ATA/ATAPI/MFM/RLL support (DEPRECATED)  --->
█   SCSI device support   --->
<M> Serial ATA and Parallel ATA drivers  --->
```

```
< > RAID Transport Class
{M} SCSI device support
-M- SCSI target support
[*] legacy /proc/scsi/ support
    *** SCSI support type (disk, tape, CD-ROM) ***
<M> SCSI disk support
<M> SCSI tape support
<M> SCSI OnStream SC-x0 tape support
<M> SCSI CDROM support
[ ]    Enable vendor-specific extensions (for SCSI CDROM)
<M> SCSI generic support
<M> SCSI media changer support
[*] Probe all LUNs on each SCSI device
[*] Verbose SCSI error reporting (kernel size +=12K)
[*] SCSI logging facility
[*] Asynchronous SCSI scanning
    SCSI Transports  --->
[*] SCSI low-level drivers  --->
[*] PCMCIA SCSI adapter support  --->
< > SCSI Device Handlers  --->
< > OSD-Initiator library
```

Figure 3.7
Menuconfig option displaying SCSI options.

For functional USB storage, you need to enable the SCSI drivers. Figure 3.7 illustrates the SCSI option necessary as part of USB mass storage.

The kernel configuration of the storage driver provides an option to enable and disable debug messages of the USB storage driver with the following menu, which is generally enabled during development activity.

```
config USB_STORAGE_DEBUG
        bool "USB Mass Storage verbose debug"
        depends on USB_STORAGE
```

Because the USB mass storage devices are based on class specification, the driver can support devices from different vendors. The following menu option enables a driver that supports loading of the USB storage driver for USB mass storage without rebuilding the module.

```
config USB_LIBUSUAL
        bool "The shared table of common (or usual) storage devices"
        depends on USB
```

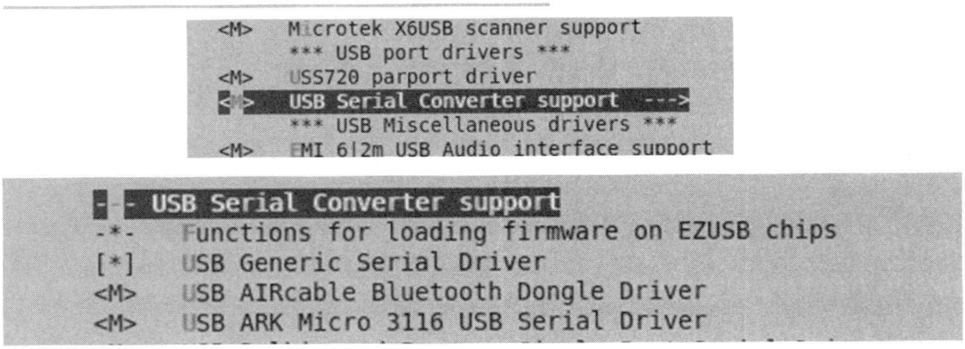

Figure 3.8
Menuconfig option displaying USB Serial option.

When configured to generate as a module, the makefile generates `usb-storage.ko`, allowing you to load and unload the module dynamically.

Serial Class

The serial class provides a driver for USB-to-serial converters and for devices that use a serial interface from user space to interact with the devices. You can refer to `Documentation/usb/usb-serial.txt` to learn the details of the serial driver.

Figure 3.8 illustrates the serial class menu when you run a `make menuconfig`.

The following configuration from the `drivers/usb/serial/Kconfig` file provides the necessary menu options to configure the USB host serial support.

```
# USB Serial device configuration
#

menuconfig USB_SERIAL
        tristate "USB Serial Converter support"
        depends on USB
```

The kernel configuration of the serial driver also provides an option to enable and disable debug messages of the USB serial driver with the following menu, which is generally enabled during development activity.

```
config USB_SERIAL_DEBUG
        tristate "USB Debugging Device"
```

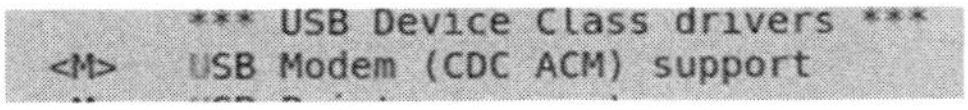

Figure 3.9
Menuconfig option displaying USB CDC option.

Sometimes you need to add serial console support to your device to emulate a terminal console over serial port. The following option enables you to set serial console support.

```
config USB_SERIAL_CONSOLE
        bool "USB Serial Console device support"
        depends on USB_SERIAL=y
```

When a USB device doesn't have a serial driver of its own, enable this generic driver so that a host can detect it at runtime. You can specify `insmod usbserial vendor=`$V\text{-}ID$ `product=`$P\text{-}ID$, where $V\text{-}ID$ and $P\text{-}ID$ are the vendor and product ID of your device.

```
config USB_SERIAL_GENERIC
        bool "USB Generic Serial Driver"
```

When it's configured to generate as a module, the makefile generates `usbserial.ko`, allowing you to load and unload the module dynamically.

CDC Ethernet Support

The other important class of USB is the Ethernet class, which is available in most of the embedded systems that support USB. This feature is needed only in a USB host system to support such devices that provide CDC Ethernet support. The following option enables a USB host to support USB CDC devices.

Figure 3.9 illustrates the CDC class menu when you run a `make menuconfig`, which is outside the USB menu option.

The following configuration from `drivers/net/usb/Kconfig` file provides the necessary menu options to configure the USB host CDC support.

```
#
# USB Network devices configuration
#
comment "Networking support is needed for USB Network Adapter support"
        depends on USB && !NET
n
```

```
menu "USB Network Adapters"
        depends on USB && NET
...
...
config USB_USBNET
        tristate "Multi-purpose USB Networking Framework"
        select MII
config USB_NET_CDCETHER
        tristate "CDC Ethernet support (smart devices such as cable modems)"
        depends on USB_USBNET
```

Miscellaneous Host Drivers

The Linux USB host subsystem provides additional features that are not USB but add a definite value to the USB subsystem. These features are part of the usbcore module and are added to the module based on the configuration option. This section covers how to configure and build these additional features with the kernel.

Debug Infrastructure

The host infrastructure provides options to configure and control debug messages that are part of the usbcore and hub drivers. The following configuration from the drivers/usb/core/Kconfig file provides the necessary menu options to configure the USB host debug support.

```
config USB_DEBUG
        bool "USB verbose debug messages"
        depends on USB
```

File Systems

The Linux USB host system extends internals to the user space as part of the file system. User space applications use these internals. The following configuration from drivers/usb/core/Kconfig file allows you to configure the USB device file system as part of the kernel.

```
config USB_DEVICEFS
        bool "USB device filesystem (DEPRECATED)"

        depends on USB
config USB_DEVICE_CLASS
        bool "USB device class-devices (DEPRECATED)"
```

```
        depends on USB
        default y
```

Power Management

A USB host system can suspend the USB devices when the bus has no activity. The Linux USB host system provides an option to suspend the devices and enables runtime power management. The following configuration from the drivers/usb/core/Kconfig file allows you to configure the USB power as part of the kernel.

```
config USB_SUSPEND
        bool "USB runtime power management (suspend/resume and wakeup)"
        depends on USB && PM_RUNTIME
```

Test Infrastructure

The host infrastructure also provides test facilities that enable you to test certain host and device features. The following configuration from the drivers/usb/misc/Kconfig file allows you to configure the USB test feature part of the kernel and generate usbtest.ko.

```
config USB_TEST
        tristate "USB testing driver"
        depends on USB
```

LINUX USB GADGET SUBSYSTEM

The next key framework of the Linux USB subsystem is the gadget driver framework or the driver framework for the USB device controller, device protocol implementation, and functional drivers of a USB device. The framework also implements the debug and gadget file system. Figure 3.10 provides an architectural view of the Linux USB gadget subsystem.

The USB controller driver implements the driver module for the USB device controller, which acts mainly as a hardware abstraction layer exporting hardware features to the above gadget layers. The gadget layer implements the USB protocol framework that interfaces the device driver layer and the class driver layer, such as storage. The class driver layer implements the functional aspect of the USB device.

The drivers/usb/gadget/Kconfig configuration file contains the various options to select gadget framework features. You can enable the USB gadget driver from

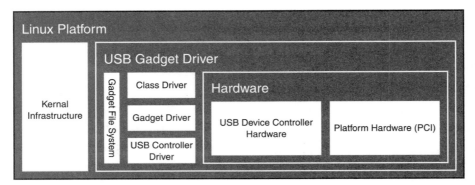

Figure 3.10
Linux USB gadget subsystem architectural view.

Figure 3.11
USB gadget support option in menuconfig.

Device Drivers, USB Support, USB Gadget Support. You can find the USB Gadget Support option inside the USB Support option of the menuconfig, as shown in Figure 3.11.

```
menuconfig USB_GADGET
        tristate "USB Gadget Support"
```

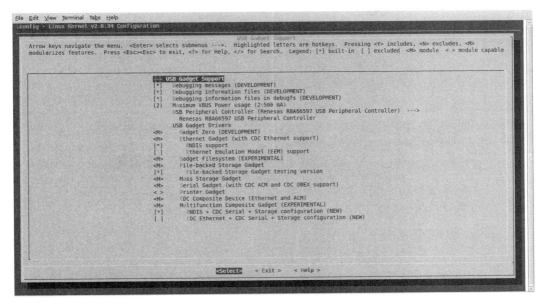

Figure 3.12
Various USB gadget options in menuconfig.

The section that follows details some of the prominent configuration options of the gadget framework. Compared to the USB host configuration, the gadget configuration is simple, with fewer options. Figure 3.12 illustrates the gadget subsystem configuration options.

The first step in configuring the gadget driver framework is to select the driver for the device controller that the platform supports. Unlike the USB host framework, the gadget framework supports only one device controller. You can select the device controller driver from the USB Peripheral Controller Support menu option, as shown in the following code that allows you to select one device controller.

```
#
# USB Peripheral Controller Support
#
# The order here is alphabetical, except that integrated controllers go
# before discrete ones so they will be the initial/default value:
#    - integrated/SOC controllers first
#    - licensed IP used in both SOC and discrete versions
```

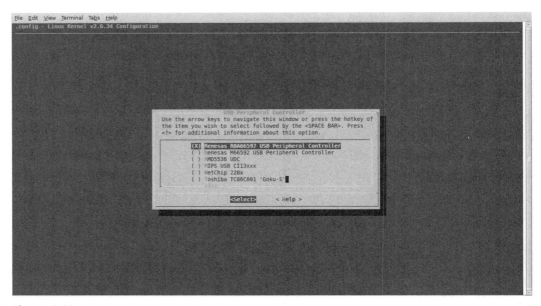

Figure 3.13
Various peripheral controller drivers available in the kernel listed by menuconfig.

```
#      - discrete ones (including all PCI-only controllers)
#      - debug/dummy gadget+hcd is last.
#
choice
       prompt "USB Peripheral Controller"
       depends on USB_GADGET
```

When you select the USB Peripheral Controller Support menu option, the menuconfig prompts you with the menu option shown in Figure 3.13, which lists the different USB controller drivers supported in the kernel. Selecting this menu option sets the USB device controller driver for the platform-supported controller.

It's important to have a debugging mechanism that provide insights on the gadget driver's activity. The gadget framework drivers provide debug information through normal print, which is enabled using the following option.

```
config USB_GADGET_DEBUG
       boolean "Debugging messages (DEVELOPMENT)"
       depends on DEBUG_KERNEL
```

Certain USB device controller drivers use the `PROC_FS` to export debug information to the user for debugging purposes. If your device controller driver uses a `PROC_FS`-based debug solution, try the following option.

```
config USB_GADGET_DEBUG_FILES
        boolean "Debugging information files (DEVELOPMENT)"
        depends on PROC_FS
```

Some USB controller drivers use `DEBUG_FS` to export debug information to the user for debugging purposes. If your device controller driver uses a `DEBUG_FS`-based debug solution, try the following option.

```
config USB_GADGET_DEBUG_FS
        boolean "Debugging information files in debugfs (DEVELOPMENT)"
        depends on DEBUG_FS
```

The USB gadget subsystem also exports the USB functionality of the user space to develop USB functional applications through the gadget file system. The following menu option enables you to enable the gadget file system. You can find more details on this in Chapter 16, "USB Virtual File Systems."

```
config USB_GADGETFS
        tristate "Gadget Filesystem (EXPERIMENTAL)"
```

The functional drivers are the next feature of the gadget subsystem. They are the implementation of class drivers. This also includes support to a composite framework that enables multifunctional USB devices. The most prominent USB class specification implemented as part of the gadget framework is listed in Table 3.2.

The composite driver framework is available in different combinations and is driven mostly by vendor-specific requirements. In the gadget configuration file, you can see various composite functionalities, mainly for devices from Nokia, Samsung, and Google's Android.

```
config USB_CDC_COMPOSITE
        tristate "CDC Composite Device (Ethernet and ACM)"
        depends on NET


config USB_G_NOKIA
        tristate "Nokia composite gadget"
        depends on PHONET
```

Table 3.2 USB Device Class Kernel Configuration

USB Class Specification	Gadget Driver Configuration

USB AUDIO class	config USB_AUDIO
	    tristate "Audio Gadget (EXPERIMENTAL)"
	    depends on SND
	    select SND_PCM

USB CDC class	config USB_ETH
	    tristate "Ethernet Gadget (with CDC Ethernet Support)"
	    depends on NET
	    select CRC32

USB RNDIS	config USB_ETH_RNDIS
	    bool "RNDIS Support"
	    depends on USB_ETH

USB Ethernet Emulation	config USB_ETH_EEM
	    bool "Ethernet Emulation Model (EEM) Support"
	    depends on USB_ETH

USB Mass Storage Class	config USB_FILE_STORAGE
	    tristate "File-Backed Storage Gadget"
	    depends on BLOCK
	config USB_MASS_STORAGE
	    tristate "Mass Storage Gadget"
	    depends on BLOCK

USB Serial port	config USB_G_SERIAL tristate "Serial Gadget (with CDC ACM and CDC OBEX Support)"

USB MIDI Audio device	config USB_MIDI_GADGET
	    tristate "MIDI Gadget (EXPERIMENTAL)"
	    depends on SND && EXPERIMENTAL
	    select SND_RAWMIDI

USB Printer devices	config USB_G_PRINTER tristate "Printer Gadget"

```
config USB_G_MULTI
       tristate "Multifunction Composite Gadget (EXPERIMENTAL)"
       depends on BLOCK && NET

config USB_G_MULTI_RNDIS
       bool "RNDIS + CDC Serial + Storage configuration"
       depends on USB_G_MULTI

config USB_G_MULTI_CDC
       bool "CDC Ethernet + CDC Serial + Storage configuration"
       depends on USB_G_MULTI
```

This section detailed various key menu options of the Linux USB subsystem of both host and device. Besides the menu options available through interfaces such as command line and menuconfig, explore the `Kconfig` and the makefile so you know the files that make up the module and can explore the correct files.

Summary

When you're working on large code bases, configuration management is the key knowledge to develop over and above knowledge of source code. The same applies to the Linux kernel so that you can effectively use the kernel's various modules. For example, if your platform supports only USB device mode, it makes sense to remove the USB host subsystem drivers. This enables you to effectively use platform resources such as memory and avoid conflicts on shared resources. The Linux USB subsystem provides comprehensive menu options so you can select required modules and skip others. You need to update the menu option when you write your own driver and integrate it with the kernel.

More Reading

To better understand the kernel configuration and to modify a configuration file, read the `Kconfig` documentation from `Documentation/kbuild/kconfig-language.txt`. You can also read about how to build the module `Documentation/kbuild/modules.txt` and the makefile `Documentation/kbuild/makefiles.txt`.

Part I

USB Host

CHAPTER 4

LINUX USB HOST DRIVER

In This Chapter

- Overview of a General USB Host Stack Architecture
- Overview of Linux USB Host Stack Architecture

The universal serial bus (USB) protocol is a host-driven system consisting of three major layers: the USB interface, the USB system, and the client software. The USB system software is implemented as part of the Linux kernel; the rest of the layer is outside the scope of this chapter. The USB system software consists mostly of the host controller driver (HCD) and a framework for the USB protocol. The system software sometimes adds functionality that is specific to the implementation, which makes the system more functional. You will learn about additional functionality that the Linux USB host stack provides in the subsequent chapters of this part.

This chapter initially explores the generic USB host software, detailing what a host stack looks like. It subsequently explores the Linux host stack architecture and provides a starting point to study the USB host stack.

OVERVIEW OF A GENERAL USB HOST STACK ARCHITECTURE

On a typical USB host system, the hardware implements most of the USB protocol and the physical layer. The system software consists of host controller

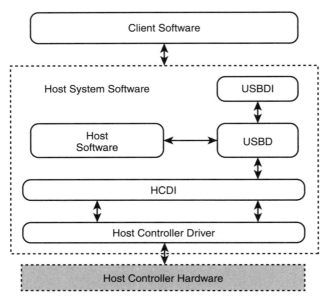

Figure 4.1
A typical USB host stack.

software and modules to manage device enumerations and data transfers, along with USB drivers that support USB devices. Figure 4.1 illustrates a typical USB host stack.

Host Software

The host software module implements the USB host protocol requirements of the USB specification. This includes detecting the attachment and removal of devices, supporting the enumeration process, and transferring data. The operating systems running on the platform for managing devices generally provide the host software.

USB Driver

The USB driver (USBD) module implements the necessary protocol interface between the client application and the system software—the USBDI—and provides the necessary interface between the HCD and the system software: the Host Controller Driver Interface (HCDI). The HCDI is designed to provide a generic interface between the HCD and the system software. This allows the system to work with any HCD without modifying the system software design. The USBD also implements the necessary infrastructure for transfer of data between the client application and the HCD.

HCD

The HCD implements the driver for Enhanced Host Controller Interface (EHCI), Open Host Controller Interface (OHCI), and other custom USB host controllers. It also provides the necessary abstraction to the hardware below. In general, the HCDs are based on the type of interface they use to connect to the main processor. On a personal computer, the host controllers primarily interface using Peripheral Component Interconnect (PCI); therefore, the HCDs are based on the PCI framework. On an embedded setup, the interfaces vary, depending on the system requirement and the interface availability.

OVERVIEW OF LINUX USB HOST STACK ARCHITECTURE

The Linux USB host stack consists of two major parts: the usbcore available in the /drivers/usb/core folder and the HCDs available in /drivers/usb/host/. The usbcore module implements both the host software and the USBD functionalities. Figure 4.2 represents the Linux USB host stack in a simple way.

usbcore

The USB system software module is named usbcore and consists of the following modules: device management, power management, USB hub driver, USB host driver, and HCD interfaces.

Device Management

As part of device management, the Linux USB subsystem implements functionalities that help manage USB devices connected to the host. The USB devices that are connected to the host share information via virtual file systems (VFSs) of Linux as part of the sysfs and procfs file systems. The devices also implement frameworks such as device notification, allowing the host system to report the addition or removal of devices to other modules.

Power Management

The USB specification defines methods to save power on USB devices and is implemented as part of the usbcore. The power management framework on

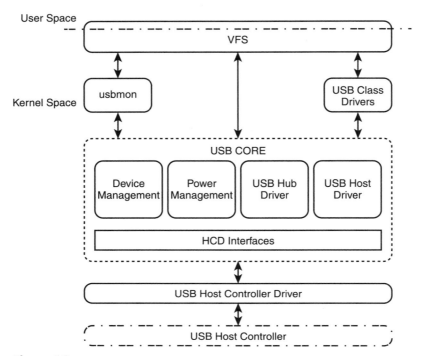

Figure 4.2
A simplistic representation of the Linux USB host stack.

Linux is part of the `usbcore`, which implements USB requirements such as remote wakeup. The power management framework also provides a VFS to manage the framework from user space.

USB Hub Driver

The USB hub driver framework implements the USB hub requirements and is part of the `usbcore`. The hub framework is responsible for resetting the device and announcing new devices to other modules.

USB Host Driver

The USB host driver framework implements USB transfers and other USB host requirements. The host driver also manages USB Request Block (URB) transfer from the class drivers to the HCDs.

HCD Interfaces

The HCD interfaces framework implements routines between the `usbcore` and the USB HCD, which facilitates URB transfer to the HCD.

Linux USB HCD

The USB HCD implements drivers for the USB host controllers. The USB host controllers are based on EHCI or OHCI specification or sometimes custom host controller implementation. The HCD implements the necessary abstraction between the hardware and the Linux USB system software: the `usbcore`.

SUMMARY

The USB host system software stack is complex compared to the device counterpart, because USB is a host-driven system. This chapter provided a brief overview of the Linux USB host architecture and a simple view of the USB host stack. The Linux USB host framework is layered and designed with clean interfaces that help you design similar software frameworks. The subsequent chapters detail the internal layers of the Linux USB host framework.

MORE READING

The USB host software architecture consists of application software and drivers that are specific to the operating systems. The application software is mostly USB-class specific; it determines the system configuration. The Linux documentation on the USB subsystem is available on `Documentation/usb`. You can read about how USB devices are notified of other modules in Chapter 5, "USB Device Notification." Chapter 6, "Device File System," offers a detailed study of the USB device file system. That's followed by USB host power management internals in Chapter 7, "Power Management," and USB hub implementation in Chapter 8, "Hub." You can take a detailed look at a generic USB host implementation in Chapter 9, "Generic Driver." Finally, you can study details of USB HCD implementation in Chapter 10, "Host Driver for Embedded Controller."

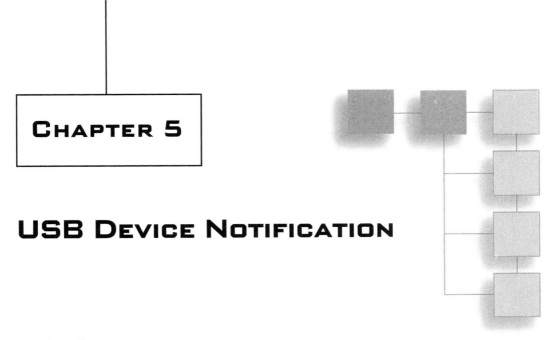

Chapter 5

USB Device Notification

In This Chapter

- Bootstrap: Notifier Chain
- Linux USB Notification

Request-reply (synchronous) and polling methods are common means of communication between software modules. Such methods reduce the performance of the system; they waste processor cycles. Asynchronous methods and publish-subscribe methods act as effective alternatives to address such performance-related issues. Linux uses publish-subscribe methods to communicate between modules. In the publish-subscribe model, the client (subscriber), which requires notification of a certain event, registers a callback function with the server (publisher). The server informs the client whenever an event of interest occurs through the registered callback. Such a model reduces the bandwidth requirement and the polling cycle requirement, because the client no longer needs to periodically request new data.

For a subsystem such as universal serial bus (USB) that supports hot plugging of devices, an effective message-passing system is important. Assume a scenario in which a USB device is plugged in to the platform, and the usbcore driver detects it. Once the USB device is configured to the usbcore, you need to create a Virtual File System (VFS) file. You then need to pass on this device addition message to the module that handles the USB file system. How does the Linux USB implement such a requirement to cater to these needs? Like a USB framework, many other modules require such notification methodology to enable them to communicate effectively. Linux provides a kernel infrastructure called the *notifier chain*; this infrastructure provides an effective mechanism for inter-module communication.

This chapter focuses on how the Linux USB subsystem passes on information with notifier chains to indicate addition or removal of a USB device. The first part of this chapter discusses the details of the Linux notification chain framework and subsequently explores the implementation of Linux-USB notification, with emphasis on its key data structures and interface methods. Later it covers the sequence of activities inside the Linux USB notification framework. Finally, to validate the understanding, there is a simple module that notifies of the addition and removal of the USB devices using the USB notification framework.

BOOTSTRAP: NOTIFIER CHAIN

Before getting into the details of the Linux USB notification framework, you need to have a basic understanding of the Linux notifier chain, because it acts as the backbone of the Linux USB notification framework. The `<kernel/notifier.c>` implements the Linux notifier chain and provides the necessary framework for the publish-subscribe model. The Linux notifier chain is like a simple linked list data structure with function pointer members. The function pointers hold the subscriber callback functions.

Based on need, the notifier chain callbacks are invoked either from a process context or from an interrupt/atomic context. Thus, the notifier chains are classified based on the context in which they execute and by the lock protection mechanism they use in the calling chain. The types of notification chains follow.

- Atomic
- Blocking
- Raw
- Sleepable Read-Copy Update (SRCU)

The Linux-USB framework uses a blocking notifier chain framework. This chapter explores only one blocking notifier chain and leaves other Linux notification chain features for you to explore on your own.

A blocking notifier chain runs in the process context. The calls in the blocking notification chain, as the name suggests, can be blocked because they run in a process context. The Linux network module uses blocking notifier chains to inform other modules of change in quality of service (QoS) value or addition of a new device. Thus, notifications that are not highly time critical can use blocking notifier chains.

The `<include/linux/notifier.h>` defines the Linux notifier chain framework's key data structures and interface definitions. The key data structure `struct notifier_block` offers a framework for the publisher module to extend events. The subscriber modules, which expect these events, register a callback for the extended events:

```
struct notifier_block {
int (*notifier_call)(struct notifier_block *, unsigned long,void *);
struct notifier_block *next;
int priority;
};
```

The `struct notifier_block` contains a function pointer for the callback functions, and the list extends provision for multiple subscribers. The `priority` field creates a sorted list of the notifier requests.

The modules (publisher) that provide notification support also have to maintain a list head to manage and traverse the notification list. The `<include/linux/notifier.h>` file defines the prototype of this blocking notifier head as `struct blocking_notifier_head`.

```
struct blocking_notifier_head {
        struct rw_semaphore rwsem;
        struct notifier_block *head;
};
```

The structure maintains a head pointer pointing to the list of subscribers and a semaphore to avoid a race condition.

The Linux notifier chains subsystem also provides interface functions to add and delete `struct notifier_block` objects to and from the head of the list. Any subscriber can add to the head of the publisher module's list by using the `block_notifier_chain_register` application programming interface (API). You can delete from the list using `blocking_notifier_chain_unregister`, where * is the type of notifier chain.

N o t e

Network drivers often use the notification chain framework.

The `blocking_notifier_chain_register` method operates like a simple linked list program. The method adds the `struct notifier_block` to the `blocking_notifier_head` based on the priority set in the notifier block:

```
int blocking_notifier_chain_register(struct blocking_notifier_head *nh, struct notifier_block *nb);
```

You can use `blocking_notifier_chain_unregister`, provided by the notifier framework, to remove the registered `struct notifier_block` callback from the list head:

```
int blocking_notifier_chain_unregister(struct blocking_notifier_head *nh, struct notifier_block *nb);
```

Once you have successfully created the notifier chain, the callbacks have to be executed when a particular event occurs. The `blocking_notifier_call_chain` interface function calls the registered callback functions. This interface function takes the notifier chain head and traverses it to call the registered functions. The other parameter, `void pointer *v`, is passed on to the subscriber with an `unsigned long val` to indicate the type of event:

```
int blocking_notifier_call_chain(struct blocking_notifier_head *nh, unsigned long val, void *v);
```

Having seen an overview of the notifier chain framework, now you'll see how the Linux USB subsystem uses the notifier chain framework for communication between different modules.

Linux USB Notification

The Linux-USB notification framework is part of the `usbcore` functionality, and its key functionality is to communicate addition or removal of a USB device/bus to other modules, such as the file system or class framework. You can find the USB notification framework's data structure definitions in `linux/usb.h` and the functional implementation in `/drivers/usb/core/notify.c`.

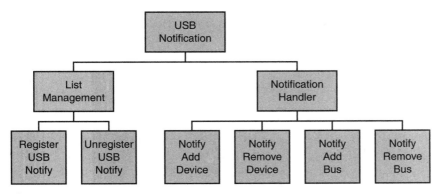

Figure 5.1
Functional breakdown of the USB notification.

A top-down breakdown of this framework would look like Figure 5.1. You can visualize this framework as routines that manage the list and routines that handle notifications.

The routines that manage the lists are exported and act as an interface. These interface functions enable modules to register their callback functions and thereby receive USB device notification.

Having seen the breakdown of the USB notification module, you'll now explore the key data structures, API, and internals.

The notification handler extends support for four events: addition of a USB device, addition of a USB bus, removal of a USB device, and removal of a USB bus. These events are defined by linux/usb.h and are illustrated next. They originate from the usbcore module and subsequently are passed to the other USB modules:

```
/* Events from the usb core */
#define USB_DEVICE_ADD          0x0001 (Represents addition of a USB device)
#define USB_DEVICE_REMOVE       0x0002 (Represents removal of a USB device)
#define USB_BUS_ADD             0x0003 (Represents addition of a USB bus)
#define USB_BUS_REMOVE          0x0004 (Represents removal of a USB bus)
```

While using a notifier chain, the first step in the process is to define a head of the notification list. The USB notification framework uses a blocking notifier chain to pass on the device notifications, because the information is not that time critical. The notify.c declares a notification list head usb_notifier_list of type struct blocking_notifier_notifier_head to maintain information on the list of callbacks registered:

```
static BLOCKING_NOTIFIER_HEAD(usb_notifier_list);
```

Other routines further use this head notification link to register and manage the notification list.

Now you'll look at the functions that act on the list. The usb_register_notify interface function adds the notifier_block passed on to the head pointer usb_notifier_list, using the blocking_notifier_chain_register function. The blocking_notifier_chain_register, which was discussed in the previous section, takes care of the insertion into the list based on the priority set in the struct notifier_block:

```
void usb_register_notify(struct notifier_block *nb)
{
    blocking_notifier_chain_register(&usb_notifier_list, nb);
}
EXPORT_SYMBOL_GPL(usb_register_notify);
```

The usb_unregister_notify interface function allows other subsystems to remove a struct notifier_block object from the usb_notifier_list, and the routine internally uses blocking_notifier_chain_unregister provided by the Linux notification subsystem to remove the struct notifier_block object.

```
void usb_unregister_notify(struct notifier_block *nb)
{
    blocking_notifier_chain_unregister(&usb_notifier_list, nb);
}
EXPORT_SYMBOL_GPL(usb_unregister_notify);
```

With these interface routines, other subscribing modules can register their notifier blocks with the USB notification subsystem. Recall from the previous sections that this subsystem publishes four notification events: USB_DEVICE_ADD, USB_DEVICE_REMOVE, USB_BUS_ADD, and USB_BUS_REMOVE. When these events occur, the publisher must notify the subscriber. To do this, the Linux notifier framework uses a blocking_notifier_call_chain interface routine. The USB notification module exports the following four routines to notify these USB events.

```
void usb_notify_add_device(struct usb_device *udev)
{
    blocking_notifier_call_chain(&usb_notifier_list, USB_DEVICE_ADD, udev);
```

```
}
void usb_notify_remove_device(struct usb_device *udev)
{
  /* Protect against simultaneous usbfs open */
  mutex_lock(&usbfs_mutex);
  blocking_notifier_call_chain(&usb_notifier_list,USB_DEVICE_REMOVE, udev);
  mutex_unlock(&usbfs_mutex);
}
void usb_notify_add_bus(struct usb_bus *ubus)
{
  blocking_notifier_call_chain(&usb_notifier_list, USB_BUS_ADD, ubus);
}
void usb_notify_remove_bus(struct usb_bus *ubus)
{
  blocking_notifier_call_chain(&usb_notifier_list, USB_BUS_REMOVE, ubus);
}
```

These four routines internally use `blocking_notifier_call_chain` to traverse the `usb_notifier_list` and invoke the subscriber's routine registered.

In the Linux USB subsystem, the subscribers of these events are device file system, class file system, and USB monitor modules. More detail on how the modules use these notifications is discussed in the respective chapters. This chapter focuses on the sequence of activities between the USB notification module and its subscribers.

The USB notification framework is part of the `usbcore` and acts as an interface between the `usbcore` and the frameworks interested in USB events, such as addition and removal of USB devices. Thus, the USB notification framework's role is to pass on information from the `usbcore` to other interested modules. The following section contains sequence diagrams to explain the sequence of activities between the USB notification framework and other modules.

The first step in getting the USB events is to register with the notification framework. The subscriber module can register its notification block using the `usb_register_notify` interface function. Figure 5.2 illustrates three frameworks of the Linux USB subsystem registering their notification blocks with the USB notification framework.

Once the registration is successful, the framework is ready to receive the USB events. When a USB device is connected to the platform, the `usbcore`'s

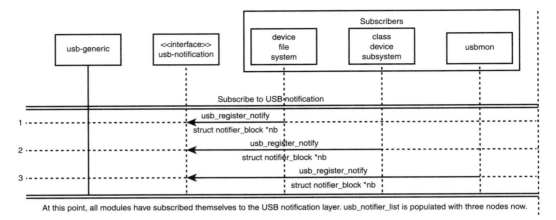

Figure 5.2
Sequence of activities when modules subscribe for USB notification.

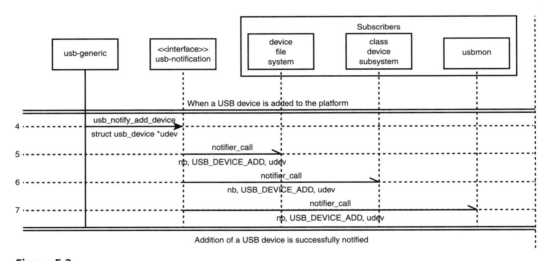

Figure 5.3
Sequence of activities when a device is added to the system.

usb-generic framework sets up the device and notifies the USB notification framework using `usb_notify_add_device` interface function. This function traverses the `usb_notification_list` using the `blocking_notifier_call_chain` function to pass on the `USB_DEVICE_ADD` information to the subscriber modules. Figure 5.3 illustrates how the USB addition event traverses to the subscriber from the usb-generic framework.

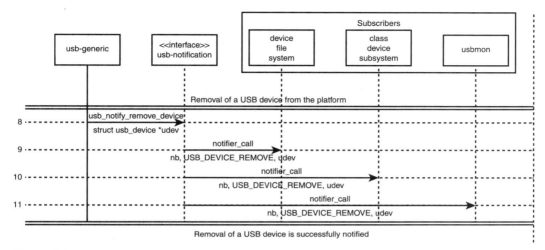

Figure 5.4
Sequence of activities when a device is removed from the system.

Similarly, the usb-generic framework handles any USB device removal as illustrated in Figure 5.4. It passes on the device removal using the usb_notify_remove_device interface function. This function internally traverses the usb_notification_list using the blocking_notifier_call_chain function to pass on the USB_DEVICE_REMOVE information to the subscriber modules.

When the modules are no longer using the USB events, they have to unsubscribe from the USB notification framework. The subscriber modules can unregister their notification block using the usb_unregister_notify interface function. Figure 5.5 illustrates three frameworks of the Linux USB subsystem unregistering their notification blocks with the USB notification framework.

Writing a Simple USB Notification-Subscriber

In the preceding sections, you learned about the USB notification framework. In this section, you learn how to use this framework to receive information about addition and removal of a USB device. To achieve this, you have to write a simple module that subscribes itself to the USB notification framework and prints a message when a device is added or removed.

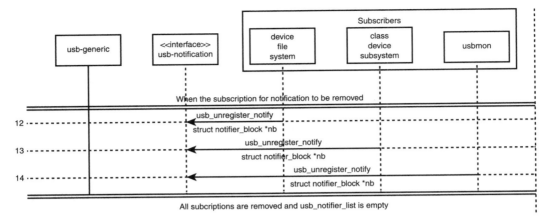

Figure 5.5
Sequence of activities when a subscriber unregisters from USB notification.

The first step in the process is to define a callback function of type int
(*notifier_call)(struct notifier_block *, unsigned long, void *), say usb_
notify_subscriber as shown later.

The callback function receives a pointer to a struct notifier_block, an
unsigned long value, and a void pointer. The struct notifier_block is the
object that was used when subscribing to the notification framework, the
unsigned long is the notification code providing information on the notification,
and the void pointer is either struct usb_device or struct usb_bus based on the
type of notification.

```
#include <linux/module.h>
#include <linux/kernel.h>
#include <linux/usb.h>
static int usb_notify_subscriber(struct notifier_block *self, unsigned long
action, void *dev)
{
        printk(KERN_INFO "usb_notify_subscriber \n");
        switch (action) {
                case USB_DEVICE_ADD:
                        printk(KERN_INFO "usb_notify_subscriber:USB
                        device added \n");
                        break;
                case USB_DEVICE_REMOVE:
```

```
                printk(KERN_INFO "usb_notify_subscriber:USB
                device removed \n");
                break;
        case USB_BUS_ADD:
                printk(KERN_INFO "usb_notify_subscriber:USB Bus
                added \n");
                break;
        case USB_BUS_REMOVE:
                printk(KERN_INFO "usb_notify_subscriber:USB Bus
                removed \n");
        }
        return NOTIFY_OK;
}
```

In the next step, declare a `struct notifier_block` type variable, say `usb_nb` as shown next. Initialize the `notifier_call` member variable of `usb_nb` with the handler function `usb_notify_hook`:

```
static struct notifier_block usb_simple_nb = {
.notifier_call = usb_notify_subscriber,
};
```

You have successfully completed the notifier framework of the simple subscriber module, and you must register or subscribe with the USB notification framework. For this, you have to use the `usb_register_notify` interface method provided by the USB notification framework to add the `usb_simple_nb` notification block. This adds `usb_simple_nb` to the head list `usb_notifier_list`. Also, you must use `usb_unregister_notify` to remove `usb_simple_nb` from the `usb_notifier_list`. You accomplish these operations from the module `init` and cleanup routines shown here:

```
int init_module(void)
{
        printk(KERN_INFO "Init USB simple subscriber.\n");
        /*
        * Register to the USB core to get notification on any addition or
        removal of USB devices
        */
        usb_register_notify(&usb_simple_nb);
        return 0;
}
void cleanup_module(void)
```

```
{
    /*
     * Remove the notifier
     */
    usb_unregister_notify(&usb_simple_nb);

    printk(KERN_INFO "Remove USB simple subscriber\n");
}
MODULE_LICENSE ("GPL");
```

Now the code is set to receive the notification from the USB subsystem on any change in device or bus status.

When a USB device is attached to the kernel, the USB subsystem receives the information. It then uses usb_notify_add_device to call the registered subscribers. In the kernel log, you should be able to see the USB device added debug message that you had printed.

Save this source code as simple_usb_subscriber.c and compile it. A sample makefile to build the source is given next. With proper kernel module build setup, a successful compilation generates simple_usb_subscriber.ko:

```
obj-m += simple_usb_subscriber.o

all:
    make -C /lib/modules/$(shell uname -r)/build M=$(PWD) modules

clean:
    make -C /lib/modules/$(shell uname -r)/build M=$(PWD) clean
```

Insert the compiled simple_usb_subscriber.ko into the kernel using insmod and verify its successful insertion from the kernel dump, as shown here using the dmesg command:

```
[ 1573.812923] Init USB simple subscriber.

[ 1592.875806] usb_notify_subscriber
[ 1592.875810] usb_notify_subscriber:USB device added

[ 1602.891349] usb_notify_subscriber
[ 1602.891355] usb_notify_subscriber:USB device removed
[ 1853.970956] Remove USB simple subscriber
```

Now the subscriber module can start receiving notification from the USB framework. Add a USB device to the computer to see a `USB device added` debug message.

SUMMARY

Although the USB notification framework is a simple part of the `usbcore`, it is vital to pass on USB events. The USB notification module effectively uses the Linux notifier subsystem as its base framework. This chapter provided an overview of the Linux notifier framework and USB notification framework followed by an example. In the next chapter, you will learn about the USB device file system and how the USB device notification framework helps the USB device file system framework create device files dynamically.

MORE READING

The USB system architecture allows hot plugging of devices to the platform. Thus, when devices are added or removed at runtime, this information needs to be passed on to other drivers in the platform. A USB notification driver module satisfies this need using the Linux notifier framework. For more on the notifier block framework, refer to `linux/notifier.h`. To understand how this USB notification is being used, read Chapter 6, "Device File System," and Chapter 18, "Debugging Using Linux USB."

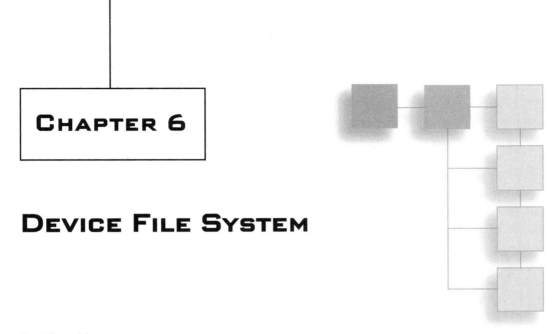

CHAPTER 6

DEVICE FILE SYSTEM

In This Chapter

- Bootstrap Essentials: Virtual File System
- Linux USB Device File System
- Creating the Linux USB File System

The Linux Virtual File System (VFS) is a thin kernel framework that provides a file system interface to the user space applications, allowing them to access the kernel internals. The Linux kernel supports different file system formats, such as Network File System (NFS) and Extended File System (EXT2, EXT3, and EXT4). The VFS provides an abstraction between different file system formats, thus creating the necessary transparency for applications to access the file information. Figure 6.1 illustrates a simplistic view of VFS inside Linux.

Linux developers are encouraged to create VFS files for the device instead of populating Linux kernel system files to share device details. The Linux USB subsystem also creates the VFS file usbfs, which produces files for universal serial bus (USB) and USB devices and allows user space applications to interact with connected USB devices.

This chapter initially explores the essential data structures and infrastructure for developing VFS. Subsequently, it explores the design and sequence of activity in the usbfs VFS implementation. This chapter concludes by implementing a simple VFS file for the Linux USB subsystem.

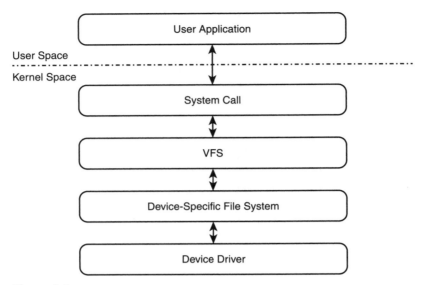

Figure 6.1
A simplistic view of VFS inside the Linux kernel.

Bootstrap Essentials: Virtual File System

In general, the Linux VFS framework provides an abstraction layer for the different file formats in the design. The Linux device model also uses the VFS framework to extend access to the devices onto the user space. The VFS framework uses four major data structure objects: dentries, files, inodes, and super blocks. These data structures are the backbone of any VFS-based implementation.

Note

> The Virtual File System Switch (VFS) is the more descriptive definition of VFS, because it switches between multiple file systems to seek information.

The super block data structure lies as the root of the file system. Any file system that is mounted is represented by a VFS `struct super_block` data structure. The definitions of the super block data structures are available as part of `include/linux/fs.h` of the kernel source package. A super block data structure typically contains a pointer to super block operations, information on block size, identifiers to the block device, and file-specific information. The `struct` `super_operations` data structure provides methods to manage an inode, beyond methods that manage the super block and collect statistics.

```
struct super_operations {
        struct inode *(*alloc_inode)(struct super_block *sb);
        void (*destroy_inode)(struct inode *);
        void (*dirty_inode) (struct inode *);
        int (*write_inode) (struct inode *, struct writeback_control *wbc);
        int (*drop_inode) (struct inode *);
        void (*delete_inode) (struct inode *);
        void (*put_super) (struct super_block *);
        void (*write_super) (struct super_block *);
        int (*sync_fs)(struct super_block *sb, int wait);
        int (*freeze_fs) (struct super_block *);
        int (*unfreeze_fs) (struct super_block *);
        int (*statfs) (struct dentry *, struct kstatfs *);
        int (*remount_fs) (struct super_block *, int *, char *);
        void (*clear_inode) (struct inode *);
        void (*umount_begin) (struct super_block *);
        int (*show_options)(struct seq_file *, struct vfsmount *);
        int (*show_stats)(struct seq_file *, struct vfsmount *);
#ifdef CONFIG_QUOTA
        ssize_t (*quota_read)(struct super_block *, int, char *, size_t, loff_t);
        ssize_t (*quota_write)(struct super_block *, int, const char *, size_t,
loff_t);
#endif
        int (*bdev_try_to_free_page)(struct super_block*, struct page*,
gfp_t);
};
```

The next important data structure is the inode or the index node, which may refer to a file or directory object. The inode holds file metadata information, such as the file length in bytes, file time–related information, and ownership. These VFS inode objects are allocated by a slab allocator from the inode cache that the kernel maintains. The inode objects represent both data files and device files and sometimes are stored on a disk.

```
struct inode_operations {
        int (*create) (struct inode *,struct dentry *,int, struct nameidata *);
        struct dentry * (*lookup) (struct inode *,struct dentry *, struct
nameidata *);
```

```
          int (*link) (struct dentry *,struct inode *,struct dentry *);
          int (*unlink) (struct inode *,struct dentry *);
          int (*symlink) (struct inode *,struct dentry *,const char *);
          int (*mkdir) (struct inode *,struct dentry *,int);
          int (*rmdir) (struct inode *,struct dentry *);
          int (*mknod) (struct inode *,struct dentry *,int,dev_t);
          int (*rename) (struct inode *, struct dentry *,
                         struct inode *, struct dentry *);
          int (*readlink) (struct dentry *, char __user *,int);
          void * (*follow_link) (struct dentry *, struct nameidata *);
          void (*put_link) (struct dentry *, struct nameidata *, void *);
          void (*truncate) (struct inode *);
          int (*permission) (struct inode *, int);
          int (*check_acl)(struct inode *, int);
          int (*setattr) (struct dentry *, struct iattr *);
          int (*getattr) (struct vfsmount *mnt, struct dentry *, struct kstat *);
          int (*setxattr) (struct dentry *, const char *,const void *,size_t,int);
          ssize_t (*getxattr) (struct dentry *, const char *, void *, size_t);
          ssize_t (*listxattr) (struct dentry *, char *, size_t);
          int (*removexattr) (struct dentry *, const char *);
          void (*truncate_range)(struct inode *, loff_t, loff_t);
          long (*fallocate)(struct inode *inode, int mode, loff_t offset,
                         loff_t len);
          int (*fiemap)(struct inode *, struct fiemap_extent_info *, u64 start,
                    u64 len);
};
```

The next important data structure of a VFS framework is struct file_
operations, which allows you to access the created files. The file operation
decides how to manage the information in the file. It offers methods to open,
read, write, and move file pointers using lseek operations. Files representing
devices may not support operations such as lseek. It is not necessary to
implement all methods.

```
struct file_operations {
        struct module *owner;
        loff_t (*llseek) (struct file *, loff_t, int);
        ssize_t (*read) (struct file *, char __user *, size_t, loff_t *);
        ssize_t (*write) (struct file *, const char __user *, size_t, loff_t *);
        ssize_t (*aio_read) (struct kiocb *, const struct iovec *, unsigned
long, loff_t);
```

```
        ssize_t (*aio_write) (struct kiocb *, const struct iovec *, unsigned
long, loff_t);
        int (*readdir) (struct file *, void *, filldir_t);
        unsigned int (*poll) (struct file *, struct poll_table_struct *);
        int (*ioctl) (struct inode *, struct file *, unsigned int, unsigned
long);
        long (*unlocked_ioctl) (struct file *, unsigned int, unsigned long);
        long (*compat_ioctl) (struct file *, unsigned int, unsigned long);
        int (*mmap) (struct file *, struct vm_area_struct *);
        int (*open) (struct inode *, struct file *);
        int (*flush) (struct file *, fl_owner_t id);
        int (*release) (struct inode *, struct file *);
        int (*fsync) (struct file *, struct dentry *, int datasync);
        int (*aio_fsync) (struct kiocb *, int datasync);
        int (*fasync) (int, struct file *, int);
        int (*lock) (struct file *, int, struct file_lock *);
        ssize_t (*sendpage) (struct file *, struct page *, int, size_t, loff_t *,
int);
        unsigned long (*get_unmapped_area)(struct file *, unsigned long, un-
signed long, unsigned long, unsigned long);
        int (*check_flags)(int);
        int (*flock) (struct file *, int, struct file_lock *);
        ssize_t (*splice_write)(struct pipe_inode_info *, struct file *, loff_t
*, size_t, unsigned int);
        ssize_t (*splice_read)(struct file *, loff_t *, struct pipe_inode_info
*, size_t, unsigned int);
        int (*setlease)(struct file *, long, struct file_lock **);
}
```

The preceding section covered the basics of the VFS framework that enable you to understand the Linux USB file system. Detailed information on all these data structures and methods is available in /Documentation/filesystems/vfs.txt from the kernel package.

The VFS infrastructure extends interface methods to add new file systems and to remove them from the kernel. The register_filesystem adds the new file system to the kernel. A successful operation returns 0, and failure returns a negative error code.

```
extern int register_filesystem(struct file_system_type *);
extern int unregister_filesystem(struct file_system_type *);
```

The `unregister_filesystem` interface method removes the file system from the kernel. Similar to `register`, a successful operation of removal returns 0, and failure returns a negative error code.

The `file_system_type` data structure used in these operations maintains the name of the file system, including getting and removing the super blocks. You can release and reuse the `file_system_type` data object once the file system is unregistered.

```
struct file_system_type {
        const char *name;
        int fs_flags;
        int (*get_sb) (struct file_system_type *, int,
                        const char *, void *, struct vfsmount *);
        void (*kill_sb) (struct super_block *);
  --cut--
};
```

Now that you've seen an overview of the essential data structures of the VFS framework, the following sections explore the Linux USB file system framework and the sequence of activities inside the USB file system.

Linux USB Device File System

The Linux USB device file system framework is part of the `usbcore` module. Its key functionality is to implement VFS files to represent the devices connected to the USB host system. The Linux USB device file system, referred to as `usbfs`, creates a `devices` file in the root of the mount path, directories to represent USB, and files to represent USB devices. The Linux USB device file system implementation is mostly implemented across the files of `usbcore`, mainly `drivers/usb/core/inode.c`, `drivers/usb/core/devices.c`, and `drivers/usb/core/devio.c`. In these files, the `inode.c` file implements the VFS framework, and the later files provide necessary file operations to allow users to access the file information.

Figure 6.2 represents a simple top-down breakdown of the Linux USB device file system. The framework consists of two main functionalities: VFS-specific operations and utility interface routines.

The VFS operations implement the necessary VFS framework, such as setting up the super blocks and inode and creating the Linux USB device files. The

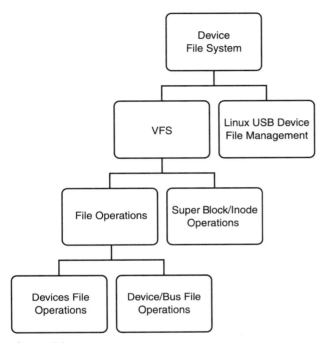

Figure 6.2
A simple top-down breakdown of the USB VFS framework.

framework creates a directory for each USB that's connected to the host and files inside the directory for each USB device connected to the bus. The framework also implements file operations to access the files created by the USB VFS framework. The framework includes utility routines that act as interfaces with the notification framework and module initialization.

The following section explores key functions and the sequence of activity in the Linux USB device file framework. The Linux USB device file framework provides interface functions `usbfs_init` and `usbfs_cleanup`. These interface function definitions are available in `drivers/usb/core/hcd.h`.

```
extern int usbfs_init(void);
extern void usbfs_cleanup(void);
```

The `usbfs_init` starts initialization and setup of the VFS framework from the `usbcore` module initialization. The `usbfs_cleanup` is called when the module exits to clean up the VFS files and notification handlers. These functions are available as part of `usbcore`'s `drivers/usb/core/inode.c` file.

During initialization, the framework registers with the USB notification to get events when new USB bus and USB devices are added to the system. The usbfs_nb notifier block defined as /drivers/usb/core/inode.c registers the usbfs_notify callback handler to collect addition and removal events from the USB bus/device.

```
static struct notifier_block usbfs_nb = {
        .notifier_call =          usbfs_notify,
};
static int usbfs_notify(struct notifier_block *self, unsigned long action, void
*dev)
{
        switch (action) {
        case USB_DEVICE_ADD:
                usbfs_add_device(dev);
                break;
        case USB_DEVICE_REMOVE:
                usbfs_remove_device(dev);
                break;
        case USB_BUS_ADD:
                usbfs_add_bus(dev);
                break;
        case USB_BUS_REMOVE:
                usbfs_remove_bus(dev);
        }
        usbfs_update_special();
        usbfs_conn_disc_event();
        return NOTIFY_OK;
}
```

The usbfs_notify receives four events that indicate the addition and removal of USB devices and USB bus. These events trigger the creation of USB files by setting up the VFS objects within the framework.

Figure 6.3 illustrates the sequence of activities during initialization and exit of the USB VFS framework. The USB VFS framework starts when the usbcore calls upon the usbfs_init. The usbfs_init function registers to the USB file system and notifier callback. The registration to the file system triggers creation of the super block objects. Similarly, during exit of the module usbcore, the usbfs_cleanup function is called, which successfully unregisters the file system and the notifier callback.

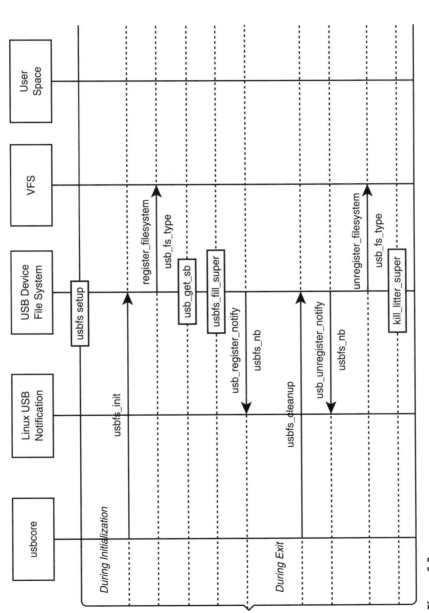

Figure 6.3
Initialization and exit sequence of Linux USB device file system.

The USB VFS framework creates a special `devices` file in the root directory of the `usbfs` mount path. Figure 6.4 captures the set of activities in the `devices` file life cycle. Other files of `usbfs` have a similar set of activities.

The `create_special_files` function creates the `devices` when the first USB bus is added. During creation, the file operation object that's required to access the file is passed on. This file operation object is updated to the inode created for the `devices` file and linked to the super block created earlier. The file operations of the `devices` file are implemented in the `drivers/usb/core/devices.c` file. When a user application reads the `devices` file, the `read` system call invokes the `usb_device_read` function registered through the `file_operations` data structure. Subsequently, the `usb_device_dump` prints to the read buffer and passes the information to the user space application.

The subsequent section explores how to create a Linux VFS based on the Linux USB device file system.

CREATING THE LINUX USB FILE SYSTEM

The Linux USB file system, referred to as the `usbfs`, mounts the USB file system from the user space. The following section explores how `usbfs` is created. The first step in the process of creating a VFS framework starts by defining the file system type and registering the file system with the kernel.

```
static struct file_system_type usb_fs_type = {
        .owner =         THIS_MODULE,
        .name =          "usbfs",
        .get_sb =        usb_get_sb,
        .kill_sb =       kill_litter_super,
};
```

The registration of the file system occurs as part of the `usbfs_init` interface function, which is called when the `usbcore` is initialized through the `usb_init` function.

```
int __init usbfs_init(void)
{
        int retval;

        retval = register_filesystem(&usb_fs_type);
        if (retval)
```

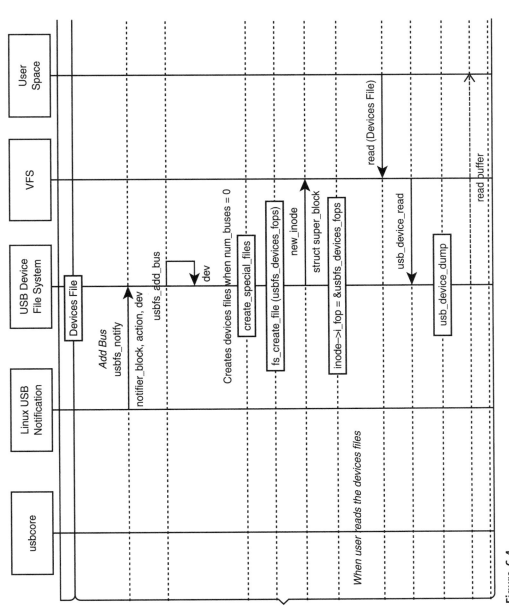

Figure 6.4
The life cycle of the devices file.

```
            return retval;
        --cut--
        --cut--
}
```

Notice the two super block callback operations registered as part of file system type data structure. These functions manage the file system's super block. The `kill_litter_super` callback is a generic function defined as part of the VFS framework, which cleans the data structure when the file is unmounted. The next step is defining the `usb_get_sb` handler function, which triggers the creation of the super block and updates the super block with usbfs-specific information.

```
static int usb_get_sb(struct file_system_type *fs_type,
        int flags, const char *dev_name, void *data, struct vfsmount *mnt)
{
        return get_sb_single(fs_type, flags, data, usbfs_fill_super, mnt);
}
```

`get_sb_single`, which the VFS framework provides, creates much of the super block. The `usbfs_fill_super` function passed on to the `get_sb_single` VFS function is called back, along with the newly created super block for updating.

You need to update the newly created super block with super block operations that are specific to the `usbfs` file system. These operations are generally used in the generic VFS framework.

```
static const struct super_operations usbfs_ops = {
        .statfs =       simple_statfs,
        .drop_inode =   generic_delete_inode,
        .remount_fs =   remount,
        .show_options = usbfs_show_options,
};
```

Generally, the super block data structures are set with a magic number to be recognized by the super block operations. The usbfs's super block is assigned with a magic number USBDEVICE_SUPER_MAGIC, as shown here:

```
#define USBDEVICE_SUPER_MAGIC   0x9fa2
static int usbfs_fill_super(struct super_block *sb, void *data, int silent)
{
        --cut--
        sb->s_blocksize = PAGE_CACHE_SIZE;
```

```
sb->s_blocksize_bits = PAGE_CACHE_SHIFT;
sb->s_magic = USBDEVICE_SUPER_MAGIC;
sb->s_op = &usbfs_ops;
sb->s_time_gran = 1;
inode = usbfs_get_inode(sb, S_IFDIR | 0755, 0);
--cut--
root = d_alloc_root(inode);
--cut--
sb->s_root = root;
--cut--
}
```

The next step in the process is creating the inode data structure for the root directory of the usbfs. The usbfs_get_inode(sb, S_IFDIR | 0755, 0) function call creates an inode for the root directory. The S_IFDIR indicates creating an inode data structure for a directory. The usbfs_get_inode function updates the inode with directory operations that are available from the VFS framework because the usbfs does not require a special directory operation. The following code from usbfs_get_inode shows the updating inode with directory operations.

```
case S_IFDIR:
        inode->i_op = &simple_dir_inode_operations;
        inode->i_fop = &simple_dir_operations;
```

Once you've set the root directory and its operations, the super block is successfully initialized. The next step is creating the files. The usbfs creates files for each bus in the host and devices that are added to the system. It uses notifier chain callbacks to create files for the devices and buses that are connected to the host. Along with these files, the usbfs creates a special devices file that lists information of the USB devices connected to the host. The create_special_files function creates the devices file and passes on the file operations usbfs_devices_fops required to handle the devices file.

```
static int create_special_files (void)
{

    --cut--

    parent = usbfs_mount->mnt_sb->s_root;
    devices_usbfs_dentry = fs_create_file ("devices",
                                    listmode | S_IFREG, parent,
```

```
                                            NULL, &usbfs_devices_fops,
                                            listuid, listgid);
        --cut--

}
```

After the successful creation of files, you need to define the file operations that provide access to the files. The `drivers/usb/core/devices.c` file implements the file operation callbacks required for the `devices` file.

```
const struct file_operations usbfs_devices_fops = {
        .llseek =       usb_device_lseek,
        .read =         usb_device_read,
        .poll =         usb_device_poll,
};
```

The `devices` file is read only. The read callback dumps information from the file to the user space. You can read Chapter 16, "USB Virtual File Systems," to learn more about the `devices` file's contents and how to use the information in the file.

SUMMARY

The Linux device drivers use the Linux kernel's VFS infrastructure to extend control of the devices to the user space. The Linux USB subsystem VFS files export information about the devices and allow you to develop an application from the user space. The next chapter explores the USB power management framework of the Linux USB host subsystem along with its usage.

MORE READING

This chapter briefly covered the Linux VFS. You can read more about the Linux VFS framework in the `Documentation/filesystems/vfs.txt` of the kernel packages. Also, you can read Chapter 16 to learn how to use the `usbfs` files. Furthermore, `Documentation/usb/proc_usb_info.txt` explains how to use the USB file system in user space.

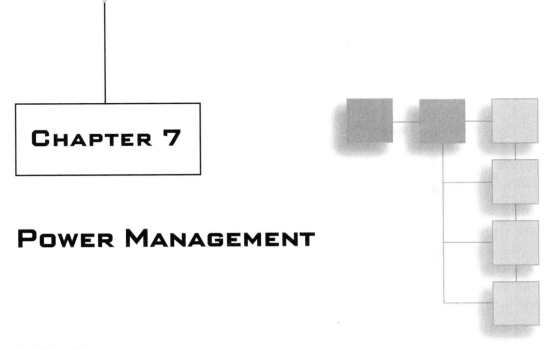

CHAPTER 7

POWER MANAGEMENT

In This Chapter

- Bootstrap Essentials: Power Management
- Linux USB Power Management
- Setting up Linux-USB Power Management

Power management is one of the key requirements for any embedded system. The USB specification defines power management methodologies for both universal serial bus (USB) devices and the USB host. A USB device saves power by going into suspended mode globally or at the interface level. The suspend occurs when there is no bus activity or sometimes depends on device class implementations. To resume a suspended host, the USB device may use remote wakeup. Not all devices support remote wakeup; that capability is passed on to the host along with the configuration descriptor.

The USB host power management depends greatly on the host system software's (Microsoft Windows and Linux) power management framework. The Linux kernel implements the necessary power management framework that enables peripheral subsystems such as the Linux USB system to effectively manage power. This chapter starts with a quick bootstrap on Linux power management, subsequently explores the Linux USB host subsystem's power management internals and sequence of activities, and finally provides a practical session on its usage.

BOOTSTRAP ESSENTIALS: POWER MANAGEMENT

Linux power management has two different models for power management: the system sleep model and the runtime power management model. In the system sleep model, the complete system goes to a low power model by interacting with various buses, devices, or class drivers. Individual drivers can also go into power save mode when the system is running, which is referred to as *runtime power management.*

The power management occurs in different phases, each having separate callbacks to be executed before starting the next phase. The phases involve bus, device, and class driver callbacks (dev->bus->pm, dev->type->pm, and dev->class->pm). During a suspend operation, the callbacks are invoked in the following order: class, device, and then bus. During resume, the order of callbacks is reversed as bus, device, and then class. The following section explores these power management operations and utility functions, which are essential for subsequent Linux USB understanding.

The first important data structure that registers power management callbacks is struct dev_pm_ops, which is defined in include/linux/pm.h of the kernel source package. The drivers that implement power management use this data structure.

Note

It is not mandatory to implement every callback.

```
struct dev_pm_ops {
        int (*prepare)(struct device *dev);
        void (*complete)(struct device *dev);
        int (*suspend)(struct device *dev);
        int (*resume)(struct device *dev);
        int (*freeze)(struct device *dev);
        int (*thaw)(struct device *dev);
        int (*poweroff)(struct device *dev);
        int (*restore)(struct device *dev);
        int (*suspend_noirq)(struct device *dev);
        int (*resume_noirq)(struct device *dev);
        int (*freeze_noirq)(struct device *dev);
        int (*thaw_noirq)(struct device *dev);
        int (*poweroff_noirq)(struct device *dev);
        int (*restore_noirq)(struct device *dev);
```

```
        int (*runtime_suspend)(struct device *dev);
        int (*runtime_resume)(struct device *dev);
        int (*runtime_idle)(struct device *dev);
};
```

The `struct dev_pm_ops` also includes the device runtime power management callbacks, which you can use at the driver level to manage power.

Note

The new runtime power management framework was introduced only in 2.6.32 of the kernel.

- `int (*runtime_suspend)(struct device *dev)`

    The `runtime_suspend` callback takes the device to a low-power suspended mode that stops communicating with the system. The `runtime_suspend` can be executed only for active devices.

- `int (*runtime_resume)(struct device *dev)`

    The `runtime_resume` callback resumes the suspended device to a normal state. You can execute the `runtime_resume` only for suspended devices. Generally, the subsystem `resume` callback is responsible for resuming the device appropriately even without the `runtime_resume`.

- `int (*runtime_idle)(struct device *dev)`

    The `runtime_idle` callback sets devices appearing to be inactive to a low-power suspended mode that stops communicating with the system. When `runtime_suspend` callback is executed for a device, the `runtime_idle` callback will not be executed for the same device.

The power management framework also defines wrapper functions to interface with the device power management callback operations. These interface functions are defined in the `include/linux/pm_runtime.h` header file and exported from `drivers/base/power/runtime.c`. Some of the key interface functions of power management are listed here.

- `nt pm_runtime_suspend(struct device *dev)`

    The `pm_runtime_suspend` method suspends the device passed on by invoking the `runtime_suspend` callback. It returns 0 when successful and appropriate error codes such as `-EBUSY` based on the device state.

- `int pm_runtime_resume(struct device *dev)`

  The `pm_runtime_resume` method resumes the device passed on by invoking the `runtime_resume` callback. It returns 0 when successful and appropriate error codes such as `-EAGAIN` based on the device state.

- `int pm_runtime_idle(struct device *dev)`

  The `pm_runtime_idle` method notifies to suspend the device by invoking the `runtime_resume` callback. It returns 0 when successful and appropriate error codes such as `-EINPROGRESS` based on the device state.

- `void pm_runtime_enable(struct device *dev)`

  When the device starts, the runtime power management is disabled for all devices. The `pm_runtime_enable` method enables runtime power management for the device by decrementing the `disable_depth` field of power management info data structure.

- `void pm_runtime_disable(struct device *dev)`

  The `pm_runtime_disable` method disables runtime power management for the device and cancels all pending power management operations. Internally, the method increments the `disable_depth` field of power management info data structure to note the disable call.

- `nt pm_runtime_set_active(struct device *dev)`

  The `pm_runtime_set_active` method sets the status of the device and its children to power management active status. This method is unsuccessful when the runtime error and disable depth fields of device info are not 0 or when the device's parent is not active and has set the Ignore Children field active. In such a case, the method returns an appropriate error code such as `-EAGAIN` or `-EBUSY` to indicate the state of the device.

  Another important data structure of the power management framework is `struct dev_pm_info`, which holds key power management framework–related information. The device data structure adds this power management info data structure as a member. One of the most often-used members is the runtime `usage_count`, which holds information about whether a callback can be executed.

```
struct dev_pm_info {
        pm_message_t            power_state;
        unsigned int            can_wakeup:1;
        unsigned int            should_wakeup:1;
        unsigned                async_suspend:1;
        enum dpm_state          status;         /* Owned by the PM core */
#ifdef CONFIG_PM_SLEEP
        struct list_head        entry;
        struct completion       completion;
        unsigned long           wakeup_count;
#endif
#ifdef CONFIG_PM_RUNTIME
        struct timer_list       suspend_timer;
        unsigned long           timer_expires;
        struct work_struct      work;
        wait_queue_head_t       wait_queue;
        spinlock_t              lock;
        atomic_t                usage_count;
        atomic_t                child_count;
        unsigned int            disable_depth:3;
        unsigned int            ignore_children:1;
        unsigned int            idle_notification:1;
        unsigned int            request_pending:1;
        unsigned int            deferred_resume:1;
        unsigned int            run_wake:1;
        unsigned int            runtime_auto:1;
        enum rpm_request        request;
        enum rpm_status         runtime_status;
        int                     runtime_error;
        unsigned long           active_jiffies;
        unsigned long           suspended_jiffies;
        unsigned long           accounting_timestamp;
#endif
};
```

The data structure also maintains the device's power management states required by the power management core, which includes the device power management and the device runtime power management. These states are defined in the include/linux/pm.h file.

```
enum dpm_state {
        DPM_INVALID,
        DPM_ON,
        DPM_PREPARING,
        DPM_RESUMING,
        DPM_SUSPENDING,
        DPM_OFF,
        DPM_OFF_IRQ,
};

enum rpm_status {
        RPM_ACTIVE = 0,
        RPM_RESUMING,
        RPM_SUSPENDED,
        RPM_SUSPENDING,
};
```

This section explored some of the key power management framework data structures that are required when using the framework. The subsequent section explores key power management functions of Linux USB host power management along with an activity diagram of the Linux USB power management framework.

Linux USB Power Management

The Linux-USB power management framework is part of the `usbcore` functionality. Its key functionality is to handle low power states within the Linux USB host framework. You can find the host power management framework's data structure definitions in `<linux/usb.h>` and the functional implementation spread across the `usbcore` module files in `<./drivers/usb/core/hcd.c>`, `<./drivers/usb/core/driver.c>`, `<./drivers/usb/core/usb.c>`, `<./drivers/usb/core/generic.c>`, and `<./drivers/usb/core/hub.c>`. The power management framework is available along the `usbcore` only when `CONFIG_USB_SUSPEND`, `CONFIG_PM_RUNTIME`, and `CONFIG_SUSPEND` are part of the Linux configuration.

Figure 7.1 illustrates a simple top-down breakdown of the Linux-USB host power management framework. You can visualize the framework consisting of USB-specific power management routines and Linux-specific power management routines.

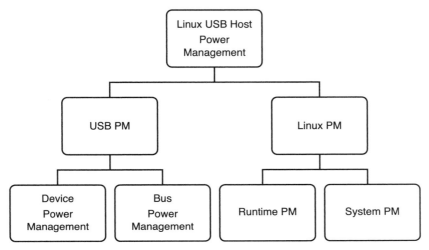

Figure 7.1
A top-down breakdown of Linux USB host power management.

The USB-specific power management routines deal with USB requirements such as power management–specific USB control transfers and host controller– and hub-specific requirements. The USB host power management also registers callback with the Linux power management framework to handle system-specific power management events such as the system low power suspend mode. The following section explores the key USB data structures, APIs, and sequence of activities of the USB host power management framework.

The USB power management framework defines `struct dev_pm_ops`–based objects `usb_bus_pm_ops` and `usb_device_pm_ops` to register callbacks to the power management core. The Linux power management core uses these callbacks to control the USB framework.

```
static struct dev_pm_ops usb_bus_pm_ops = {
        .runtime_suspend =      usb_runtime_suspend,
        .runtime_resume =       usb_runtime_resume,
        .runtime_idle =         usb_runtime_idle,
};
static const struct dev_pm_ops usb_device_pm_ops = {
        .prepare =      usb_dev_prepare,
        .complete =     usb_dev_complete,
        .suspend =      usb_dev_suspend,
```

```
.resume =        usb_dev_resume,
.freeze =        usb_dev_freeze,
.thaw =          usb_dev_thaw,
.poweroff =      usb_dev_poweroff,
.restore =       usb_dev_restore,
};
```

The USB power management framework supports the automatic suspend and resume feature of idle devices. To enable another host USB framework to use this feature, the Linux USB host power management framework exports interface routines. These routines enable other USB modules to communicate suspend and resume requirements to the usbcore.

- int usb_enable_autosuspend(struct usb_device *udev)

  The usb_enable_autosuspend interface routine enables a USB device for power management. It sets the autosuspend_disabled flag to 0 to enable auto suspend. The suspend takes place when the device becomes idle and the auto suspend delay expires.

- int usb_disable_autosuspend(struct usb_device *udev)

  The usb_disable_autosuspend routine prevents the USB device from going to low power suspend mode by setting the autosuspend_disable flag's value to true.

- int usb_autopm_get_interface(struct usb_interface *intf);

- int usb_autopm_get_interface_async(struct usb_interface *intf);

  Both these _get interface routines increment the power management's usage counter and auto resume if the device is suspended. The major difference between the two interface routines is that the async method can operate in an atomic context.

- void usb_autopm_put_interface(struct usb_interface *intf);

- void usb_autopm_put_interface_async(struct usb_interface *intf);

  The _put interface routines decrement the power management usage counter of the device and try auto-suspending the device if the usage counter is 0. Like the previous sync routine, you can execute this sync routine in an atomic context.

- `void usb_autopm_get_interface_no_resume(struct usb_interface *intf);`
- `void usb_autopm_put_interface_no_suspend(struct usb_interface *intf);`

The `no_resume` and `no_suspend` interface routines increment and decrement the device's power management usage counter. You can execute these routine in an atomic context.

Over and above these interface routines, the auto suspend and auto resume framework is controlled by module parameters. You can modify these module parameters from user space to control the power management activity. The following section explores the auto suspend and auto resume sequence of activities followed by system power management of the host controller.

Figure 7.2 illustrates an abstract activity of the USB runtime power management setup. The power management activity starts with registration of the power management callbacks with the Linux power management core. After a successful registration, the Linux USB framework activates the runtime framework using interface functions `pm_runtime_set_active` and `pm_runtime_enable` of the power management framework.

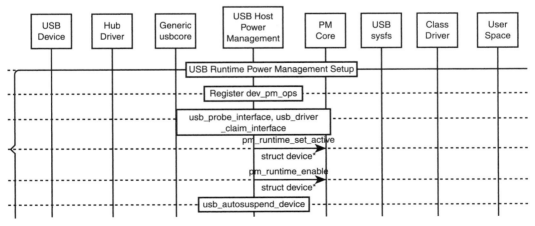

Figure 7.2
Initialization sequence of USB runtime power management.

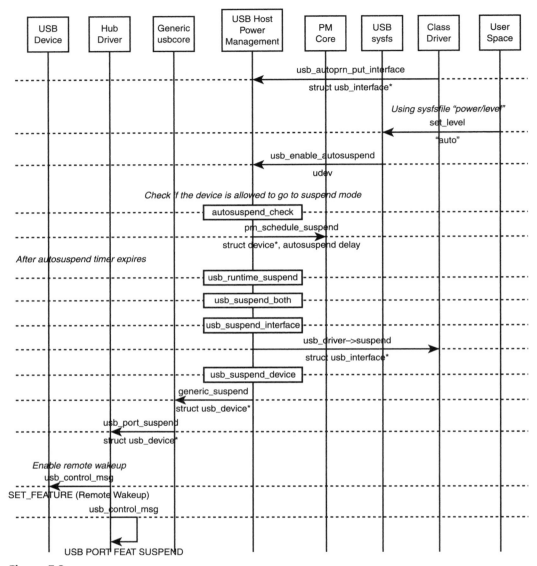

Figure 7.3
Sequence of activities during runtime suspend of a device.

Once the auto power management framework is registered and properly set up, you can manage the framework from user space by writing to the necessary files. Two major files, power/autosuspend and power/level, are necessary to suspend and resume a USB device. Figure 7.3 illustrates the sequence of activities that

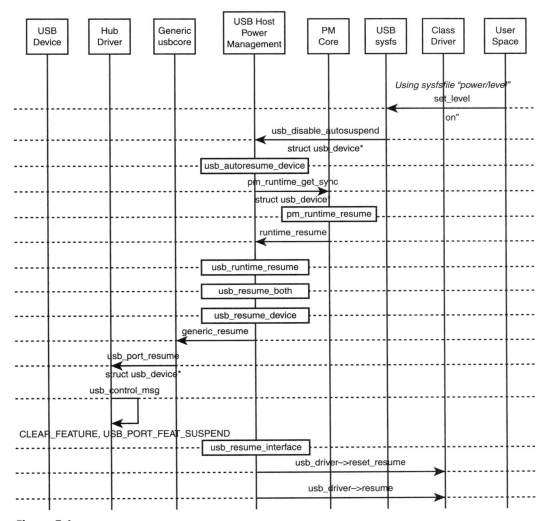

Figure 7.4
Sequence of activities during a runtime resume of a device.

occurs when suspending a USB device using auto suspend. During the process, only USB interfaces and the device activities are suspended.

A USB device can resume activity either from user space by writing to power/file or by remote wakeup activity. Figure 7.4 illustrates the sequence of activities that occurs when a USB device is activated through power/file. The resume operation is started by writing "on" to the power/level of the USB device.

The Linux USB host framework also includes system power management, which is executed with a similar sequence of activities. In a system power management activity, the suspend operation powers down the host controllers using host controller driver power management operations along with the USB connected device. The major difference in suspending a host controller is that the power management framework invokes hcd_bus_suspend instead of usb_port_suspend. To resume, the hcd_bus_resume is invoked instead of usb_port_resume. The hcd_bus_suspend and hcd_bus_resume internally invoke the host controller driver's bus_suspend(ex: ehci_bus_suspend) and bus_resume(ex: ehci_bus_resume) callbacks. These host controller power management frameworks are available as part of the host controller driver files in drivers/usb/host/*.

Having explored the runtime and system-level power management, the next section discusses the procedure to control USB devices using runtime power management with a practical session.

Setting Up Linux-USB Power Management

You can control the USB power management framework through the parameters exported by the usbcore and through the sysfs file from the user space. The USB power management framework is part of the usbcore module, and the autosuspend parameter is available in the following path.

root@rajaram-laptop:/sys/module/usbcore/parameters/# cat autosuspend

The autosuspend holds a default value of 2. The device goes to suspend mode after 2 seconds of idleness. You can modify the suspend time by updating the autosuspend parameter. When the autosuspend parameter is set with the value -1, the auto suspend operation is disabled.

There are other sets of files in the power directory of the USB device's sysfs directory /sys/bus/usb/devices. Linux 2.6.34 contains three main files to manage runtime power from user space: wakeup, level, and autosuspend.

- wakeup. This file indicates whether the device supports the remote wakeup mechanism. If this file is empty, the device does not support remote wakeup. Normally when the device supports remote wakeup, the file contains enabled or disabled.

- level. This file indicates whether the device can be auto suspended. When the file contains "on", it indicates that the device should be resumed and further auto suspend is not allowed. The other value auto allows the device to auto suspend and auto resume.

- autosuspend. This file indicates the number of seconds the device can remain idle before the kernel auto suspends it. It performs the same role as the usbcore's autosuspend module parameter. A negative value -1 written to the autosuspend file disables the auto suspend operation.

Having explored different options to control a USB device's power, the following section covers two different suspend/resume scenarios: auto suspend and USB activity when the complete system suspends.

The first scenario analyzes the activity of a single USB device's suspend and resume by capturing the USB transaction using usbmon and the kernel log. In the sample setup, a USB human interface device (HID) is connected to bus number 5 and device number 3. Capture the transaction in the 5u file as shown here.

```
root@rajaram-laptop:/sys/kernel/debug/usb/usbmon# cat 5u
```

When the auto suspend environment is properly set, the device goes to suspend mode after the stipulated time. You can resume the device by pressing any keys or by writing "on" to the level file in the power folder of the device.

```
root@rajaram-laptop:/sys/devices/pci0000:00/0000:00:1d.0/usb5/5-2/power# ls
-l
total 0
-r--r--r-- 1 root root 4096 2010-12-18 15:08 active_duration
-rw-r--r-- 1 root root 4096 2010-12-18 15:48 autosuspend
-r--r--r-- 1 root root 4096 2010-12-18 15:08 connected_duration
-rw-r--r-- 1 root root 4096 2010-12-18 15:08 control
-rw-r--r-- 1 root root 4096 2010-12-18 15:46 level
-rw-r--r-- 1 root root 4096 2010-12-18 15:08 persist
-rw-r--r-- 1 root root 4096 2010-12-18 15:46 wakeup
root@rajaram-laptop:/sys/devices/pci0000:00/0000:00:1d.0/usb5/5-2/power#
echo "on" > level
```

The usbmon and kernel logs capture this successful suspend and resume; the following section analyzes them. When the auto suspend timeout occurs, notice that the USB host sends a SET_FEATURE with remote wake to the device. Along with that, the host suspends the port using the SetPortFeature(PORT_SUSPEND) request, as shown in the log. At this point, after the two commands you might notice the power to your device going off to a suspended mode.

```
f69d2780 3679249639 C Ii:5:003:1 -2:8 0
f3d68a80 3679249721 S Co:5:003:0 s 00 03 0001 0000 0000 0 (SET_FEATURE)
f3d68a80 3679252636 C Co:5:003:0 0 0
f3d68a80 3679252655 S Co:5:001:0 s 23 03 0002 0002 0000 0
(SetPortFeature(PORT_SUSPEND)
f3d68a80 3679252662 C Co:5:001:0 0 0
```

Now when you look into the kernel log message using the dmesg command, observe the following log confirming auto suspend, which is a log message of the usb_port_suspend interface function.

```
[ 1200.001530] uhci_hcd 0000:00:1d.0: release dev 3 ep81-INT, period 8, phase 4,
93 us
[ 1200.004535] usb 5-2: usb auto-suspend
[ 1278.856178] hub 5-0:1.0: state 7 ports 2 chg 0000 evt 0004
```

The resume operation starts when you begin using the device, perhaps pressing a key if the USB device is a keyboard. Notice the usbmon capturing the host sending a Get Status request and subsequently Clear Feature for remote wakeup, which brings the device back to normal operation.

```
f5ecf100 3533577355 S Ci:5:003:0 s 80 00 0000 0000 0002 2 <(Get Status)
f5ecf100 3533581318 C Ci:5:003:0 0 2 = 0200 (Indicates remote wakeup)
f5ecf100 3533581361 S Co:5:003:0 s 00 01 0001 0000 0000 0 (Clear Feature remote
wakeup)
f5ecf100 3533584314 C Co:5:003:0 0 0
```

Also notice the log from the usb_port_resume using dmesg, as shown here.

```
[ 1278.856207] uhci_hcd 0000:00:1d.0: port 2 portsc 01a5,01
[ 1278.873041] usb 5-2: usb wakeup-resume
[ 1278.873077] usb 5-2: finish resume
[ 1278.879170] uhci_hcd 0000:00:1d.0:
```

The previous scenario analyzed selective suspension of the USB device. In a typical embedded platform, it is more likely to go to complete system suspend. The following section analyzes the data that usbmon captures when the system is suspended and resumed.

```
f3d6c300 2771040672 S Ci:5:001:0 s a3 00 0000 0002 0004 4 <
f3d6c300 2771040689 C Ci:5:001:0 0 4 = 03030000
```

```
f3d6c300 2771040703 S Ci:5:003:0 s 80 00 0000 0000 0002 2 <
f3d6c300 2771044688 C Ci:5:003:0 0 2 = 0200
f3d6c300 2771044722 S Co:5:003:0 s 00 01 0001 0000 0000 0
f3d6c300 2771047681 C Co:5:003:0 0 0
f69d2780 2771047710 S Ii:5:003:1 -115:8 4 <
f69d2780 2771052681 C Ii:5:003:1 0:8 4 = 02000000
f69d2780 2771052754 S Ii:5:003:1 -115:8 4 <
f69d2780 2771060673 C Ii:5:003:1 0:8 4 = 00000000
f69d2780 2771060748 S Ii:5:003:1 -115:8 4 <
f69d2780 2788091584 C Ii:5:003:1 -2:8 0
f3d91880 2788288758 S Co:5:001:0 s 23 03 0002 0002 0000 0
f3d91880 2788288765 C Co:5:001:0 0 0
f68f9580 2788344058 C Ii:5:001:1 -2:128 0
---cut---
---cut---
f3cfe200 2811478237 S Co:5:000:0 s 00 05 0003 0000 0000 0 (Set Address)
f3cfe200 2811480640 C Co:5:000:0 0 0
f3cfe080 2811498230 S Ci:5:003:0 s 80 06 0100 0000 0012 18 < (Get Descriptor)
f3cfe080 2811503641 C Ci:5:003:0 0 18 = 12010002 00000008 ca15c300 12050002 0001
f3cfe080 2811503651 S Ci:5:003:0 s 80 06 0200 0000 0022 34 <
f3cfe080 2811511641 C Ci:5:003:0 0 34 = 09022200 010100a0 31090400 00010301 02-
000921 10010001 22480007 05810304
f3cfe080 2811511650 S Co:5:003:0 s 00 09 0001 0000 0000 0
f3cfe080 2811514640 C Co:5:003:0 0 0
f3cfe080 2811514650 S Ci:5:003:0 s 80 00 0000 0000 0002 2 <
f3cfe080 2811518639 C Ci:5:003:0 0 2 = 0000
f3cfe080 2811518648 S Co:5:003:0 s 21 0a 0000 0000 0000 0
f3cfe080 2811521640 C Co:5:003:0 0 0
```

With a system suspend, notice that the resume resets the device and performs another enumeration.

```
[52353.772354] ehci_hcd 0000:00:1a.7: GetStatus port 1 status 001005 POWER
sig=se0 PE CONNECT
[52353.828063] usb 1-1: reset high speed USB device using ehci_hcd and address 2
[52353.832054] usb 6-1: finish reset-resume
[52353.832082] usb 5-2: finish reset-resume
[52353.884221] ehci_hcd 0000:00:1a.7: port 1 high speed
```

A complete log of the system suspend with host controller transactions is available on the CD-ROM. You can further explore the USB activities when system suspend and resume occur.

SUMMARY

Power management is essential for embedded systems, especially if they're battery operated. The beginning of this chapter explored data structures of the Linux power management framework that are essential to understanding the Linux USB power management framework, followed by details of the Linux USB host power management framework. This chapter concluded with details on configuring Linux USB host power management from user space. The next chapter explores the hub system software requirements and their implementation.

MORE READING

The USB specification defines the power management requirements for a USB system. You need to understand the power management framework of the Linux kernel; `Documentation/power/*.txt` offers further insights. In addition to these, `Documentation/usb/power-management.txt` and `Documentation/usb/persist.txt` provide information on the Linux USB power management framework.

CHAPTER 8

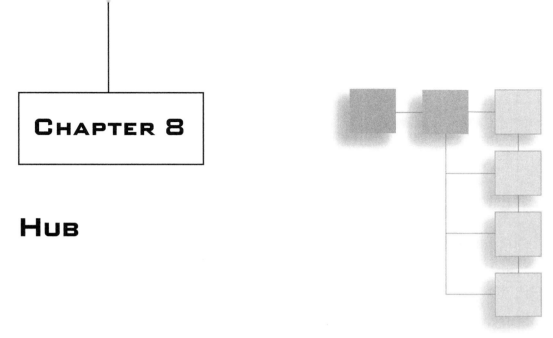

HUB

In This Chapter

- Bootstrap Essentials: Linux USB Hub
- Linux USB Hub Framework

The universal serial bus (USB) standard supports up to 127 physical device connections by a host. But a typical host computer supports a limited number of ports and thus can connect only a few devices. The USB specification defines a device model referred to as a *hub device* that allows a host to extend its port and connect multiple devices. A USB host controller is integrated with a root hub to provide one or more attachment points. Figure 8.1 illustrates a typical host, root hub, hub, and device relationship.

The Linux USB framework supports a USB hub as part of the usbcore module and provides a virtual root hub framework for host controllers. The Linux USB hub framework provides functionalities required by Chapter 11, "Hub Specification," of the USB 2.0 specification, such as hub event and change requests. The framework also plays a role in the enumeration process, such as setting the address, connection/disconnection, and reset, as well as in On-the-Go (OTG) functionality and power management of the Linux USB host functionality.

The next sections explore essential data structures required for the Linux USB hub framework. That's followed by the functionalities and activity sequence of the hub framework with other Linux USB host framework subsystems.

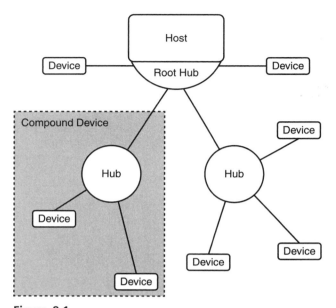

Figure 8.1
A USB host, hub, and device relationship at the physical level. (REF Figure 5-5 USB 2.0 Specification)

BOOTSTRAP ESSENTIALS: LINUX USB HUB

The hub provides the necessary electrical interface between the USB device and the USB host. The Linux USB hub framework offers hub functionalities; the key data structure of the framework is available in `drivers/usb/core/hub.h`. The data structures `struct usb_hub_descriptor` and `struct usb_tt` manage hub-related transactions, and `struct usb_hub` in `drivers/usb/core/hub.c` is used for internal information.

The hub descriptors are derived from the general USB Device Framework descriptors defined in Chapter 9 of the USB specification. The hub descriptors are defined in Chapter 11 of the USB specification. They define hub device characteristics and number of hub ports supported by the hub.

The USB Specification Table 11-13 describes the USB hub descriptor in detail. The following data structure `struct usb_hub_descriptor` defined in `drivers/usb/core/hub.h` contains this information about the hub descriptor.

```
struct usb_hub_descriptor {
        __u8  bDescLength;
        __u8  bDescriptorType;
```

The `bNbrPorts` member contains information on the number of downstream-facing ports the hub supports.

```
__u8  bNbrPorts;
__le16 wHubCharacteristics;
__u8  bPwrOn2PwrGood;
__u8  bHubContrCurrent;
```

The `DeviceRemovable` member variable indicates whether a port has a removable device attached. The Linux USB framework defines `USB_MAXCHILDREN` in `include/linux/usb.h`. The Linux USB framework supports 31 devices.

```
__u8   DeviceRemovable[(USB_MAXCHILDREN + 1 + 7) / 8];
__u8   PortPwrCtrlMask[(USB_MAXCHILDREN + 1 + 7) / 8];
} __attribute__ ((packed));
```

A hub is responsible for managing full-/low-speed devices when operating in high-speed mode; the Transaction Translator (TT) portion of the hub performs this function. This data structure is visible only in the hub framework to hub and high-speed host controller driver (HCD) framework.

```
struct usb_tt {
```

The `hub` member variable represents an upstream high-speed hub.

```
struct usb_device      *hub;
```

The multimember variable indicates the usage of TT from the HCD framework.

```
int                    multi;
```

The `think_time` member variable holds the Think Time value in nanoseconds as defined by USB Hub specification.

```
unsigned               think_time;
spinlock_t             lock;
struct list_head       clear_list;
struct work_struct     clear_work;
};
```

The Linux USB hub framework uses a data structure within the framework to manage events and other requests. Figure 8.2 illustrates the events, change information, and control information for the device. The `struct usb_hub` defined in `drivers/usb/core/hub.c` provides an infrastructure to store the information represented in the figure. The hub daemon `khubd` of the hub framework then manages this information.

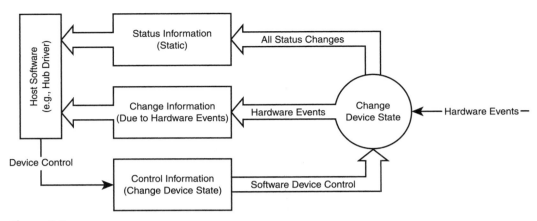

Figure 8.2
Hub events and system software relationship. (REF Figure 11-20 USB 2.0 Specification)

```
struct usb_hub {
--cut--
--cut--
        struct list_head          event_list;
        unsigned long             event_bits[1];
        unsigned long             change_bits[1];

        unsigned long             busy_bits[1];

        unsigned long             removed_bits[1]

        struct usb_hub_descriptor *descriptor;
        struct usb_tt             tt;
--cut--
--cut--
};
```

Having covered the essential data structures for the hub framework, the following section explores the key exported interface functions of the Linux USB hub framework.

- void usb_set_device_state(struct usb_device *udev, enum usb_device_ state new_state)

    This interface function allows usbcore and the host controller driver (HCD) framework to change a device's current state to the specified state. The function receives the new state and pointer to the device for which the state has to be applied. You must perform the state change with lock protection any time the device switches to `USB_STATE_NOTATTACHED`. Another framework should not directly set the state. It should use this interface function.

- `int usb_hub_clear_tt_buffer(struct urb *urb)`

This interface function clears the control/bulk TT state in a high-speed hub. A high-speed host controller driver informs the hub driver that some split control or bulk transaction failed and requires clearing the internal state of a transaction translator. This interface function is invoked from an interrupt context.

- `int usb_reset_device(struct usb_device *udev)`

This interface function resets a USB device after informing the registered interface drivers. The function performs a port reset, reassigns the device's address, and sets up the configuration. When there is a change in the descriptor value after the reset, the hub framework is informed as if the device has been disconnected and then reconnected. Internally, the `usb_reset_and_verify_device` performs the USB port reset to reinitialize a device.

- `void usb_queue_reset_device(struct usb_interface *iface)`

This interface function resets a USB device in an atomic context. The reset via this method is delayed to a work queue but is functionally equivalent to calling `usb_reset_device`.

LINUX USB HUB FRAMEWORK

The Linux USB hub framework is part of the `usbcore` module that is implemented in the file `drivers/usb/core/hub.c`. Some of the hub protocol and driver data structure definitions are part of `drivers/usb/core/hub.h`, and some are visible to host controller drivers. The hub framework implements a hub daemon, a kernel thread, namely `khubd`, which is responsible for handling hub events. The `usbcore` hub framework contains four functionalities, as illustrated in Figure 8.3.

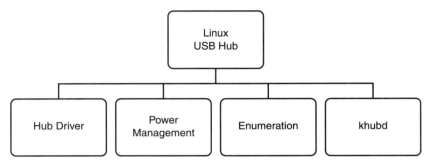

Figure 8.3
A generic breakdown of the Linux USB hub framework.

One important functionality of the hub framework is management of hub events and state changes through khubd. During initialization, this framework creates a kernel thread (khubd) that waits in an infinite loop to manage hub events. The framework also implements the hub driver that probes and identifies hub devices. The framework contributes to device enumeration and manages the enumeration state machine. It also provides infrastructure support for runtime power management, as discussed in the previous chapter. The subsequent section explores the sequence of activities that are internal to the hub framework.

The hub framework defines a struct usb_driver as part of the usbcore, which represents a USB hub device. The driver is registered with the usbcore module using the usb_register interface function during the usbcore initialization. The registered probe routine identifies a hub and successfully configures the device, after which you can manage the hub device.

```
static struct usb_driver hub_driver = {
        .name =             "hub",
        .probe =            hub_probe,
        .disconnect =       hub_disconnect,
        .suspend =          hub_suspend,
        .resume =           hub_resume,
        .reset_resume =     hub_reset_resume,
        .pre_reset =        hub_pre_reset,
        .post_reset =       hub_post_reset,
        .ioctl =            hub_ioctl,
        .id_table =         hub_id_table,
        .supports_autosuspend = 1,
};
```

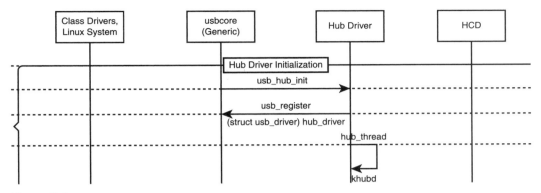

Figure 8.4
Initialization sequence of Linux USB hub framework.

Figure 8.4 illustrates the activities that occur during the hub framework initialization. The usbcore module starts the hub initialization, which involves the hub framework registering the hub USB driver with the usbcore module and starting the khubd to manage the events.

Another important feature often used at the application level is the USB device reset, which is managed in the hub framework. Figure 8.5 illustrates a simplified reset sequence whose key functions are represented in the sequence flow. The hub driver invokes the pre_reset callback before resetting the device and invokes the post_reset callback; the driver provides both. The driver learns about the reset through these callbacks.

Another important aspect that the hub framework manages is enumeration and device state management. Figure 8.6 illustrates the sequence of activities during the enumeration process.

The process starts with a state change in the hub's port, which the hub_port_ connect_change function manages. After successful enumeration, the hub framework adds the device to the kernel through the device_add interface function of the kernel device framework. The driver that matches the device takes control, and the device is brought to the configuration state. The enumeration

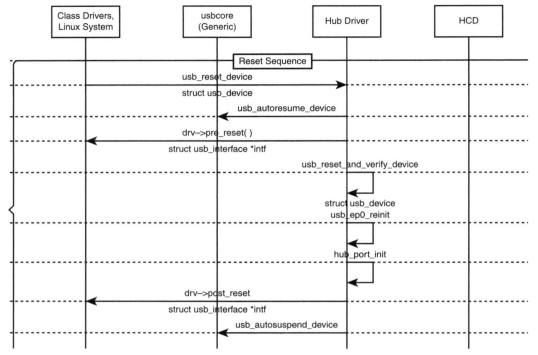

Figure 8.5
A simplified reset sequence involving the hub.

process for OTG devices is part of this path you can explore to improve the sequence.

The core functionality of the hub framework is the handling of events. Figure 8.7 illustrates the flow of activities inside the khubd while handling events.

The khubd waits in an infinite loop for any hub activity, which is notified through a kick_khubd interface routine. This allows the hub thread to come out of the wait state and process the new event using hub_events. After successful processing, the khubd thread hub_thread again waits for new events.

This section captured the basic functionalities of the hub framework.

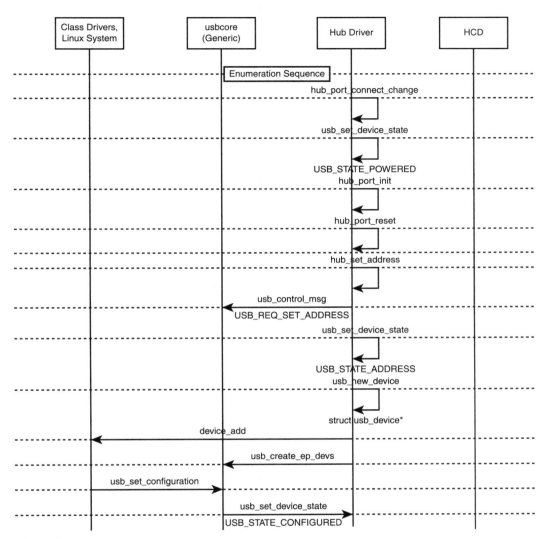

Figure 8.6
A simplified enumeration sequence involving the hub.

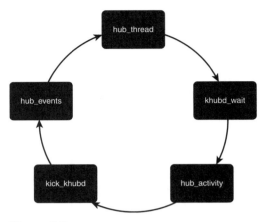

Figure 8.7
A simplified khubd activity flow.

Summary

The hub is one of the key functionalities in the USB topology, providing the electrical interface between a USB device and a USB host. This chapter explored the Linux USB framework's hub functionality and the essential data structures of the hub framework. The hub framework offers functionalities such as device reset to other frameworks, perhaps user space applications, through the usbfs file system. The hub framework includes a debugging framework that announces new devices. Check out the usbcore menu options listed at drivers/usb/core/Kconfig.

```
config USB_ANNOUNCE_NEW_DEVICES
        bool "USB announce new devices"
        depends on USB
        default N
        help
```

Chapter 9, "Generic Driver," explores the usbcore module functionality that provides the framework to manage Linux USB host functionality.

More Reading

To better understand the USB hub activity, read Chapter 11 of the USB 2.0 specification. You can explore the Linux USB hub framework for additional details on the enumeration, reset, and support to the OTG framework. You can also explore the hub driver implementation that supports interaction with the hub device and the khubd implementation.

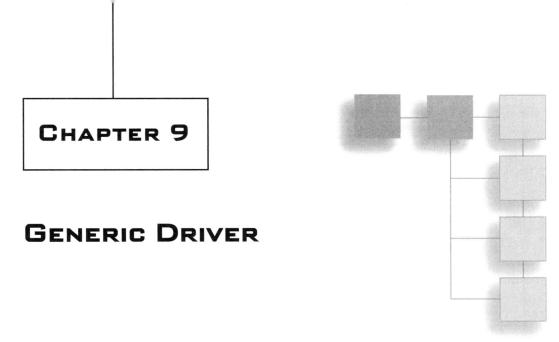

CHAPTER 9

GENERIC DRIVER

In This Chapter

- Bootstrap Essentials: Linux USB Generic Driver
- Linux USB usbcore-generic Driver Framework
- Developing a USB Device Driver

The universal serial bus (USB) host system software is responsible for managing control and data flow between the host and devices, power management, and enumeration. The USB host system software is complex, and the design is specific to the operating system. In Linux, the USB host system software module is referred to as usbcore, which implements these host functionalities. Previous chapters explored features such as power management, the hub, and other miscellaneous functionalities, such as the device file system. This chapter explores the framework that implements control and data flow of part of the system software along with the framework that develops class drivers. Figure 9.1 is a simple representation of this framework within the Linux USB host system.

Because this part of the usbcore module is responsible for most of the USB host functionality, we provide a hypothetical name for this framework, say, usbcore-generic for ease of reference. Initially, this chapter details the data structures required for the usbcore-generic framework. Subsequently, it explores the sequence of activities within the usbcore-generic framework. The chapter

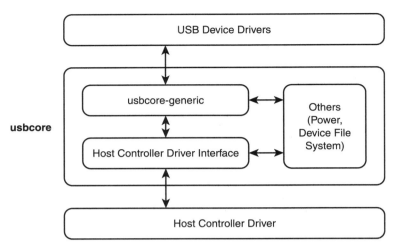

Figure 9.1
A conceptual representation of the usbcore-generic framework.

concludes by exploring a simple implementation of a driver based on the usbcore-generic framework.

BOOTSTRAP ESSENTIALS: LINUX USB GENERIC DRIVER

The usbcore's generic driver framework is responsible for managing the device, the device drivers, and the flow of information. The usbcore-generic framework uses the key data structures struct usb_device_driver, struct usb_driver, struct usb_bus, and struct usb_device, which are available as part of include/linux/usb.h. The framework also exports interface routines and provides callbacks to manage the functionalities. This section explores the data structures and the interface functions of the usbcore-generic driver framework.

The struct usb_device_driver structure identifies a USB device driver to the usbcore module. The Linux USB framework declares a usb_device_driver object usb_generic_driver in drivers/usb/core/generic.c that acts in USB device identification.

struct usb_device_driver {

The name field gives a unique name to the driver, which is normally the same as the module name.

const char *name;

The `probe` routine of the `struct usb_device_driver` identifies whether a particular driver is ready to associate and manage a USB device. The routine returns 0 on success and a negative value on failure.

```
int (*probe) (struct usb_device *udev);
```

The `disconnect` callback routine is called when a USB device is removed or the driver to it is unloaded and the device is no longer accessible.

```
void (*disconnect) (struct usb_device *udev);
```

The `suspend` and `resume` callbacks are part of the power management framework. They suspend/resume the device when the system is undergoing power management.

```
        int (*suspend) (struct usb_device *udev, pm_message_t message);
        int (*resume) (struct usb_device *udev, pm_message_t message);

   --cut--
}
```

The `struct usb_driver` structure registers the USB interface driver with the `usbcore` framework.

```
struct usb_driver {
```

The `name` field provides a unique identifier for the USB driver, generally based on the functionality it supports.

```
const char *name;
```

The `probe` callback routine identifies and associates the interface of a USB device with the USB driver. When the probe is successful, it returns 0; when it fails, it returns a negative error value.

```
int (*probe) (struct usb_interface *intf,
              const struct usb_device_id *id);
```

You use the `disconnect` routine when an interface is no longer accessible and the device is disconnected. The routine cleans up on exit and releases associated resources.

```
void (*disconnect) (struct usb_interface *intf);
```

The drivers use the `ioctl` callback routine to share information with user space applications.

```
int (*ioctl) (struct usb_interface *intf, unsigned int code,
              void *buf);
```

The following callback interface functions are part of the power management framework and are called when the system suspends or resumes. With reset_ resume, the callback is invoked when the suspended device is reset instead of resumed.

```
int (*suspend) (struct usb_interface *intf, pm_message_t message);
int (*resume) (struct usb_interface *intf);
int (*reset_resume)(struct usb_interface *intf);
```

The pre_reset method is called before a device is reset. This callback is invoked by the reset routine usb_reset_device(), which is part of the hub framework.

```
int (*pre_reset)(struct usb_interface *intf);
```

The post_reset callback is called after a device is reset. This callback is invoked by the reset routine usb_reset_device(), which is part of the hub framework.

```
int (*post_reset)(struct usb_interface *intf);
```

The USB drivers use the id_table member to support hot plugging. This must be set so that the driver's probe function is called.

```
        const struct usb_device_id *id_table;
--cut--

}
```

In the previous data structure, the member's name, probe(), disconnect(), and id_table should be set before usage; other fields are optional.

When a USB device is successfully probed and identified, you need data structures to represent it. The host controller driver uses struct usb_bus to represent and manage host controller information.

```
struct usb_bus {
        struct device *controller;      /* host/master side hardware */
        int busnum;                     /* Bus number (in order of reg) */
        const char *bus_name;           /* stable id (PCI slot_name etc) */
        u8 uses_dma;                    /* Does the host controller use DMA? */
        u8 otg_port;                    /* 0, or number of OTG/HNP port */
        unsigned is_b_host:1;           /* true during some HNP role switches */
        unsigned b_hnp_enable:1;        /* OTG: did A-Host enable HNP? */
        unsigned sg_tablesize;          /* 0 or largest number of sg list entries */
```

```
        int devnum_next;                /* Next open device number in
                                         * round-robin allocation */

        struct usb_devmap devmap;       /* device address allocation map */
        struct usb_device *root_hub;    /* Root hub */
        struct usb_bus *hs_companion;   /* Companion EHCI bus, if any */
        struct list_head bus_list;      /* list of busses */

        int bandwidth_allocated;        /* on this bus: how much of the time
                                         * reserved for periodic (intr/iso)
                                         * requests is used, on average?
                                         * Units: microseconds/frame.
                                         * Limits: Full/low speed reserve 90%,
                                         * while high speed reserves 80%.
                                         */
        int bandwidth_int_reqs;         /* number of Interrupt requests */
        int bandwidth_isoc_reqs;        /* number of Isoc. requests */

#ifdef CONFIG_USB_DEVICEFS
        struct dentry *usbfs_dentry;    /* usbfs dentry entry for the bus */
#endif

#if defined(CONFIG_USB_MON) || defined(CONFIG_USB_MON_MODULE)
        struct mon_bus *mon_bus;        /* non-null when associated */
        int monitored;                  /* non-zero when monitored */
#endif
};
```

The important data structure is `struct usb_device`, which the kernel uses to represent a USB device. This data structure holds the USB device's essential information, including the descriptors and endpoint details.

```
struct usb_device {
```

The `devnum` member variable holds the number assigned to the device.

```
int             devnum;
```

The `devpath` member variable holds a string value that represents a device ID.

```
char            devpath [16];
```

The state member variable holds the state information of the device. The state of the device is set using the interface function usb_set_device_state. The state can hold values such as USB_STATE_NOTATTACHED, USB_STATE_ATTACHED, USB_STATE_POWERED USB_STATE_ADDRESS, and USB_STATE_CONFIGURED.

```
enum usb_device_state    state;
```

The speed member variable holds the speed information of the device. It can hold values such as USB_SPEED_LOW, USB_SPEED_FULL, USB_SPEED_HIGH, and USB_SPEED_UNKNOWN.

```
enum usb_device_speed    speed;
--cut--
--cut--
```

The data structure also holds descriptor and endpoint information retrieved from the USB device.

```
struct usb_device_descriptor descriptor;
struct usb_host_config *config;
struct usb_host_config *actconfig;
struct usb_host_endpoint *ep_in[16];
struct usb_host_endpoint *ep_out[16];
--cut--
--cut--

};
```

Having explored the key infrastructure data structures, you'll now look at the interface methods that manage these drivers.

- int usb_register_driver(struct usb_driver *, struct module *,const char *);

  This method registers a USB interface driver with the USB core. It returns 0 when successful and a negative value on failure.

- void usb_deregister(struct usb_driver *);

  This method unlinks a USB interface driver from the usbcore. The method also updates the USB device file system indicating the unlink.

- int usb_register_device_driver(struct usb_device_driver *,struct module *);

This method registers a USB device driver with the USB core. This method returns 0 when successful and a negative value on failure.

- `void usb_deregister_device_driver(struct usb_device_driver *);`

This method unregisters a USB device driver from the `usbcore`.

- `int usb_register_dev(struct usb_interface *intf, struct usb_class_driver *class_driver);`

This method registers a USB interface driver with the USB core. The difference from the former is that this method should be called by all USB drivers that use the USB major number. This function also creates a USB class device in the `sysfs` tree. This method returns 0 when successful and a negative value on failure.

- `void usb_deregister_dev(struct usb_interface *intf,struct usb_class_driver *class_driver);`

This method unlinks a USB interface driver from the `usbcore`. This method is distinct from the former one in that all drivers that use the USB major number should call it. This function removes the USB class device from the `sysfs` tree.

The previous paragraphs explored essential data structures and methods that manage the `usbcore-generic` infrastructure of `usbcore`. Next you'll explore the essentials for performing data transfers.

The USB Request Block (URB) holds all relevant information to execute a USB transaction and deliver the data and status.

```
struct urb {
        --cut--
        --cut--
```

The `dev` member holds a pointer to the USB device associated with the URB.

```
struct usb_device *dev;
struct usb_host_endpoint *ep;
```

The `pipe` member holds information of the endpoint number, direction, type, and more.

```
unsigned int pipe;
```

The `status` member is valid for non-ISO transfer. It holds the status of a particular request.

```
int status;
unsigned int transfer_flags;
```

The `transfer_buffer` member points out data that is part of the transaction. This buffer is used for the data stage of control transfers.

```
void *transfer_buffer;
dma_addr_t transfer_dma;
struct usb_sg_request *sg;
int num_sgs;
```

The `transfer_buffer_length` member indicates the size of the transfer buffer.

```
u32 transfer_buffer_length;
```

The `actual_length` member is used in non-ISO completion functions and holds information about actual bytes transferred.

```
u32 actual_length;
```

The `setup_packet` member performs control transfers and points to 8 bytes of setup data. The `transfer_buffer` is read or written to in a data phase.

```
    unsigned char *setup_packet;
  --cut--
  --cut--
};
```

Now that you have an overview of the URB data structure, the following explores the interface functions that are necessary for URB management.

- `void usb_init_urb(struct urb *urb);`

  This method initializes a URB so that the USB subsystem can use it. If you create URB with `usb_alloc_urb()`, it's not necessary to call this method.

- `struct urb *usb_alloc_urb(int iso_packets, gfp_t mem_flags);`

  This method creates a new URB for a USB driver to use. Internally it calls `usb_init_urb` to initialize the URB data structure. On successful allocation, the method returns a URB pointer; when no memory is available, `NULL` is returned.

- `void usb_free_urb(struct urb *urb)`

This method frees the memory allocated after a transaction.

Note

The transfer buffer associated with the URB is not freed unless the `URB_FREE_BUFFER` transfer flag is set.

- `struct urb *usb_get_urb(struct urb *urb);`

This method increments the reference count of URB whenever the URB is transferred from a device driver to a host controller driver.

- `int usb_submit_urb(struct urb *urb, gfp_t mem_flags);`

This method submits an asynchronous transfer request for an endpoint. The URBs can be submitted in interrupt context. When `submit` is successful, it returns 0; when it fails, it returns a negative value.

- `int usb_unlink_urb(struct urb *urb);`

This method aborts or cancels a previously submitted URB for an endpoint. When successful in the cancellation of URB, the completion handler is called with a status code indicating that the request has been cancelled.

- `void usb_kill_urb(struct urb *urb);`

The method cancels a transfer request, and the method waits for it to finish. The method guarantees that all completion handlers are finished and the URB is completely idle and available for reuse.

Linux USB usbcore-generic Driver Framework

The `usbcore-generic` layer provides the essential framework to implement USB device drivers above the `usbcore` module and manage the device. It sits on top of the Host Controller Driver Interface (HCDI) within the `usbcore` module and acts as an interface to the preceding software layers. The source of the framework is available in the folder `/drivers/usb/core`. Files such as `/drivers/usb/core/urb.c`, `/drivers/usb/core/generic.c`, `/drivers/usb/core/driver.c`, `/drivers/usb/core/usb.c`, and `/drivers/usb/core/message.c` can be visualized

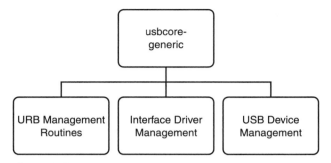

Figure 9.2
A simple breakdown of the usbcore-generic framework.

as part of this framework. Figure 9.2 shows a simple breakdown of the usbcore-generic layer of the usbcore module.

You can visualize the usbcore-generic framework as composed of three important functionalities: URB management, USB device driver management, and USB device management. The usbcore-generic framework includes essential data structures and routines that manage URBs submitted from the device drivers and user space applications. Along with the hub and host controller driver (HCD) framework, the usbcore core performs device enumeration. After a successful enumeration, the devices are managed using the struct usb_device and struct usb_bus data structures. The framework also provides routines that handle interface driver requirements and registration.

With these functionalities in the usbcore-generic framework, you need to understand two important activities of the usbcore-generic framework: the USB driver registration with usbcore-generic, and the life cycle of URB and how data flows between class driver/user applications in the host to USB devices.

Figure 9.3 illustrates the device driver registration with the usbcore using the usb_register interface function.

As part of registration, usbcore-generic updates the kernel device driver with its callback methods for probe and disconnect. Subsequently, it registers the device driver with the kernel framework. After a successful registration, the registration routing updates the USB device file system.

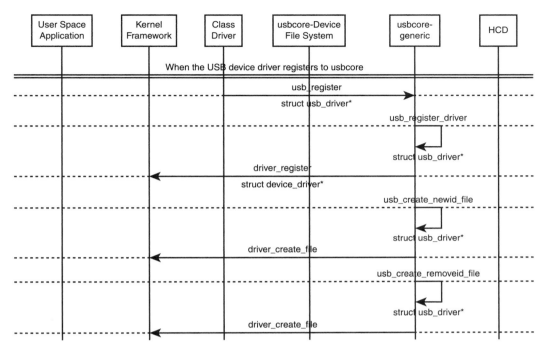

Figure 9.3
Sequence of activity when interface driver registers.

When a device detail matches the `struct usb_driver` information, the kernel framework invokes the callback method `usb_probe_interface` registered by the `usbcore-generic` framework, as illustrated in Figure 9.4.

This probe routine in turn invokes the callback registered by the USB driver. The USB driver prepares the device driver and associates it with the interface.

The `usbcore-generic` framework `usb_unbind_interface` method is called by the kernel framework, as illustrated in Figure 9.5, when the device is disconnected or unbound.

When a USB device unbind is triggered by the kernel framework, the `usbcore-generic` framework disconnects the interface and cancels the URB queue of the interface. Once the queue is cleared, the device data structure is set to `NULL` using the `usb_set_intfdata` interface. The interface data structure's state is then set to `USB_INTERFACE_UNBOUND`.

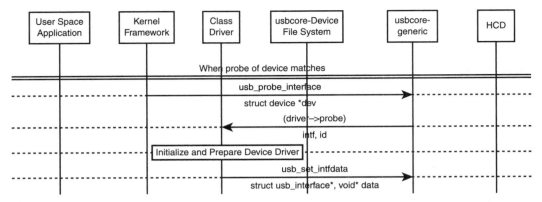

Figure 9.4
Sequence of activity on a successful probe of the interface driver.

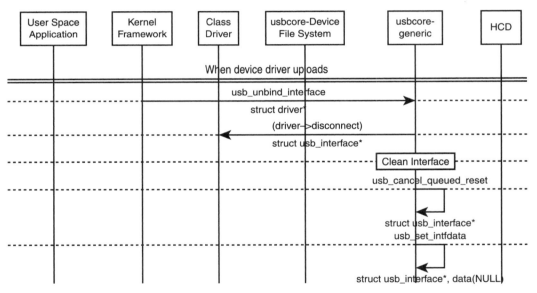

Figure 9.5
Sequence of activity when a driver unbinds.

The next important activity is the submission of URB by the class driver or the user space application through the device file system. Figure 9.6 illustrates a submit URB operation initiated from the user space.

The usbcore-generic framework allocates the URB, updates it with the necessary information, and submits it to the HCDI using usb_hcd_submit_urb. The URB

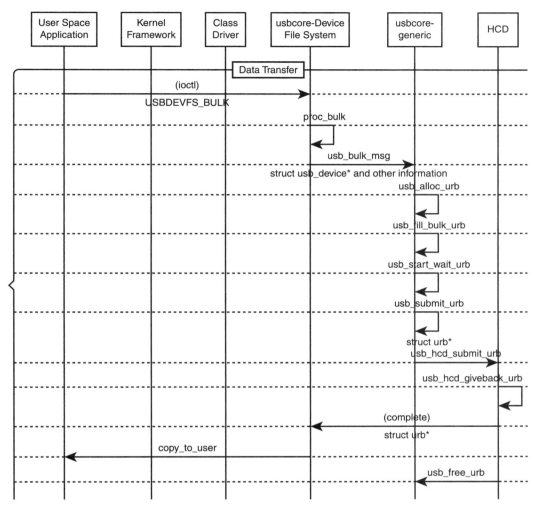

Figure 9.6
Sequence of activity during a data transfer over URB.

update differs based on the transfer type because transfers such as ISO and interrupt require time information. The completion is invoked, and the URBs are cleaned in the HCDI framework. The data for the user space application is copied to the appropriate buffer for the completion routine.

Note

Don't sleep in a completion routine, as it is called for hardware interrupt processing. You have to do minimal work within the completion routine by acquiring spinlocks.

Having explored the essential framework of the usbcore and the internals, the following section explains how to develop a USB device driver and integrate it with usbcore.

Developing a USB Device Driver

Many USB device driver implementations are available in the Linux USB framework. The usbfs, usbtest, and class drivers are the prominent device drivers of the many that exist. There is also a skeleton USB device driver, drivers/usb/usb-skeleton.c, within the kernel. The following analyzes the development of the device driver using the skeleton driver.

The first step in the development of the USB device driver is declaration and initialization of the struct usb_driver callback methods, as shown here.

```
static struct usb_driver skel_driver = {
    .name =      "skeleton",
    .probe =     skel_probe,
    .disconnect =   skel_disconnect,
    .suspend =   skel_suspend,
    .resume =    skel_resume,
    .pre_reset =    skel_pre_reset,
    .post_reset =   skel_post_reset,
    .id_table = skel_table,
    .supports_autosuspend = 1,
};
```

In the preceding initialization, the probe, disconnect, and id_table are the mandatory fields that are necessary to grab and release the device.

```
static struct usb_device_id skel_table [] = {
    { USB_DEVICE(USB_SKEL_VENDOR_ID, USB_SKEL_PRODUCT_ID) },
    { }                    /* Terminating entry */
};
MODULE_DEVICE_TABLE(usb, skel_table);
```

The `id_table` holds information to match the device of interest to the device driver, generally the vendor ID and the product ID.

Once the `struct usb_driver` is properly initialized, you can register it with the `usbcore` module using the `usb_register` interface function. This enables the kernel device framework to call back the probe function when the `id_table` matches.

```
static int __init usb_skel_init(void)
{
    int result;

    /* register this driver with the USB subsystem */
    result = usb_register(&skel_driver);
--cut--
}
```

When the device driver exits or is unloaded from the kernel, remove the driver entry from the `usbcore` module using `usb_deregister`.

```
static void __exit usb_skel_exit(void)
{
    /* deregister this driver with the USB subsystem */
    usb_deregister(&skel_driver);
}
```

After defining the entry and exit routine, you need to create the probe function of the device driver. The probe routine performs the necessary initialization required for the device driver and sets the interface to the driver using the `usb_set_intfdata` interface function. After all these successful steps, the device driver or the interface driver is registered with the `usbcore` module using the `usb_register_dev` interface routine.

```
static int skel_probe(struct usb_interface *interface, const struct usb_
device_id *id)
{
--cut--
--cut--
    dev = kzalloc(sizeof(*dev), GFP_KERNEL);
    if (!dev) {
        err("Out of memory");
        goto error;
```

```
        }
--cut--
--cut--

    dev->udev = usb_get_dev(interface_to_usbdev(interface));
    dev->interface = interface;

    iface_desc = interface->cur_altsetting;
    for (i = 0; i < iface_desc->desc.bNumEndpoints; ++i) {
        endpoint = &iface_desc->endpoint[i].desc;

--cut--
    usb_set_intfdata(interface, dev);

    /* we can register the device now, as it is ready */
    retval = usb_register_dev(interface, &skel_class);
--cut--
--cut--
    }
```

A successful registration allows the driver to take control of the interface and start communicating with the device.

When the device is disconnected or becomes unbound, the disconnect callback method is invoked. The disconnect callback should release the acquired resources and return the interface taken earlier. After successful release of resources, the driver should be deregistered from the usbcore using the interface functions.

```
static void skel_disconnect(struct usb_interface *interface)
{
--cut--
--cut--
    dev = usb_get_intfdata(interface);
    usb_set_intfdata(interface, NULL);

    /* give back our minor */
    usb_deregister_dev(interface, &skel_class);
--cut--
--cut--
    }
```

All other callback methods of the `struct usb_driver` are optional and specific to the functionality and the device they support.

Summary

The Linux USB `usbcore-generic` framework implements key functionalities of the USB host system software. This chapter covered some of the basic functionalities of the `usbcore` functionality. This framework within the `usbcore` module interacts with device drivers and manages USB devices by storing device and bus information in their respective data structures.

Chapter 10, "Host Driver for Embedded Controller," explains the role of the HCD and how it interacts with the `usbcore`.

More Reading

One of the main frameworks within the `usbcore` module is URB management, which you can learn more about in `Documentation/usb/URB.txt`. The Linux USB host framework supports URB transfer on direct memory access (DMA); see `Documentation/usb/dma.txt` for more information. If you want to control a USB device, whether connected or not, refer to `Documentation/usb/authorization.txt`. This authorization feature is used mainly in wireless USB devices. You can read more about the `usbcore` data structures and application programming interfaces (APIs) at http://www.lrr.in.tum.de/Par/arch/usb/usbdoc.

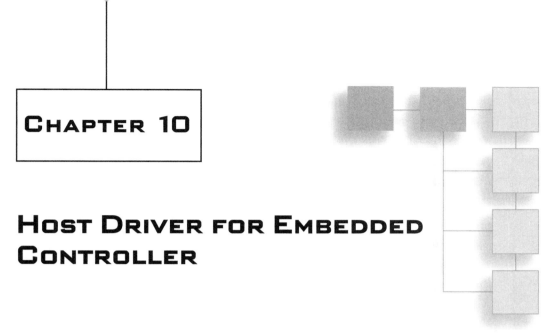

CHAPTER 10

HOST DRIVER FOR EMBEDDED CONTROLLER

In This Chapter

- Bootstrap Linux USB HCD
- Linux USB HCD
- Sample Implementation of USB HCD

This host controller hardware is compliant and implements universal serial bus (USB) host control interface (HCI) specifications defined by vendors such as Intel and Compaq. The software portion of the HCI acts as an interface to the system software. The host controller driver (HCD) is the lowermost layer of the USB host framework that directly interacts with the host controller hardware. On Linux, the HCD acts as an interface between the usbcore and the host controller hardware. It integrates the host controller hardware with the platform and allows the layers above it to manage and communicate with the connected USB device.

This chapter explores the Linux USB HCD framework that is essential for a developer to bring up his host controller hardware. It begins by discussing the essential data structures and interface functions of the Linux USB HCD. Then it explores the functional modules of the HCD and the sequence of activities that occurs inside the HCD. It concludes with a sample implementation of an HCD.

Bootstrap Linux USB HCD

The HCD framework implements a driver for USB host controllers and driver interfaces required by the Linux USB usbcore framework. The HCD framework also integrates the USB host controller to the platform. That's why the framework includes the necessary functionality to integrate the USB controller with the platform. Most of the HCDs are developed based on the platform driver framework. Check out Chapter 12, "Peripheral Device Controller Driver," to understand the basics of the platform driver framework. This section explores the essential HCD data structures and interface methods.

The essential data structures for the HCD driver are struct hc_driver and struct usb_hcd, which are defined in include/linux/usb/hcd.h.

The struct hc_driver structure has methods that serve as an interface between the usbcore and the HCD. The data structure also contains a member to describe the driver and the product.

```
struct hc_driver {
        const char      *description;
        const char      *product_desc;
        size_t          hcd_priv_size;
```

The HCD uses the irq member variable to register its interrupt request (IRQ) handler.

```
irqreturn_t      (*irq) (struct usb_hcd *hcd);
```

The flags member holds information on the version of USB that the HCD supports.

```
int      flags;
```

These interface methods initialize the HCD and the root hub drivers. They generally reset the power of the host controller hardware.

```
int      (*reset) (struct usb_hcd *hcd);
int      (*start) (struct usb_hcd *hcd);
```

This interface method allows the host controller functionality generally invoked by the usbcore when the HCD is removed.

```
void      (*stop) (struct usb_hcd *hcd);
```

This interface method powers down the host controller and is invoked as part of the platform driver's shutdown operation. The HCD framework provides usb_hcd_platform_shutdown as the wrapper function.

```
void    (*shutdown) (struct usb_hcd *hcd);
```

This interface method gets the frame number required during isochronous (ISO) transactions. The HCD framework provides the wrapper function usb_get_current_frame_number to invoke this function.

```
int     (*get_frame_number) (struct usb_hcd *hcd);
```

These interface functions manage the input/output (I/O) requests. The HCD framework provides usb_hcd_submit_urb and usb_hcd_unlink_urb methods for enqueue and dequeue, respectively.

```
int     (*urb_enqueue)(struct usb_hcd *hcd,
                        struct urb *urb, gfp_t mem_flags);
int     (*urb_dequeue)(struct usb_hcd *hcd,
                        struct urb *urb, int status);
```

This interface method synchronizes with the HCD to ensure that the endpoint state is freed from the hardware. The HCD framework provides the usb_hcd_disable_endpoint interface method to use this callback. Call usb_hcd_flush_endpoint before disabling the endpoint.

```
void    (*endpoint_disable)(struct usb_hcd *hcd,
            struct usb_host_endpoint *ep);
```

This interface method resets an endpoint's state. The callback method is invoked using the usb_hcd_reset_endpoint wrapper function.

```
void    (*endpoint_reset)(struct usb_hcd *hcd,
            struct usb_host_endpoint *ep);
```

These interface methods offer root hub support. The latter method, hub_control, handles control transfers that are directed to the hub. You can access the hub_status_data method using the usb_hcd_poll_rh_status interface function; you invoke hub_control using the rh_call_control function.

```
int     (*hub_status_data) (struct usb_hcd *hcd, char *buf);
int     (*hub_control) (struct usb_hcd *hcd,
```

```
                    u16 typeReq, u16 wValue, u16 wIndex,
                    char *buf, u16 wLength);
```

These interface methods are part of the host power management framework to suspend and resume the host controller. They are interfaced using hcd_bus_ suspend and hcd_bus_resume, respectively.

```
int     (*bus_suspend)(struct usb_hcd *);
int     (*bus_resume)(struct usb_hcd *);
```

This interface function is used as part of an On-the-Go (OTG) implementation to start enumeration after a reset. The HCD framework provides usb_bus_ start_enum as a wrapper function for this method.

```
int     (*start_port_reset)(struct usb_hcd *, unsigned port_num);
```

These interface methods release the port when there is a change in the physical or logical connection on a hub interface. The HCD framework's hub_port_ con nect_change method uses these callback methods.

```
void    (*relinquish_port)(struct usb_hcd *, int);
int     (*port_handed_over)(struct usb_hcd *, int);
```

The hub_tt_work function of the HCD framework uses this interface method for the transaction details of the host controller.

```
void    (*clear_tt_buffer_complete)(struct usb_hcd *,
                    struct usb_host_endpoint *);
```

These interface functions manage USB device allocation and release. They are like the constructors and destructors of the USB device data structure. Internally, the HCD framework provides usb_alloc_dev and hub_free_dev to enable use of these methods.

```
int     (*alloc_dev)(struct usb_hcd *, struct usb_device *);
void    (*free_dev)(struct usb_hcd *, struct usb_device *);
```

Other methods are introduced in this HCD for extensible HCI (xHCI) controllers, which are for USB3 devices and are beyond the scope of this book.

The next two important data structures are struct usb_bus, defined in include/ linux/usb.h, and struct usb_hcd, defined in drivers/usb/core/hcd.h. They maintain the necessary information for the HCD. The HCD is referred to as the *bus* on the Linux framework. It holds information on the devices connected to it.

Some other key interface functions act like an HCDI between the HCD and the `usbcore` framework along with the preceding callback functions.

- `int usb_hcd_submit_urb(struct urb *urb, gfp_t mem_flags)`

  The transfer of USB data to and from the host is using the USB Request Block (URB) data structure. This acts as an interface for the `usb_submit_urb` method and provides access to the host controller through the `urb_enqueue` callback.

- `int usb_hcd_unlink_urb(struct urb *urb, int status)`

  This interface function allows the `usbcore` to cancel a URB submission and unlink it from the URB queue. `usb_unlink_urb` invokes this interface function to abort and cancel URB submissions.

- `void usb_hcd_giveback_urb(struct usb_hcd *hcd, struct urb *urb,int status);`

  This interface function returns the information collected for the URB request to the driver. This interface hands over the URB from the HCD to the device driver using the `usb_hcd_giveback_urb` interface function.

- `struct usb_hcd *usb_create_hcd(const struct hc_driver *driver,struct device *dev, const char *bus_name)`

  This interface function allocates and initializes a `struct usb_hcd` data structure and returns `NULL` if memory is unavailable. The host drivers use this interface function on a successful probe to allocate a `struct usb_hcd` data structure.

- `int usb_add_hcd(struct usb_hcd *hcd,unsigned int irqnum, unsigned long irqflags)`

  This interface function initializes `struct usb_hcd` with necessary resources such as memory and interrupts and registers the bus. The function calls the HCD's reset and start routines.

- `void usb_remove_hcd(struct usb_hcd *hcd)`

  This interface function is invoked during the shutdown process. It releases resources allocated during the `usb_add_hcd` function and then invokes the HCD driver's stop function.

- `int usb_hcd_link_urb_to_ep(struct usb_hcd *hcd, struct urb *urb)`

  The HCD `enqueue` function calls this function to add a URB to the end-point queue. The function returns 0 on success and a negative value on failure indicating the reason for the failure.

- `void usb_hcd_unlink_urb_from_ep(struct usb_hcd *hcd, struct urb *urb)`

  This interface function is called to remove a URB from an endpoint queue. The function returns 0 on success and a negative value on failure indicating the reason for the failure.

This section explored some of the essential data structures and interfaces required to implement an HCD. Check out the other definitions available at `drivers/usb/core/hcd.h`. The following section explores the HCD internals and the sequence of activity between the HCD and the `usbcore`.

Linux USB HCD

The Linux USB HCD is the lowermost part of the USB host framework that interacts with the USB host controller hardware. The USB host driver implements USB host specifications that the controller hardware supports. The Linux USB host driver is available in the `drivers/usb/host/` folder. Its interface with the `usbcore` is through `/drivers/usb/core/hcd.c`.

Figure 10.1 illustrates a simple breakdown of the functions of an HCD.

The USB host consists of three major functionalities to make a complete framework: platform drivers, HCDI, and HCD. The two former modules are interface functionalities for hardware and the `usbcore` module, respectively. The USB host controller hardware integrates with the platform hardware through glue hardware logic. Glue logic is a custom logic circuitry that interfaces integrated circuits. The hardware glues are supported through the platform driver routines. In a normal USB host system, interfaces such as PCI act as glue logic to interfaces. In an embedded system, the USB controllers are interfaced through a less complex bus interface controller to GPIO pins and drivers.

A USB HCD is developed for every USB host controller. To control the HCD from `usbcore`, the `usbcore` uses interface routines that invoke the necessary callbacks of the HCD. The main functionality of the HCD is to implement

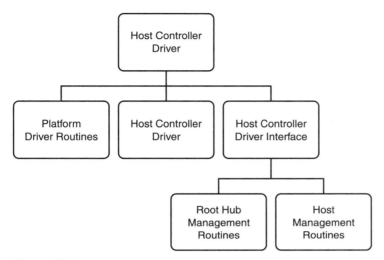

Figure 10.1
A simple breakdown of the Linux USB HCD.

specifications such as the Enhanced Host Controller Interface (EHCI), Universal Host Controller Interface (UHCI), and Open Host Controller Interface (OHCI). Elaborating on these specifications and its Linux implementation is beyond the scope of this book. You are encouraged to explore the implementation on your own at `drivers/usb/host/ehci-hcd.c`, `drivers/usb/host/uhci-hcd.c`, or `drivers/usb/host/ohci-hcd.c`.

Now that you've seen the functionalities of the HCD, the following section explores the sequence of activities when the host controller is loaded and a USB transfer occurs. Figure 10.2 illustrates the sequence of activities when an HCD loads.

After successful registration of the platform driver, the probe callback of the platform driver creates the HCD object, initializes it, and starts it. If the invocation is successful, the HCD is ready for communication.

Figure 10.3 illustrates a sequence of activities that occurs when a USB transaction starts from the class driver of the Linux USB host framework.

The transfer starts from the class driver with the submission of a URB with a callback to obtain the result of the URB submission. The class driver uses

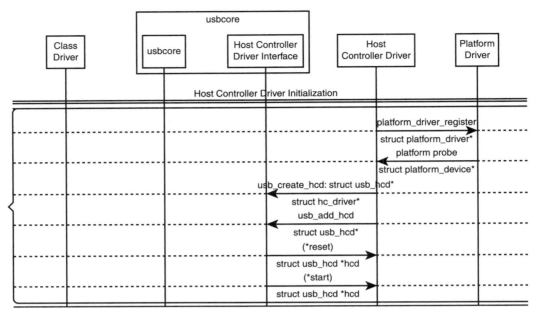

Figure 10.2
Sequence of activities when an HCD loads.

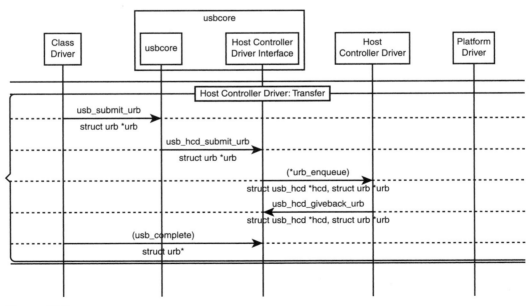

Figure 10.3
Sequence of activities when a Linux USB host framework performs transfers.

usbcore's interface function `usb_submit_urb` to submit its URB request. The usbcore subsequently uses the `usb_hcd_submit_urb` HCDI function. This abstraction allows the usbcore to interact with different HCDs. Once the URB request is handled by the HCD, it returns the status to the usbcore through `usb_hcd_giveback_urb`, which internally invokes the callbacks registered as part of the URB. The action request via the URB is highly specific to the HCD.

There are additional sequences of activities, such as cancellation of the URB request and control transfers, that are left for you to further explore. The next section briefly explores the implementation of an HCD using the knowledge gained in this section.

SAMPLE IMPLEMENTATION OF USB HCD

This section explores a sample implementation of an HCD and its platform driver, which is required to interface the host controller with the platform hardware. The Linux USB framework provides a dummy HCD driver, which is a simulation of an HCD available in `drivers/usb/gadget/dummy_hcd.c`. The dummy HCD driver sits on top of the dummy platform driver, and an HCD usually sits on top of a driver-based interface and is interfaced with the platform. For example, in a normal PC setup, USB host controllers interface to the main processor using Peripheral Component Interconnect (PCI); hence, the HCD sits on top of a PCI driver.

Thus, the first step in the process is defining the struct `platform_driver` object, say `dummy_hcd_driver`, and initializing the platform driver with the necessary callbacks. The second step is to register the driver with the kernel using `platform_driver_register` in the platform `init` routine. In a typical embedded setup, this platform driver is responsible for integrating the HCD with the hardware by grabbing essential resources from the platform.

```
static struct platform_driver dummy_hcd_driver = {
        .probe          = dummy_hcd_probe,
        .remove         = dummy_hcd_remove,
        .suspend        = dummy_hcd_suspend,
        .resume         = dummy_hcd_resume,
        .driver         = {
                .name   = (char *) driver_name,
                .owner  = THIS_MODULE,
```

```
        },
};
```

The third step in the process is to create an HCD driver on a successful platform driver probe. Other platform routines such as suspend or resume do not play a direct role in the management of the HCD but are necessary for responding to platform requests.

The probe invokes `usb_create_hcd` to create a `struct usb_hcd` object. The `usb_create_hcd` registers a `struct hc_driver` object `dummy_hcd` with callbacks to HCD.

```
static int dummy_hcd_probe(struct platform_device *pdev)
{
        --cut--
        hcd = usb_create_hcd(&dummy_hcd, &pdev->dev, dev_name(&pdev->dev));
        if (!hcd)
                return -ENOMEM;
        the_controller = hcd_to_dummy (hcd);
        retval = usb_add_hcd(hcd, 0, 0);

        --cut--

        return retval;
}
```

The `dummy_hcd` registers the necessary callbacks to make the HCD. The HCDI uses the callbacks to manage the host controller.

```
static const struct hc_driver dummy_hcd = {
        .description =          (char *) driver_name,
        .product_desc =         "Dummy host controller",
        .hcd_priv_size =        sizeof(struct dummy),
        .flags =                HCD_USB2,
        .start =                dummy_start,
        .stop =                 dummy_stop,
        .urb_enqueue =          dummy_urb_enqueue,
        .urb_dequeue =          dummy_urb_dequeue,
        .get_frame_number =     dummy_h_get_frame,
        .hub_status_data =      dummy_hub_status,
        .hub_control =          dummy_hub_control,
```

```
        .bus_suspend =              dummy_bus_suspend,
        .bus_resume =              dummy_bus_resume,
};
```

A successful probe creates a controller driver and further invokes the usb_add_hcd to initialize the HCD framework. The usb_add_hcd initializes the usb_hcd driver and starts the host controller by invoking the callback.

You can refer to the dummy_hcd source in drivers/usb/gadget/dummy_hcd.c to learn the functional implementation of the dummy host controller implementation. Generally, the HCD implementation follows one of the host controller specifications implemented in drivers/usb/host/ehci-hcd.c, drivers/usb/host/ehci-hub.c, drivers/usb/host/uhci-hcd.c, drivers/usb/host/uhci-hub.c, drivers/usb/host/ohci-hcd.c, or drivers/usb/host/ohci-hub.c. Detailing these drivers is beyond the scope of this book. I encourage you to explore the implementation because you might be required to develop your own HCD rather using the standard HCI drivers, as with r8a66597-hcd.c.

Once you are ready with the HCD and the platform driver, it's time to build the driver along with other kernel modules. You can place your driver in the drivers/usb/host folder and update the Kconfig and the makefile in the same folder to build the necessary HCD module.

Because the dummy HCD is used to evaluate the gadget framework, the configuration to build the dummy HCD module is available as part of the gadget menuconfig. The following snippet from drivers/usb/gadget/Kconfig allows you to build the dummy HCD module.

```
config USB_GADGET_DUMMY_HCD
        boolean "Dummy HCD (DEVELOPMENT)"
        depends on USB=y || (USB=m && USB_GADGET=m)
        select USB_GADGET_DUALSPEED
        help
```

After successful selection of the configuration, you can make the module using a normal kernel build command such as make modules. A successful build generates the dummy HCD module dummy_hcd.ko in the drivers/usb/gadget folder. Normally, host drivers are kept in the drivers/usb/host folder. A successful kernel build generates the HCD module you selected.

Summary

The HCD is the lowermost layer of the USB host driver; thus, this layer interacts with USB host controller hardware. Most of the host controllers comply with one of the specifications, namely ECHI, OHCI, or UHCI. Sometimes, however, USB controllers deviate from these specifications and require separate drivers. In a platform, USB host controllers become glued to the platform hardware using interfaces such as PCI or General Purpose Input/Output (GPIO). Therefore, the HCDs are developed on top of these PCI drivers or platform drivers. Once you develop the driver for the glue, you can use the already-implemented HCI drivers (perhaps the EHCI driver) and minimize the development effort.

More Reading

You can obtain more information on EHCI and UHCI from http://www.intel. com/technology/usb/spec.htm. You can read further details about OHCI at http://www.compaq.com/productinfo/development/openhci.html. The Linux documentation also provides information on ECHI and OHCI Linux imple- mentation in `Documentation/usb/ehci.txt` and `Documentation/usb/ohci.txt`. In addition, you should explore the Linux HCI implementation (`drivers/usb/host`) to broaden your understanding of the HCDs.

Part II

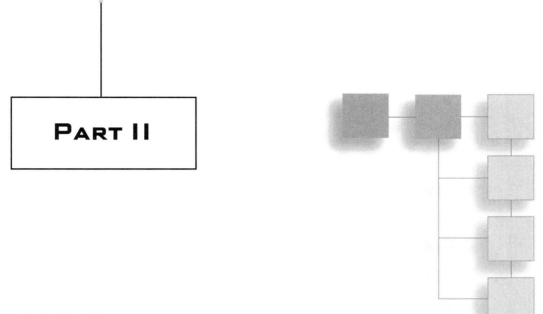

USB Device

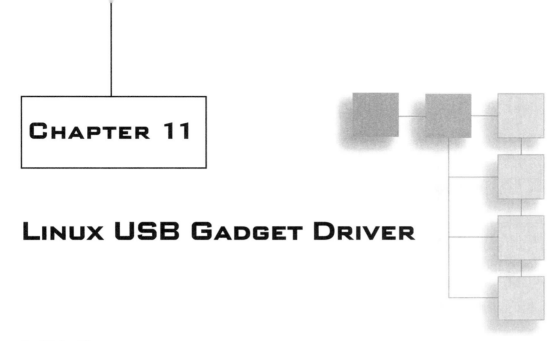

CHAPTER 11

LINUX USB GADGET DRIVER

In This Chapter

- Overview of USB Device Stack Architecture
- Overview of Linux USB Gadget Driver Architecture

The universal serial bus (USB) host-device relationship is master/slave, which means the host controls the communication, and the device responds to the host's request. Thus, the USB device implementation is simpler than the USB host implementation. This chapter starts with a software architecture overview of a generic USB device stack. This enables you to understand different layers and requirements of a USB device stack. The subsequent sections of the chapter explore the Linux USB gadget architecture, providing an overview of the gadget stack.

OVERVIEW OF USB DEVICE STACK ARCHITECTURE

The USB device controller hardware implements the physical and link layers. The USB software subsystem takes care of the rest of the functionality, which includes USB protocol and device functionality. In general, you can visualize a USB device stack as a simple three-layer implementation containing a firmware driver for the USB device controller, a USB device driver generally known as Chapter—9 implementation, and a USB class driver layer.

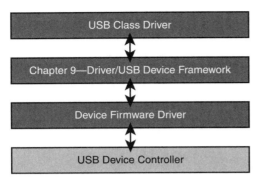

Figure 11.1
A generic USB device software architecture.

Figure 11.1 illustrates a typical USB software stack architecture. It consists of three major parts: a device firmware driver, a Chapter—9 driver, and a USB class driver.

Device Firmware Driver

The USB device firmware driver implements hardware-specific routines that allow access to the registers, memory space, and interrupts. Generally, the registers help configure the device endpoints, control the interrupts, and control the USB activity. The firmware driver exports the facilities that the USB controller provides to the upper layers. The device firmware layer is specific to the controller for which the firmware driver is written. The firmware driver can also implement service routines for the USB interrupts and interrupt events.

Chapter—9: Driver/USB Device Framework

The USB device framework, or the Chapter—9 driver layer, acts as an interface between the upper class drivers and the endpoints in the device controller through the firmware driver. This layer also implements the state machine defined by the USB specification during the enumeration process. Thus, the typical functions of this layer are to support the USB enumeration process and to transfer data from the upper layers.

USB Class Driver

The USB class driver layer implements the application functionality of the device, which is generally independent of the USB protocol. This layer is sometimes called the *functional module* of the USB system. The class driver defines the behavior of the device and provides necessary device data, such as device configuration information, to the lower layers to set up the device. For example, if you are implementing a mass storage class driver, you require bulk in/bulk out endpoints along with an optional interrupt endpoint. But in the case of the audio class driver, you require isochronous endpoints. Thus, the lower two layers offer a framework for the USB protocol and USB device controller, and the class driver uses it to provide a functional device. Some of the most well-known class drivers defined by the USB community are the mass storage class, Media Transfer Protocol, and human interface device (HID) class.

With your limited understanding of what a USB device stack looks like, you will explore the Linux USB gadget subsystem overview in the following section.

OVERVIEW OF LINUX USB GADGET DRIVER ARCHITECTURE

On Linux, the USB device stack is known as the *Linux-USB gadget driver*, which provides the essential infrastructure to develop a driver for a USB device controller. The gadget driver framework shares some of the data structures and application programming interface (API) styles of the Linux USB host driver. The gadget driver also adapts a similar approach in the input/output (I/O) transfer queue. This enables the gadget framework to support On-the-Go (OTG) devices, which can also act as minimalistic hosts.

Similar to the USB device software architecture (Figure 11.1), the Linux-USB gadget has three major modules: the USB controller driver, the gadget driver, and the class driver. Figure 11.2 illustrates how the USB gadget driver module fits into a Linux platform.

USB Controller Driver

The USB controller driver layer acts as a hardware abstraction layer (HAL) for the USB device controller, exporting the hardware to the layers above. This layer's functionality is similar to the device firmware driver. Like the device firmware driver, the Linux USB gadget subsystem's USB controller driver

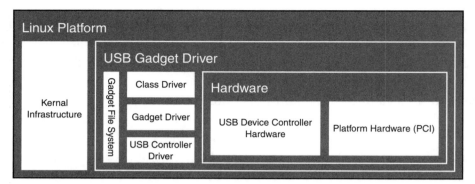

Figure 11.2
A simple representation of the Linux USB gadget driver framework.

implements hardware-specific routines that allow access to the registers, memory space, and interrupts. You can explore more about the USB controller driver in Chapter 12, "Peripheral Device Controller Driver."

Gadget Driver

The gadget driver is similar to the Chapter—9 driver/USB device framework discussed in the previous section. The gadget layer handles most of the USB protocol-specific requirements and passes on requests that are class specific. This layer sits in between the hardware layer and the class layer and provides necessary USB protocol abstraction. You can explore more on gadget driver in Chapter 13, "Gadget Driver."

Class Driver

The class driver or the functional driver implements the actual device functionality. The gadget driver handles most of the USB functionality, but the gadget layer passes on a request specific to a class. The class driver handles USB-specific requests as well, along with the functional implementation. The USB Device Working Group (DWG) defines various USB class specifications, which you can reference at http://www.usb.org/developers/devclass_docs#approved. Chapter 13 goes into the class driver in more detail.

SUMMARY

The Linux USB gadget subsystem is a simple three-layer architecture implementing the USB device specification. This chapter provided a brief overview of the Linux USB gadget stack, which will help you understand the next three chapters.

MORE READING

This chapter captured a simple generic architecture of a USB device stack. Collect USB stack architecture from different vendors and compare it to the architectures in this chapter. You can also refer to http://www.linux-usb.org/gadget/ for an overview of the Linux USB device stack. The Linux documentation `Documentation/usb/gadget_serial.txt` offers additional reading opportunity on the gadget architecture.

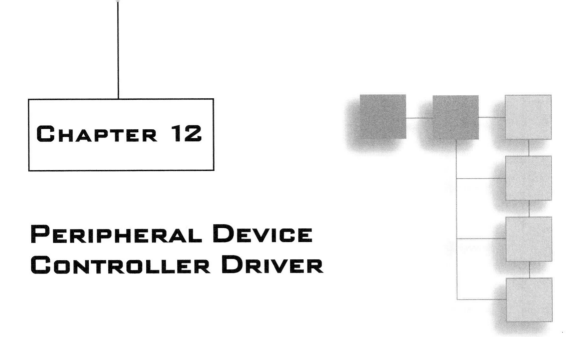

CHAPTER 12

PERIPHERAL DEVICE CONTROLLER DRIVER

In This Chapter

- Bootstrap Essentials: Platform Driver
- Linux USB Peripheral Controller Driver
- USB Device Controller Driver

On the Linux USB gadget subsystem, the USB peripheral device controller (PDC) driver is the lowermost driver layer and is closer to the hardware. This layer interacts with the USB PDC hardware and extends the hardware features to other driver layers. Thus, it acts as an interface for the USB driver layers and the platform drivers to control the USB device controller. You need to have a complete understanding of the USB PDC and the platform to develop the USB PDC driver.

Interestingly, the USB PDC driver performs minimal tasks that are USB specific, because most of the USB-specific tasks are done in either the hardware or the USB layers above the PDC driver. Therefore, the functionality of the USB PDC driver is similar to any other kernel module that interacts directly with the hardware. Depending on the platform setup, a USB device controller is connected to the platform hardware through any of the different interfaces available in the platform. The PDC driver uses the platform driver framework or the PCI driver framework as the base to develop the driver.

From a top-level overview, the PDC driver's major functionality is to allocate necessary resources such as memory and interrupt requests (IRQs) when the platform probe for the device is successful and release the allocated resources when the device is disconnected. Thus, a successful PDC driver allows the USB controller to be ready for the other USB driver layers and frees up the platform resources.

This chapter further explores the Linux platform driver framework that you should know before developing PDC driver. The subsequent sections explore the functional breakdown of the PDC driver, the activity flow of the driver, and a sample PDC driver implementation.

BOOTSTRAP ESSENTIALS: PLATFORM DRIVER

The USB device controller hardware connects to the platform using proprietary interfaces. It is important to develop the device driver with minimum complexity. The Linux platform driver is a pseudo-bus generic driver model that connects to proprietary interfaces with a simple driver framework. The platform driver framework offers direct access to the platform hardware bus. Most of the USB PDC driver is developed based on the platform driver framework. The following sections explore the basics of the platform driver framework that enable you to understand and develop a USB PDC driver.

The `linux/platform_device.h` file contains definitions and declarations of the platform driver framework. The platform driver exports its functionality through two major data structures: the struct `platform_device` and the struct `platform_driver`.

The struct `platform_device` data structure represents the device with members to identify the device and fields to represent sets of resources such as IRQ and memory allocated to the device. The Name field helps to identify the resources allocated once the probing is successful.

```
struct platform_device {
        const char      * name;
        int             id;
        struct device   dev;
        u32             num_resources;
        struct resource * resource;
};
```

Generally, the `struct platform_device` is installed as part of module initialization and registered onto the platform driver framework. The platform driver framework then passes the `struct platform_device` object with the resource allocated to the driver using the probe method, where the resources are remapped to the device driver data structures.

The next key data structure is the `struct platform_driver`. It is similar to the standard Linux driver model, which provides methods to identify and manage the device. You have to register handler routines specific to the device to handle calls from the platform driver framework. Of these handler routines, the probe and the remove methods are sufficient for a device driver to be functional.

```
struct platform_driver {
    int (*probe)(struct platform_device *);
    int (*remove)(struct platform_device *);
    void (*shutdown)(struct platform_device *);
    int (*suspend)(struct platform_device *, pm_message_t state);
    int (*resume)(struct platform_device *);
    struct device_driver driver;
};
```

After successful initialization of the `struct platform_driver` with methods specific to the device, you need to register the methods with the platform driver framework. You use the `platform_driver_register` method to register the `struct platform_driver` methods to the platform driver framework.

```
int platform_driver_register(struct platform_driver *);
```

When the hardware is not hot pluggable and needs detection during the booting of the kernel, you must use the `platform_driver_probe` method. This method is ideal for platform drivers, which are for controllers integrated with the platform hardware. This method works similarly to the `platform_driver_register`, except hardware is not probed when another device is connected after the kernel bootup.

```
int platform_driver_probe(struct platform_driver *driver, int (*probe)(struct platform_device *))
```

Note

Using the `platform_driver_probe` method reduces the runtime memory footprint. Also, the driver isn't probed if another device is registered.

When you write a device driver, cleaning and freeing up the resource is part of the device driver job. You can use the `platform_device_unregister` method of the platform driver framework to clean and free up the allocated resources.

```
void platform_device_unregister(struct platform_device *);
```

Once the device is successfully probed, the device driver must claim the resource allocated to the device by the platform framework. The platform driver framework provides the interface method `platform_get_resource` to retrieve the resource that the platform framework allocates. The types of resources that can be retrieved are shown here.

```
#define IORESOURCE_TYPE_BITS    0x00000f00        /* Resource type */
#define IORESOURCE_IO           0x00000100
#define IORESOURCE_MEM          0x00000200
#define IORESOURCE_IRQ          0x00000400
#define IORESOURCE_DMA          0x00000800
struct resource *platform_get_resource(struct platform_device *,unsigned int
type, unsigned )
struct resource *platform_get_resource_byname(struct platform_device *,un
signed int,const char *)
```

When successful, the method returns the resource allocated to the device; on failure, a negative error number is returned. The platform framework also provides interface routines to get the IRQ assigned to the device.

```
int platform_get_irq(struct platform_device *dev, unsigned int num)
int platform_get_irq_byname(struct platform_device *dev, const char *name)
```

When a resource is named, you can retrieve it by its name. `platform_get_resource_byname` and `platform_get_irq_byname` allow you to get the resource by name.

The PDC driver is closely associated with hardware; requesting an IRQ and installing an IRQ handler is an essential part of the driver layer. The Linux driver framework provides the `request_irq` interface function declared in `<linux/interrupt.h>` for installing IRQ handlers. The function returns 0 when the handler is installed successfully and a negative error code when installation fails. When the device is no more in use, the IRQ should be made available for the other driver. You have to use `free_irq` to release the IRQ shared by the device.

```
int __must_check request_irq(unsigned int, irq_handler_t handler,unsigned
lo ng, const char *, void *);
void free_irq(unsigned int irq, void *dev_id);
```

The PDC driver might require other data structures and interface methods. The condition is based on how the USB PDC is connected to the platform. But the platform driver framework satisfies most of the platform setup. The "More Reading" section at the end of this chapter provides additional information about the other frameworks used to develop the USB PDC driver.

LINUX USB PERIPHERAL CONTROLLER DRIVER

The PDC driver layer is part of the USB gadget driver framework, and its key functionality is to act as a hardware abstraction layer. The `drivers/usb/gadget` folder of the kernel contains the USB PDC driver implementation. The PDC driver files are named based on the USB PDC they are developed for. These drivers interact with the platform, grab the hardware resources, and export the hardware resources to other gadget driver layers. Figure 12.1 shows a breakdown of the PDC driver.

The PDC driver contains four major functionalities: platform initialization/exit, USB device controller setup, device controller management, and interrupt handling. The PDC driver is responsible for registering the device controller

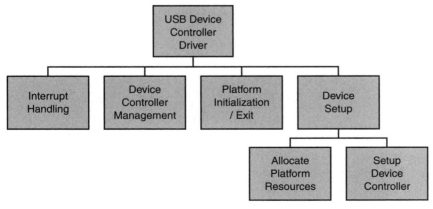

Figure 12.1
Functional breakdown of the PDC driver.

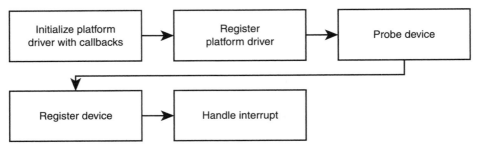

Figure 12.2
The typical control flow of the PDC driver.

with the platform framework when the gadget module is loaded and performing proper exit by releasing the resources allocated during initialization. Remember that the platform registration is specific to the way the device controller is interfaced with the platform hardware. Once the platform registration is successful, the PDC driver is responsible for setting up the device hardware and handling the interrupts. The PDC driver also provides routines to manage the USB device controller power and other hardware features.

Figure 12.2 illustrates the typical control flow of the PDC driver. The first step is to initialize platform driver callbacks and then register the driver to the platform driver framework. The driver's probe method is called when the device is connected to the platform. The probe method confirms the device and registers it to the kernel. Once the device is successfully registered, it is ready to handle USB activity.

The probe function does the major work of the PDC driver. Figure 12.3 dissects the probe method and represents its control flow. The first step in the probe method is to allocate required banks. After successful allocation of memory, you perform an ioremap so that the bus memory is accessible in central processing unit (CPU) space. The next step in the probe method is to map the interrupt of the USB controller to the device controller driver. The request_irq function helps attach the interrupt handler to the USB device controller interrupt. After registration of the interrupt routines, the probe sets up the different endpoints and buffer sizes of the device controller and passes them to the upper gadget driver. The setup includes initializing USB Request Block (URB) queues.

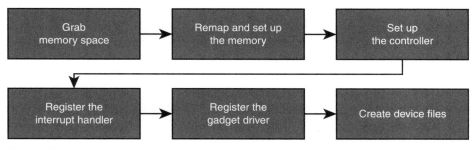

Figure 12.3
The typical flow of the PDC driver's probe routine.

After successful setup, registration, and activation of the USB device, the interrupt service routine that is registered in the probe starts receiving the transfer. The interrupt routine and the other device controller management routines are specific to the hardware.

USB DEVICE CONTROLLER DRIVER

From the preceding discussion, you know that the PDC driver acts like a hardware abstraction layer to export the hardware functionalities to the layers above. To develop this layer, you need a thorough understanding of the USB device controller and the way the device controller hardware is interfaced with the platform. The example setup uses the Renesas USB controller. This section details the development based on this driver, which is already in Linux, so you can easily reference the source.

You can start the PDC driver with a data structure that represents the device controller to the other layers when the PDC driver is successful. This data structure generally contains member variables to represent the gadget data structure, members to represent the endpoints, and other resources of the device controller. The `struct r8a66597` defined in `<drivers/usb/gadget/ r8a66597-udc.h >` is used in the example setup to represent the r8a66597 USB device controller.

From the data structure, notice that the `struct r8a66597` stores gadget, endpoint, and other resource details. This data structure can also hold information specific to your implementation, which you need in the other gadget driver layers. An object of this data structure is passed across the USB gadget driver to manipulate.

```
struct r8a66597 {
        spinlock_t              lock;
        unsigned long           reg;
        struct r8a66597_platdata        *pdata;

                struct usb_gadget               gadget;
        struct usb_gadget_driver        *driver;
        struct r8a66597_ep      ep[R8A66597_MAX_NUM_PIPE];
        struct r8a66597_ep      *pipenum2ep[R8A66597_MAX_NUM_PIPE];
        struct r8a66597_ep      *epaddr2ep[16];
        struct timer_list       timer;
        struct usb_request      *ep0_req;       /* for internal request */
        u16                     ep0_data;       /* for internal request */
        u16                     old_vbus;
        u16                     scount;
        u16                     old_dvsq;

        unsigned char bulk;
        unsigned char interrupt;
        unsigned char isochronous;
        unsigned char num_dma;

        unsigned irq_sense_low:1;
};
```

The next step in the process is to register the device to the Linux platform. This is specific to the way the device controller is connected to the platform. As discussed in the previous section, when the devices are connected to the platform using proprietary connections like General Purpose Input/Output (GPIO), the driver is based on platform driver framework. You will also see Peripheral Component Interconnect (PCI) driver framework–based drivers in the drivers/usb/gadget folder. Thus, this declaration is specific to the way the device controller is interfaced to the platform.

In this example setup, the device controller requires a platform driver framework, and the driver declares a struct platform_driver–based object r8a6657_driver. The r8a6657_driver is named to help you easily identify the device and driver when loaded.

```
static const char udc_name[] = "r8a66597_udc";

static struct platform_driver r8a66597_driver = {
        .remove =            __exit_p(r8a66597_remove),
        .driver        = {
                .name = (char *) udc_name,
        },
};
```

The r8a6657 driver registers a remove handler to clean up the allocated resources when the device is removed.

```
static int __exit r8a66597_remove(struct platform_device *pdev)
{
        struct r8a66597            *r8a66597 = dev_get_drvdata(&pdev->dev);

        del_timer_sync(&r8a66597->timer);
        iounmap((void *)r8a66597->reg);
        free_irq(platform_get_irq(pdev, 0), r8a66597);
        r8a66597_free_request(&r8a66597->ep[0].ep, r8a66597->ep0_req);
        kfree(r8a66597);
        return 0;
}
```

The next step in the development is to register the struct platform_driver object to the platform driver framework. The platform registration is generally part of the module init routine of the driver. In the example setup, because the device controller hardware is not hot pluggable, it uses the platform_driver_ probe interface method. Recall from the "Bootstrap Essentials: Platform Driver" section that this platform_driver_probe interface is for devices that are not hot pluggable.

```
static int __init r8a66597_udc_init(void)
{
        return platform_driver_probe(&r8a66597_driver, r8a66597_probe);
}
module_init(r8a66597_udc_init);

static void __exit r8a66597_udc_cleanup(void)
{
```

```
                platform_driver_unregister(&r8a66597_driver);
}
module_exit(r8a66597_udc_cleanup);
```

After a successful device registration of the platform driver with the platform framework, the probe routine `r8a66597_probe` detects the device. The probe routine prepares the PDC driver and the device controller for the next stage. One of the key functionalities of the probe routine is to map the platform resources. Some of the key resources that are mapped are the IRQ and the I/O memory. The resource mapping is done to the device data structure's members, which are later used by other gadget driver layers.

```
static int __init r8a66597_probe(struct platform_device *pdev)
{
        unsigned long irq_trigger;

        res = platform_get_resource(pdev, IORESOURCE_MEM, 0);
        if (!res) {
                ret = -ENODEV;
                printk(KERN_ERR "platform_get_resource error.\n");
                goto clean_up;
        }
        ires = platform_get_resource(pdev, IORESOURCE_IRQ, 0);
        irq = ires->start;
        irq_trigger = ires->flags & IRQF_TRIGGER_MASK;

        if (irq < 0) {
                ret = -ENODEV;
                printk(KERN_ERR "platform_get_irq error.\n");
                goto clean_up;
        }

        reg = ioremap(res->start, resource_size(res));
        if (reg == NULL) {
                ret = -ENOMEM;
                printk(KERN_ERR "ioremap error.\n");
                goto clean_up;
        }
```

After mapping the platform resource, the driver obtains control of the device controller hardware. The probe routine now can initialize the device controller hardware and set it up for USB activity. The other part of the probe routine is specific to the device controller. You can explore it from the source available in the kernel.

```
ret = request_irq(irq, r8a66597_irq, IRQF_DISABLED | IRQF_SHARED,
                        udc_name, r8a66597);
```

The platform IRQ is mapped to the PDC driver handler routine `r8a66597_irq` using the `request_irq` interface function. Once the IRQ is successfully mapped, the PDC driver starts receiving the IRQ and handles the USB transfers.

You can refer to other routines of the `r8a66597` PDC driver at `drivers/usb/gadget/ r8a66597-udc.h`.

SUMMARY

The peripheral device controller driver is the only layer of the gadget driver that directly interacts with the USB device hardware. Although the implementation framework is the same, it varies for each USB controller and the way it is integrated with the platform. You have to carefully read the data sheet of the USB controller and the platform hardware details before implementing this driver layer. In the next chapter, you read about the gadget layer, which sits on top of the PDC layer. The gadget layer handles USB-specific device operations and is independent of the USB controller hardware being used.

MORE READING

You can collect more information on the Linux platform driver framework from the Linux kernel documentation `Documentation/driver-model/platform.txt`. When your platform adds extra glue logic to interact with the device controller hardware, additional driver frameworks such as GPIO are required to control the hardware. You can read more about the GPIO framework from the Linux kernel documentation `Documentation/gpio.txt`.

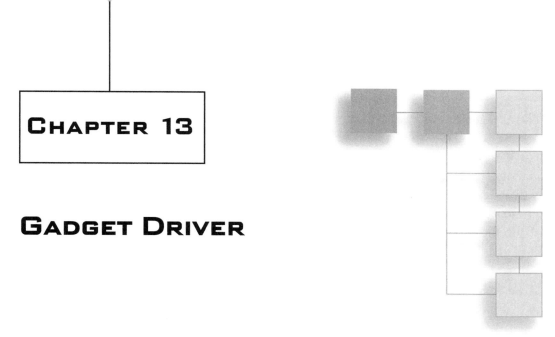

CHAPTER 13

GADGET DRIVER

In This Chapter

- Bootstrap Essentials: Gadget Driver
- Gadget Driver: Design
- Gadget Driver: Implementation

The gadget driver is an important infrastructure in the USB gadget subsystem. It is built in a flexible way that allows the upper class or the functional driver to manage the system effectively. The gadget framework is the core of the Linux USB gadget subsystem; it provides a framework for the USB device framework, as described by USB Specification (Chapter 9). It also performs other USB device management operations that are specific to the implementation. The gadget driver provides the framework required for a USB device to operate and expects intelligence of configuring the device from the class driver or the upper layer. Such a design offers flexibility to develop class drivers with different device configurations and functionality.

This chapter first explores the essential gadget data structures defined by the gadget driver. From there, it discusses the gadget framework's flow of activity and the way other layers use the gadget framework. Finally, this chapter analyzes a gadget driver implementation with a practical example.

Bootstrap Essentials: Gadget Driver

The gadget driver relies on four major data structures: `struct usb_gadget` to represent a gadget device, `struct usb_ep` to manage the device hardware, `struct usb_gadget_driver` to manage the device function, and `struct usb_request` to manage USB transfers. These data structures hold key information for the gadget layer and methods that extend the gadget infrastructure to other layers. These data structures and methods are defined in `include/linux/usb/gadget.h` of the Linux kernel source. The next section explores the methods that these key data structures extend.

USB Gadget Data Structure and Methods

The `struct usb_gadget` represents the USB device within the gadget layer. The `struct usb_gadget` uses methods to perform hardware-specific operations and maintains gadget-related information, such as endpoint lists. Thus, this data structure acts as an abstraction of the hardware. Its members are mostly read only.

```
struct usb_gadget {
        const struct usb_gadget_ops     *ops;
        struct usb_ep                   *ep0;
        struct list_head                ep_list;
        enum usb_device_speed           speed;
        unsigned                        is_dualspeed:1;
        unsigned                        is_otg:1;
        unsigned                        is_a_peripheral:1;
        unsigned                        b_hnp_enable:1;
        unsigned                        a_hnp_support:1;
        unsigned                        a_alt_hnp_support:1;
        const char                      *name;
        struct device                   dev;
};
```

Notice that `struct usb_gadget` defines only a basic set of gadget information. When you are developing a gadget layer for a USB device, you might need additional gadget-related information. You can define a data structure that is a superset of `struct usb_gadget`, which can hold additional information.

The `struct usb_gadget` declares the `struct usb_gadget_ops` member to export the hardware-specific operations. These gadget operations extend gadget features to the upper layers through wrapper functions. The following section details the gadget operations.

```
struct usb_gadget_ops {
        int        (*get_frame)(struct usb_gadget *);
        int        (*wakeup)(struct usb_gadget *);
        int        (*set_selfpowered) (struct usb_gadget *, int is_selfpowered);
        int        (*vbus_session) (struct usb_gadget *, int is_active);
        int        (*vbus_draw) (struct usb_gadget *, unsigned mA);
        int        (*pullup) (struct usb_gadget *, int is_on);
        int        (*ioctl)(struct usb_gadget *,
                                unsigned code, unsigned long param);
};
```

- `int        (*get_frame)(struct usb_gadget *)`

  This callback method returns the current frame number if the controller supports retrieval of the USB frame number. The `usb_gadget_frame_number` acts as the interface function. When the capability is not available, a negative value is returned.

- `int        (*wakeup)(struct usb_gadget *)`

  This callback method sends a wakeup notification to the USB host that the device hardware is connected to. The `usb_gadget_wakeup` serves as an interface function to the callback that performs the necessary hardware-specific operation. A device supporting this feature must inform the USB host through the USB descriptors. If the operation is successful, 0 is returned; if the operation fails, a negative value is returned.

- `int        (*set_selfpowered) (struct usb_gadget *, int is_selfpowered)`

  This callback method sets the device as self-powered. Interface functions `usb_gadget_set_selfpowered` and `usb_gadget_clear_selfpowered` enable and disable the device to and from the self-powered state, respectively. This operation affects the device status and is indicated by the peripheral device controller (PDC) driver. If the operation is successful, 0 is returned; if the operation fails, a negative value is returned.

- `int     (*vbus_session) (struct usb_gadget *, int is_active)`

  This callback method notifies the device controller that VBUS is powered. Interface functions `usb_gadget_vbus_connect` and `usb_gadget_vbus_disconnect` communicate when the VBUS session starts and ends. This method is necessary for a driver when an external transceiver (or General Purpose Input/Output [GPIO]) that detects a VBUS power session starts. The operation returns 0 on success and a negative value on failure.

- `int     (*vbus_draw) (struct usb_gadget *, unsigned mA)`

  This callback method conveys the device controller's VBUS power usage. The interface function `usb_gadget_vbus_draw` acts as a wrapper used by gadget drivers during `SET_CONFIGURATION` to indicate how much power a device may consume. The operation returns 0 on success and a negative value on failure.

- `int     (*pullup) (struct usb_gadget *, int is_on)`

  This callback method controls the USB device connection to the host through software. It is wrapped by the `usb_gadget_connect` interface function to enable D+ pull-up. The host starts enumerating this gadget when the pull-up and a VBUS session are active. To disconnect the USB connection, use the `usb_gadget_disconnect` interface function. Not all hardware supports hardware control of connection and disconnection.

- `int     (*ioctl)(struct usb_gadget *,unsigned code, unsigned long param)`

  This callback method sends an input/output control (IOCTL) if it's implemented. The operation returns 0 on success and a negative value on failure.

USB Endpoint Data Structure and Methods

The next important functionality in the gadget layer is endpoint management. The endpoint data structure extends methods to manage the device endpoints. One of the foremost and important functionalities is data queue management. The `struct usb_ep` extends a layer for data management and certain buffer management that is specific to the endpoint. Inside the gadget layer based on the endpoint available in the hardware, each endpoint is assigned an instance of the struct usb_ep data structure.

```
struct usb_ep {
        void                        *driver_data;
        const char                  *name;
        const struct usb_ep_ops     *ops;
        struct list_head            ep_list;
        unsigned                    maxpacket:16;
};
```

The struct usb_ep declares a struct usb_ep_ops member to export endpoint-specific operations. These endpoint operations allow the upper layers to control and manage an endpoint. The following section details the endpoint operations.

```
struct usb_ep_ops {
        int (*enable) (struct usb_ep *ep,
                const struct usb_endpoint_descriptor *desc);
        int (*disable) (struct usb_ep *ep);
        struct usb_request *(*alloc_request) (struct usb_ep *ep,
                gfp_t gfp_flags);
        void (*free_request) (struct usb_ep *ep, struct usb_request *req);
        int (*queue) (struct usb_ep *ep, struct usb_request *req,
                gfp_t gfp_flags);
        int (*dequeue) (struct usb_ep *ep, struct usb_request *req);
        int (*set_halt) (struct usb_ep *ep, int value);
        int (*set_wedge) (struct usb_ep *ep);
        int (*fifo_status) (struct usb_ep *ep);
        void (*fifo_flush) (struct usb_ep *ep);
};
```

- int (*enable) (struct usb_ep *ep, const struct usb_endpoint_descriptor *desc)

    This callback method provides the necessary infrastructure to configure an endpoint by upper class driver layers. This is required when a configuration is set or interfaces are changed and requires successful setting up of endpoint for transfers. A successful endpoint enable returns 0, and a failure returns a negative code. The gadget layer provides an interface function usb_ep_enable to access the callback.

Enabling endpoints is specific to the implementation and the device controller. The functionality involves setting up the endpoint types and enabling an interrupt that is specific to the endpoints.

- `int (*disable) (struct usb_ep *ep)`

This callback method provides the necessary infrastructure to disable an endpoint. This method frees all pending transactions; you also cannot use the endpoint before enabling it again. The gadget layer provides an interface function `usb_ep_disable` to access this callback. On successful completion, the callback returns 0; on failure, it returns a negative error code.

- `struct usb_request *(*alloc_request) (struct usb_ep *ep, gfp_t gfp_flags)`

This callback method provides the necessary infrastructure to allocate memory and returns a `usb_request` object. The implementation is specific to a USB controller. A successful return from this callback is based on the resource availability in the system and the way an endpoint is designed to be served. On successful allocation, it returns the `struct usb_request` object; on failure, it returns `NULL`. The gadget layer provides an interface `usb_ep_alloc_request` wrapper function to access this callback.

- `void (*free_request) (struct usb_ep *ep, struct usb_request *req)`

This callback method provides the necessary infrastructure to free the memory allocated by a previous `alloc_request`. When a class driver does not require a USB request, it should return the memory to the gadget driver. The gadget layer provides an interface function `usb_ep_free_request` wrapper function to access this callback.

- `int (*queue) (struct usb_ep *ep, struct usb_request *req, gfp_t gfp_flags)`

This callback method provides the necessary infrastructure to transfer data through the device controller and queue the USB transfer requests. After successful completion or cancellation of the data transfer, the callback triggers the completion routine. The gadget layer provides an interface function `usb_ep_queue` for the class drivers to queue the data. Once a gadget driver submits a request, that request cannot be examined or modified until it is given back to that gadget driver through the completion callback. On successful completion, the callback returns 0; on failure, it returns a negative error code.

- `int (*dequeue) (struct usb_ep *ep, struct usb_request *req)`

  This callback method provides the necessary infrastructure to remove a USB request from an endpoint queue. After successful removal, it invokes the completion routine for the USB request with parameter `ECONNRESET`. The gadget layer provides an interface function `usb_ep_dequeue` for the class drivers to remove the data that was queued earlier. A successful completion returns 0; failure returns a negative error code.

- `int (*set_halt) (struct usb_ep *ep, int value)`

  This callback method provides the necessary infrastructure to halt a particular endpoint when there is a transaction error. On successful completion, the callback returns 0; with an error, a negative error code is returned. The gadget layer provides an interface function `usb_ep_set_halt` with a parameter value of 0 to set halt and an interface function of `usb_ep_clear_halt` to clear halt with a parameter value of 1.

- `int (*fifo_status) (struct usb_ep *ep)`

  This callback method provides the necessary infrastructure for the class driver to query the status of hardware first in, first out (FIFO) for any garbage or unhandled bytes. You can use this method for error recovery or precise handling. This callback returns the number of bytes left out if the hardware is using or supporting FIFO. A negative error number is returned if the callback is not supported. The gadget layer provides the interface function `usb_ep_fifo_status` to access this callback.

- `void (*fifo_flush) (struct usb_ep *ep)`

  This callback method provides the necessary infrastructure for the class driver to clear any garbage or unhandled bytes in the FIFO. The gadget layer provides the interface function `usb_ep_fifo_flush` to access this callback.

Gadget Driver Data Structure and Methods

The next important data structure is `struct usb_gadget_driver`, which acts as a core interface between the class drivers. The class driver defines the methods to suit its functionality. It helps handling of setup packets, allocating resources for the functional driver and handling resume and suspension notification.

```
struct usb_gadget_driver {
        char                    *function;
        enum usb_device_speed   speed;
        int                     (*bind)(struct usb_gadget *);
        void                    (*unbind)(struct usb_gadget *);
        int                     (*setup)(struct usb_gadget *,
                                        const struct usb_ctrlrequest *);
        void                    (*disconnect)(struct usb_gadget *);
        void                    (*suspend)(struct usb_gadget *);
        void                    (*resume)(struct usb_gadget *);
        /* FIXME support safe rmmod */
        struct device_driver    driver;
};
```

- `int (*bind)(struct usb_gadget *)`

  This callback method binds the necessary hardware such as endpoints and buffers by the gadget driver. The upper functional layer or class driver layer implements the `bind` callback. In the `bind` function, the class driver prepares itself with the necessary resources for the subsequent class-specific operations. You should invoke this method from a context that can be blocked.

- `void (*unbind)(struct usb_gadget *)`

  This callback method unbinds the resource allocated to the `bind` callback. The upper functional layer or class driver layer implements this callback. You should invoke this method from a context that can be blocked.

- `int (*setup)(struct usb_gadget *, const struct usb_ctrlrequest *)`

  This callback method passes on the setup requests that are meant for the class driver. The gadget framework handles most of the Endpoint Zero (ep0) requests, such as descriptor management. Class-specific operations and management of configurations or interfaces are passed on to the class drivers through this callback method. This method is called in the interrupt context and cannot be blocked.

- `void (*disconnect)(struct usb_gadget *)`

This callback method notifies the class driver of the disconnection event. The `disconnect` callback is implemented by the upper functional layer or class driver layer to handle a host disconnection. This is called in the interrupt context and cannot be blocked.

- `void (*suspend)(struct usb_gadget *)`

This callback method notifies the class driver of the USB host's suspend event. The upper functional layer or class driver layer implements the `suspend` callback. The gadget framework invokes this callback to inform the class driver to take appropriate action for a suspend event. This is called in the interrupt context and cannot be blocked.

- `void (*resume)(struct usb_gadget *)`

This callback method notifies the class driver of the USB host's resume event. The upper functional layer or class driver layer implements the `suspend` callback, and the gadget framework invokes this callback to inform the class driver to take appropriate action for a resume event. This is called in the interrupt context and cannot be blocked.

Over and above these data structures and the callback, the gadget framework exports two interface functions for the functional layer to interact with the gadget driver layer. These functions are the start and exit methods of the gadget driver framework.

- `int usb_gadget_register_driver(struct usb_gadget_driver *driver)`

This method starts the gadget driver and sets up the gadget subsystem for data transfers. This interface method is responsible for invoking the `bind` callback and subsequently powering up the gadget controller hardware. You can invoke this method in a blocking context.

- `int usb_gadget_unregister_driver(struct usb_gadget_driver *driver)`

This method does just the opposite of `usb_gadget_register_driver`. This method removes the gadget driver and powers down the USB device controller. This method is responsible for unbinding the gadget driver from the controller driver. You should invoke this method from a context that can be blocked.

USB Request Data Structure

The gadget and functional drivers use `struct usb_request` for transfer of information to the PDC driver. The data structure holds essential information for transfers.

```
struct usb_request {
        void                    *buf;
        unsigned                length;
        dma_addr_t              dma;
        unsigned                no_interrupt:1;
        unsigned                zero:1;
        unsigned                short_not_ok:1;
        void                    (*complete)(struct usb_ep *ep,
                                        struct usb_request *req);
        void                    *context;
        struct list_head        list;
        int                     status;
        unsigned                actual;
};
```

Following are a few of the important fields:

- The `complete` member variable is a callback routine that obtains the status of a USB request once the request is completed.

- The `length` member variable holds the length of data that is expected or sent.

- The `status` member variable indicates the status of the USB request transfer.

- The `actual` member variable holds the actual length of data received or sent.

Gadget Driver Utility Functions

The gadget framework provides utility functions that facilitate selection of endpoints based on the descriptor that the class driver provides. These utility functions are available in `drivers/usb/gadget/epautoconf.c`, and their definitions are available in `include/linux/usb/gadget.h`.

- `struct usb_ep *usb_ep_autoconfig(struct usb_gadget *,`
  `struct  usb_endpoint_descriptor *)`

  This method automatically selects endpoints for the interface based on the descriptor. Internally, the function traverses the endpoint list for free endpoints matching the descriptor. On success, this function returns an unclaimed `struct usb_ep` object; on failure, it returns a `NULL` pointer.

- `void usb_ep_autoconfig_reset(struct usb_gadget *)`

  This method resets previously auto-configured gadget endpoints. Internally, it clears states such as `ep->driver_data` and the record of assigned endpoints used by `usb_ep_autoconfig()`.

Having described the essential data structures of the gadget driver framework, the next section explores the sequence of activity inside the gadget driver framework.

GADGET DRIVER: DESIGN

The gadget driver implementation is part of the Linux USB gadget subsystem; its implementation is generally coupled along with the PDC driver implementation. These files are usually named after the USB device controller they are developed for and are placed in `drivers/usb/gadget/`. The data structures required for the gadget framework are defined in `include/linux/usb/gadget.h`.

The functionality of the gadget framework can be broadly classified into three major categories based on the operations performed. Figure 13.1 illustrates this broad classification of the gadget driver framework.

You can map the data structures and their callbacks in the previous section to each block in Figure 13.1 for easy interpretation of the functionality that the block implements. Because the previous section detailed the callbacks, this section focuses on the sequence of activities inside the gadget driver at key stages.

gadget register

The first activity in the gadget framework starts with registration of the `struct usb_gadget_driver` object using the `usb_gadget_register_driver` interface

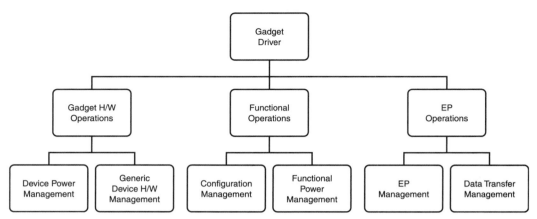

Figure 13.1
A broad breakdown of the gadget driver framework.

function by a class driver. The `usb_gadget_register_driver` interface function is responsible for setting up and starting the USB device controller. Figure 13.2 illustrates the sequence of activities when the gadget driver starts, triggered by the `_init` function.

Notice that the `module_init` function of the class driver starts with invocation of the `usb_gadget_register_driver` interface function. In this interface function, the `bind` callback is invoked, and the control returns to the class driver. The class driver selects the necessary endpoints based on the functionality it implements. The `usb_ep_autoconfig` interface function that the gadget framework exports is used to select the necessary endpoint. After successful selection of endpoints, the class driver allocates a buffer for Endpoint Zero using `usb_ep_alloc_request` to support enumeration. The class driver performs all these activities in the `bind` callback. Once the `bind` method is successful, the `usb_gadget_register_driver` activates Endpoint Zero and subsequently powers up the PDC to start the enumeration process.

gadget unregister

When the class module exits, the gadget driver that was registered during module initialization must be removed. The `module_exit` function invokes the `usb_gadget_unregister_driver` to remove the methods that were registered

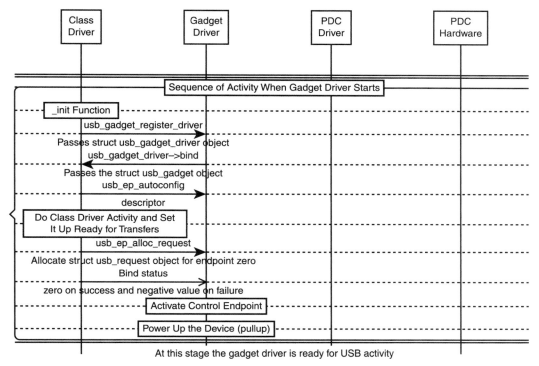

Figure 13.2
Sequence of activities triggered during initial stages.

earlier. Figure 13.3 illustrates the sequence of activities when the gadget driver exits.

This `usb_gadget_unregister_driver` interface function initially disconnects the class driver activity, subsequently disables endpoints, and powers down the hardware. Then the interface function invokes the `unbind` interface function and passes on the control to the class driver. The driver cleans up class activity and frees up any previous `usb_request` allocation.

USB Enumeration

Once the gadget driver enables Endpoint Zero, the host starts the enumeration process, and the device starts to respond. Figure 13.4 illustrates the sequence of activity that occurs in Endpoint Zero.

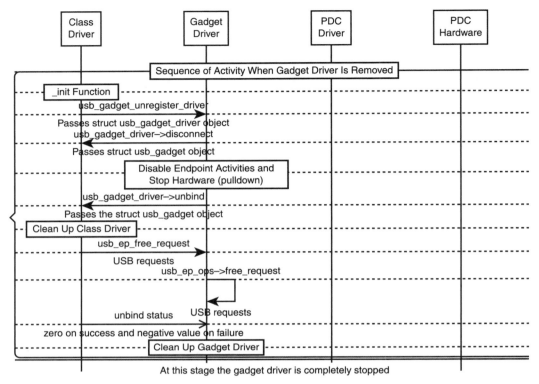

Figure 13.3
Sequence of activities triggered during module exit.

When the PDC driver receives an Endpoint Zero interrupt, the gadget driver handles the basic control request and passes on class-specific control requests to the class driver through the setup callback. Some of the control requests have a data phase, which requires data to be transferred to the host. For example, a Get Descriptor requires a response to the host. In such scenarios, the class driver allocates a struct usb_request object, updates the response, and queues it to the gadget framework for transfer.

The second section of the sequence diagram illustrates the activity after a successful enumeration. At this stage, the host selects a particular interface for further activity. When the Set Interface control request is received, the class driver enables the particular endpoints using the usb_ep_enable interface function. After successfully enabling the endpoints, the class driver allocates a struct usb_request object and gets ready for OUT transfer.

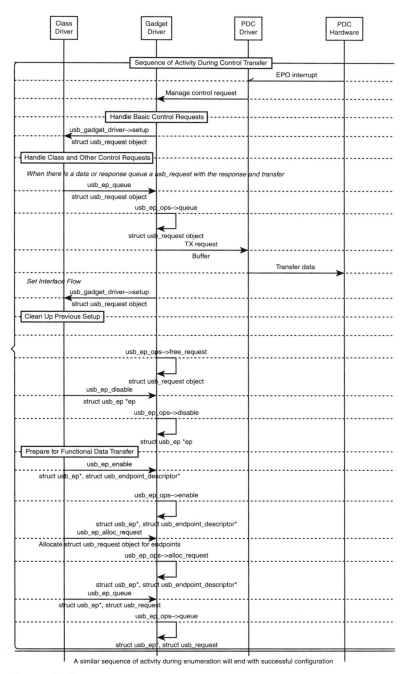

Figure 13.4
Sequence of activities in Endpoint Zero.

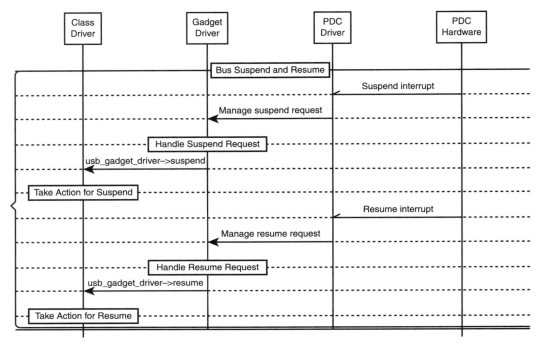

Figure 13.5
Sequence of activities triggered during suspend and resume.

Power Management

The gadget driver framework extends interfaces to pass on USB power management events, such as suspension and resumption of bus activity. Figure 13.5 illustrates the sequence of activity that passes on the suspend and resume events.

The PDC driver receives the USB suspend and resume events through interrupts and passes them on to the gadget driver. The gadget driver invokes the callbacks suspend and resume of the struct usb_gadget_driver, which passes on the events to the class driver.

OUT Transfer

When the USB enumeration is successful with a set interface, the USB gadget subsystem goes to a receive state. Figure 13.6 illustrates the sequence of activity that occurs during an OUT transfer.

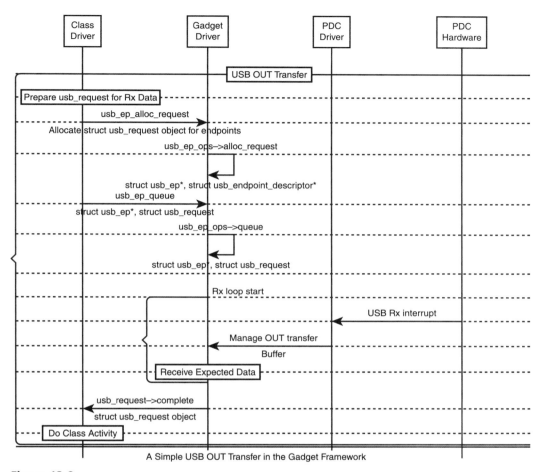

Figure 13.6
Sequence of activities in USB OUT transfer.

Once the configuration is successful, the class driver prepares itself for data transfer. It allocates the necessary buffer and requests a `struct usb_request` object; subsequently, it queues it to the gadget framework using `usb_ep_queue`. The class driver is aware of the size of data expected and sets it as part of the `struct usb_request` it submits to the gadget framework where it is queued. The gadget framework receives the data requested as part of the interrupt routine. Once the data that's requested is collected, the control is passed back to the class driver through a complete routine. The `struct usb_request` now holds the data received, actual read data, and the state of the request. The class driver then extracts the information from the request and processes it.

IN Transfer

When the USB host starts the communication through an IN transfer, the device must respond to the host's request. Figure 13.7 illustrates the sequence of activities that occurs during an IN transfer.

The class driver prepares the data to be transmitted and maps to the struct usb_request allocated using usb_ep_alloc_request. The class driver then queues the usb_request to the gadget framework for transfer. After that, the gadget framework transfers the data using the hardware driver. Once the transfer is

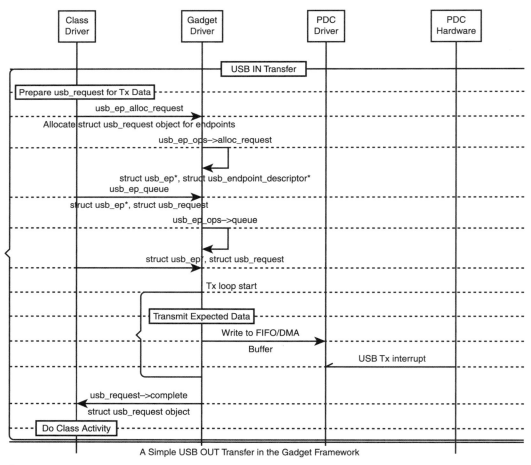

Figure 13.7
Sequence of activities in USB IN transfer.

completed, the gadget driver invokes the complete callback to pass on the transfer status to the class driver.

The preceding sections presented the sequence of activities for the Linux USB gadget framework in typical/ideal conditions. You can explore the other control path that occurs during an erroneous scenario. The next section explores an actual gadget driver implementation.

GADGET DRIVER: IMPLEMENTATION

To develop a gadget driver, you need to understand the hardware, because certain parts of the gadget driver are specific to underlying USB device controller hardware. The following section explores the gadget driver implementation in continuation with Chapter 12's PDC driver implementation for the Renesas USB controller. The following code analysis is based on `drivers/usb/gadget/r8a66597-udc.c` from the kernel source.

The first step in the process is to define callbacks for the key data structures `struct usb_ep_ops` and `struct usb_gadget_ops`, which allow you to control the gadget hardware. It is not necessary for the gadget driver to support all these callbacks of the endpoint and gadget data structures; the nonsupport could be the result of unavailability in hardware feature.

```
static struct usb_ep_ops r8a66597_ep_ops = {
        .enable         = r8a66597_enable,
        .disable        = r8a66597_disable,
        .alloc_request  = r8a66597_alloc_request,
        .free_request   = r8a66597_free_request,
        .queue          = r8a66597_queue,
        .dequeue        = r8a66597_dequeue,
        .set_halt       = r8a66597_set_halt,
        .set_wedge      = r8a66597_set_wedge,
        .fifo_flush     = r8a66597_fifo_flush,
};
static struct usb_gadget_ops r8a66597_gadget_ops = {
        .get_frame              = r8a66597_get_frame,
}
```

These data structures are registered to the `struct usb_gadget` defined in `struct r8a66597` during the `probe` function of the PDC driver. The next step is to implement the exported interface functions, namely the `usb_gadget_register_driver` and the `usb_gadget_unregister_driver`. The previous section illustrated the sequence of activity of these two interface functions. The `usb_gadget_register_driver` as illustrated in Figure 13.2 is responsible for binding the gadget driver and powering up the gadget controller. Also, note that the `struct usb_gadget_driver` object passed to the `usb_gadget_register_driver` by the functional driver should support two basic callbacks—`bind` and `setup`—for the gadget driver to be functional.

```
int usb_gadget_register_driver(struct usb_gadget_driver *driver)
{
        --cut--
        if (!driver
                        || driver->speed != USB_SPEED_HIGH
                        || !driver->bind
                        || !driver->setup)
                return -EINVAL;
        --cut--
        retval = driver->bind(&r8a66597->gadget);
        if (retval) {
                printk(KERN_ERR "bind to driver error (%d)\n", retval);
                device_del(&r8a66597->gadget.dev);
                goto error;
        }
        r8a66597_bset(r8a66597, VBSE, INTENB0);
        --cut--
}
EXPORT_SYMBOL(usb_gadget_register_driver);
```

As illustrated in Figure 13.3, `usb_gadget_unregister_driver` unbinds the gadget driver from the functional driver and powers down the gadget controller.

```
int usb_gadget_unregister_driver(struct usb_gadget_driver *driver)
{
     --cut--
       if (driver != r8a66597->driver || !driver->unbind)
               return -EINVAL;
       --cut--
       driver->unbind(&r8a66597->gadget);
       init_controller(r8a66597);
       disable_controller(r8a66597);
```

```
        device_del(&r8a66597->gadget.dev);
        r8a66597->driver = NULL;
        return 0;
}
EXPORT_SYMBOL (usb_gadget_unregister_driver);
```

The next important function is to handle the control request sent over Endpoint Zero. Handling of the control request is generally part of interrupt service routines. As illustrated in Figure 13.4, the gadget driver framework handles part of the control requests and passes control to the class driver callback registered through the setup callback.

```
static void irq_control_stage(struct r8a66597 *r8a66597)
__releases(r8a66597->lock)
__acquires(r8a66597->lock)
{
        --cut--
        case CS_WRND:
        if (setup_packet(r8a66597, &ctrl)) {
                spin_unlock(&r8a66597->lock);
                if (r8a66597->driver->setup(&r8a66597->gadget, &ctrl)
                        < 0)
                        pipe_stall(r8a66597, 0);
                spin_lock(&r8a66597->lock);
        }
        --cut--
}
```

The next step is to implement the callbacks declared as endpoint and gadget operations. Most of these operations are specific to the underlying hardware. This section covers only queue and de-queue implementation, because most other callbacks are specific to the hardware. The queue and de-queue are simple list management routines that hold the requests from the functional drivers. On the r8a66597-udc.c, these two callbacks are implemented as r8a66597_queue and r8a66597_dequeue.

```
static int r8a66597_queue(struct usb_ep *_ep, struct usb_request *_req,
                                gfp_t gfp_flags)
{
        struct r8a66597_ep *ep;
        struct r8a66597_request *req;
```

```
        unsigned long flags;
        int request = 0;
        ep = container_of(_ep, struct r8a66597_ep, ep);
        req = container_of(_req, struct r8a66597_request, req);
        if (ep->r8a66597->gadget.speed == USB_SPEED_UNKNOWN)
                return -ESHUTDOWN;
        spin_lock_irqsave(&ep->r8a66597->lock, flags);
        if (list_empty(&ep->queue))
                request = 1;
        list_add_tail(&req->queue, &ep->queue);
        req->req.actual = 0;
        req->req.status = -EINPROGRESS;
        if (ep->desc == NULL)    /* control */
                start_ep0(ep, req);
        else {
                if (request && !ep->busy)
                        start_packet(ep, req);
        }
        spin_unlock_irqrestore(&ep->r8a66597->lock, flags);
        return 0;
}
static int r8a66597_dequeue(struct usb_ep *_ep, struct usb_request *_req)
{
        struct r8a66597_ep *ep;
        struct r8a66597_request *req;
        unsigned long flags;
        ep = container_of(_ep, struct r8a66597_ep, ep);
        req = container_of(_req, struct r8a66597_request, req);
        spin_lock_irqsave(&ep->r8a66597->lock, flags);
        if (!list_empty(&ep->queue))
                transfer_complete(ep, req, -ECONNRESET);
        spin_unlock_irqrestore(&ep->r8a66597->lock, flags);
        return 0;
}
```

These two functions act as the essential backbone of the gadget framework for
OUT and IN transfer. You can explore other callbacks from r8a66597-udc.c
along with the datasheet r8a66597 to better understand the sequence of activities
carried out in the driver framework.

Summary

The gadget driver framework provides an essential infrastructure to support the USB device requirement as defined by the USB specification. It is designed such that the functional driver has full control managing the device, with the infrastructure provided by the gadget driver.

In the next chapter, you explore the functional driver implementation over the gadget driver framework and the composite framework designed to support multiple functional layers above the gadget driver.

More Reading

The gadget driver positioned between the functional driver and the PDC driver is responsible for the USB device management. It uses many Linux infrastructures, such as DMA management and list management. Read `Documentation/DMA-API.txt` before you program a gadget driver that supports DMA transfers. You might also want to read about spinlock at `Documentation/spinlocks.txt`.

Comprehensive coverage of the gadget driver framework is available as `gadget.pdf` on the CD that accompanies this book.

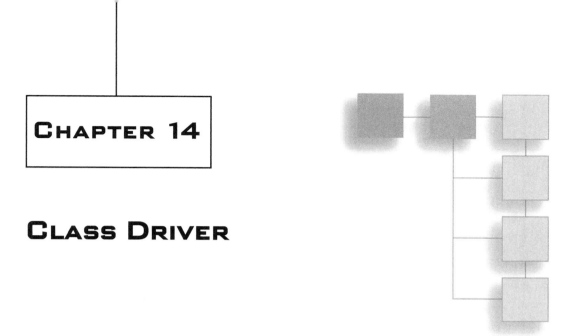

CHAPTER 14

CLASS DRIVER

In This Chapter

- Bootstrap Essentials: Class Drivers
- Class Driver: Design
- Simple Composite Class Driver: Loopback

Universal serial bus (USB) devices are often referred to along with the functionality they support, such as USB audio device or USB storage device. The USB device's functionality is implemented in the class driver layer. These classes are defined by the USB working group and are available in http://www.usb.org/developers/devclass_docs#approved. Sometimes a device can support more than one functional driver and is referred to as a *composite device.*

Linux supports simple functional drivers that provide a single functionality, such as mass storage devices. Lately, the Linux gadget framework has introduced a composite framework that enables the gadget framework to support multiple functionalities. Figure 14.1 illustrates the role of the class driver along with gadget and peripheral device controller (PDC) drivers in the Linux USB gadget subsystem.

The composite framework is placed between the functional driver and the gadget driver, as illustrated in Figure 14.2.

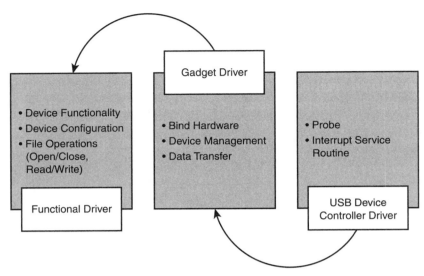

Figure 14.1
Interaction between different layers of the gadget subsystem.

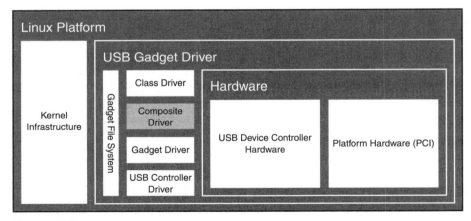

Figure 14.2
Composite gadget subsystem.

This chapter initially explores the essential data structures for class drivers and the composite framework and subsequently explores the internal flow of the composite functional driver. Finally, it analyzes a simple composite functional driver implementation.

Bootstrap Essentials: Class Drivers

The class driver is responsible for managing the functional aspects of the USB device determined by the USB descriptors. The important data structures that the class driver uses are the descriptor data structures. These data structures are defined in the `include/linux/usb/ch9.h` file of the kernel source.

The data structures `struct usb_device_descriptor`, `struct usb_config_descriptor`, `struct usb_interface_descriptor`, and `struct usb_endpoint_descriptor` are passed on to the gadget driver by the class driver. The descriptor as defined by Chapter 9 of the USB specification allows a description of the device to the host.

```
struct usb_device_descriptor {
        __u8   bLength;
        __u8   bDescriptorType;
        __le16 bcdUSB;
        __u8   bDeviceClass;
        __u8   bDeviceSubClass;
        __u8   bDeviceProtocol;
        __u8   bMaxPacketSize0;
        __le16 idVendor;
        __le16 idProduct;
        __le16 bcdDevice;
        __u8   iManufacturer;
        __u8   iProduct;
        __u8   iSerialNumber;
        __u8   bNumConfigurations;
} __attribute__ ((packed));
struct usb_config_descriptor {
        __u8   bLength;
        __u8   bDescriptorType;
        __le16 wTotalLength;
        __u8   bNumInterfaces;
        __u8   bConfigurationValue;
        __u8   iConfiguration;
        __u8   bmAttributes;
        __u8   bMaxPower;
} __attribute__ ((packed));
struct usb_interface_descriptor {
        __u8   bLength;
```

```
        __u8   bDescriptorType;
        __u8   bInterfaceNumber;
        __u8   bAlternateSetting;
        __u8   bNumEndpoints;
        __u8   bInterfaceClass;
        __u8   bInterfaceSubClass;
        __u8   bInterfaceProtocol;
        __u8   iInterface;
} __attribute__ ((packed));
struct usb_endpoint_descriptor {
        __u8   bLength;
        __u8   bDescriptorType;
        __u8   bEndpointAddress;
        __u8   bmAttributes;
        __le16 wMaxPacketSize;
        __u8   bInterval;
        /* NOTE:  these two are _only_ in audio endpoints. */
        /* use USB_DT_ENDPOINT*_SIZE in bLength, not sizeof. */
        __u8   bRefresh;
        __u8   bSynchAddress;
} __attribute__ ((packed));
```

Another important framework is the optional composite driver framework, which sits on top of the gadget driver and provides a framework to build multifunction devices. To support multiple functions, the composite framework provides methods to add functionalities, configurations, and data structures to maintain them. The composite framework uses two data structures to manage the framework: struct usb_function and struct usb_configuration. It is defined in include/linux/usb/composite.h. The struct usb_function holds information and callbacks of a function in the composite driver; similarly, the struct usb_configuration maintains details on the gadget configurations.

```
struct usb_function {
        const char                      *name;
        struct usb_gadget_strings       **strings;
        struct usb_descriptor_header    **descriptors;
        struct usb_descriptor_header    **hs_descriptors;
        struct usb_configuration        *config;
        int  (*bind)(struct usb_configuration *,struct usb_function *);
        void (*unbind)(struct usb_configuration *, struct usb_function *);
```

```
        int   (*set_alt)(struct usb_function *,unsigned interface, unsigned
alt);
        int (*get_alt)(struct usb_function *,unsigned interface);
        void  (*disable)(struct usb_function *);
        int (*setup)(struct usb_function *,const struct usb_ctrlrequest *);
        void  (*suspend)(struct usb_function *);
        void (*resume)(struct usb_function *)
        struct list_head                list;
};
struct usb_configuration {
        const char                 *label;
        struct usb_gadget_strings        **strings;
        const struct usb_descriptor_header **descriptors;
        int   (*bind)(struct usb_configuration *);
        void (*unbind)(struct usb_configuration *);
        int   (*setup)(struct usb_configuration *,const
        struct usb_ctrlrequest *);
        u8                      bConfigurationValue;
        u8                      iConfiguration;
        u8                      bmAttributes;
        u8                      bMaxPower;
        struct usb_composite_dev      *cdev;
        struct list_head       list;
        struct list_head       functions;
        u8                      next_interface_id;
        unsigned               highspeed:1;
        unsigned               fullspeed:1;
        struct usb_function *interface[MAX_CONFIG_INTERFACES];
};
```

The functionality of these callbacks is similar to the gadget callbacks, as explained in the previous chapter. The composite framework also defines interface functions to register and adds the composite information with the gadget framework.

- `int usb_composite_register(struct usb_composite_driver *);`

  This function acts as an interface to register class drivers using the composite driver framework. It is a wrapper above the gadget interface registration function `usb_gadget_register_driver` by the composite driver framework. When the function is successful, it returns 0; when it fails, it returns a negative value.

■ `void usb_composite_unregister(struct usb_composite_driver *);`

This function acts as an interface to unregister class drivers using the composite driver framework. This is a wrapper above the gadget interface registration function `usb_gadget_unregister_driver` by the composite driver framework. When the function is successful, it returns 0; when it fails, it returns a negative value.

■ `int usb_add_function(struct usb_configuration *, struct usb_function *)`

This method adds a function to a configuration and calls the `bind` method to allocate resources such as interface IDs and endpoints. It runs in a single-threaded context. When the function is successful, it returns 0; when it fails, it returns a negative value.

■ `int usb_add_config(struct usb_composite_dev *, struct usb_configuration *)`

This method adds a configuration to a device and binds the configurations with global resources, including string IDs and per-configuration resources such as interface IDs and endpoints. It runs in a single-threaded context. When the function is successful, it returns 0; when it fails, it returns a negative value.

Now that you've seen the important data structure of the functional drivers, the subsequent section details the internal activity of the composite framework and the functional driver.

CLASS DRIVER: DESIGN

The functional driver layer sits on top of the gadget driver layer implementing actual USB device functionality. The functional driver is also referred to as the *class driver*. The USB group defines the USB device functionality through USB class specifications. Like other layers of the gadget subsystem, the functional driver source is available in `drivers/usb/gadget/`, and the source files are named based on the class or function they support.

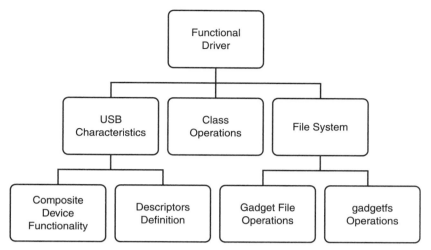

Figure 14.3
A simple breakdown of the Linux USB gadget functional layer.

Figure 14.3 provides a simple breakdown of the function layer of the gadget subsystem.

From Figure 14.3, you can infer that the functional layer consists of routines that decide the USB characteristics. One routine manages the USB descriptors, a set of routines manages the storage or mouse functionality that the USB device implements, and other routines interact with Linux file systems to export the internal data structure to user space as `gadgetfs`.

The other important framework of the functional layer is the composite driver framework, which is optional.

With the given infrastructure, you can build a composite device, supporting multiple functions. The composite infrastructure can support single configuration and multiconfiguration devices supporting multiple functions not necessarily having more than one function per configuration. Figure 14.4 illustrates the functional breakdown of the composite driver framework.

The composite framework provides methods to add configuration and functionalities and data structures to maintain them. The subsequent section concentrates only on the composite framework and the sequence of activity

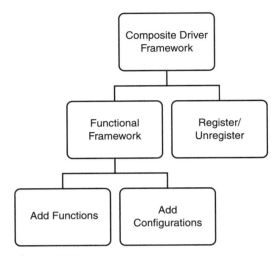

Figure 14.4
A simple breakdown of the Linux USB gadget composite driver layer.

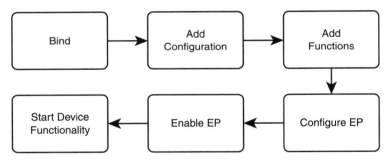

Figure 14.5
A simple control flow of the composite driver.

that occurs in the composite framework. Figure 14.5 provides a simple flow of control when the composite layer is used.

The composite flow consists of three sequences of activity different from a class driver layer: registering the gadget framework using the composite framework, adding the configuration to the functional layer, and adding functions to the configuration. The next section explores these activities in detail.

Figure 14.6 illustrates a typical sequence of calls that occur during function initiation and exit. In the composite framework, a composite driver acts as the interface between the functional driver and the gadget driver.

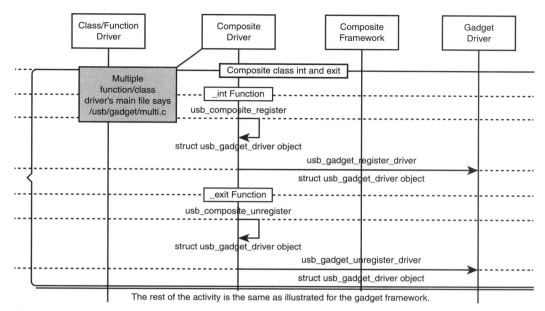

Figure 14.6
Sequence of activities during composite driver initialization.

The composite driver module registers the `struct usb_composite_driver` to the composite framework. The composite framework in turn registers to the gadget framework for further activity; a similar sequence is followed when unregistering.

The next sequence of activity triggered after a successful registration is binding of the driver with the gadget driver. With a composite driver, the `bind` callback adds the composite driver configuration to the composite framework, as shown in Figure 14.7.

The configuration then binds the functions it intends to support using `add_function`, as illustrated in Figure 14.8.

Once the functions are added successfully, the device is ready for enumeration. The host decides which configuration to choose from the composite driver. Then the routine specific to the functionality implemented takes over the functional driver flow. The next section explores the composite driver.

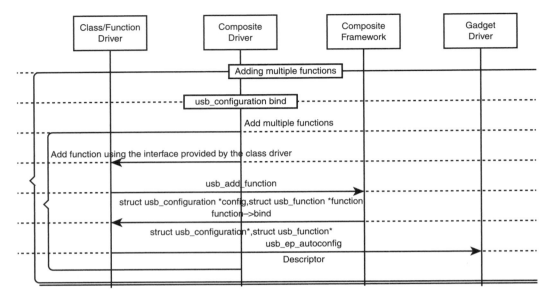

Figure 14.7
Sequence of activities during composite add configuration.

Simple Composite Class Driver: Loopback

To enable you to better understand the flow of the composite driver function, the following section explores the loopback composite function, which is part of the gadget framework as `drivers/usb/gadget/f_loopback.c`. In the gadget source, the Gadget Zero (`drivers/usb/gadget/zero.c`) composite driver module uses the loopback functional driver.

You can start the setup of the `struct usb_configuration` data structure as the first step in developing the composite framework. Generally, a functional driver exports interface functions to facilitate the addition of `struct usb_configuration`. The `f_loopback.c` functional driver creates a `struct usb_configuration` object `loopback_driver`, as shown here.

```
static struct usb_configuration loopback_driver = {
        .label            = "loopback",
        .strings          = loopback_strings,
        .bind             = loopback_bind_config,
        .bConfigurationValue = 2,
```

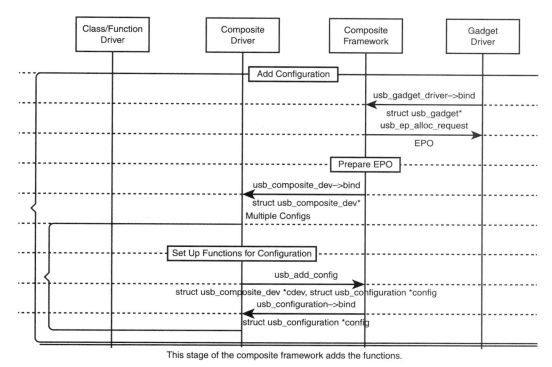

Figure 14.8
Sequence of activities during composite add functions.

```
        .bmAttributes    = USB_CONFIG_ATT_SELFPOWER,
        /* .iConfiguration = DYNAMIC */
};
```

The next step is to define the interface function that enables a composite driver to add the configuration. Adding the USB configuration is part of the composite driver `bind` function of the composite driver, as illustrated in Figure 14.7. The loopback composite function extends `loopback_add in f_loopback.c` as the interface function, which is invoked from `zero_bind` in `drivers/usb/gadget/zero.c`

```
int __init loopback_add(struct usb_composite_dev *cdev)
{       --cut--
     return usb_add_config(cdev, &loopback_driver);
}
```

A successful registration of the `struct usb_configuration` invokes its `bind` callback. The `bind` callback of the configuration is responsible for adding the composite functions, as illustrated in Figure 14.7. The configuration `bind` callback successfully initializes the `struct usb_function` data structure and invokes `add_function`. In the loopback functional driver `loopback_bind_config`, add the function to the gadget framework.

```
static int __init loopback_bind_config(struct usb_configuration *c)
{
        struct f_loopback       *loop;
        int                     status;
        loop = kzalloc(sizeof *loop, GFP_KERNEL);
        if (!loop)
                return -ENOMEM;
        loop->function.name = "loopback";
        loop->function.descriptors = fs_loopback_descs;
        loop->function.bind = loopback_bind;
        loop->function.unbind = loopback_unbind;
        loop->function.set_alt = loopback_set_alt;
        loop->function.disable = loopback_disable;
        status = usb_add_function(c, &loop->function);
        if (status)
                kfree(loop);
        return status;
}
```

The next step in the process is to implement the `bind` callback of the functional driver. The bind process involves configuring the endpoints of the device that is required for the functionality of the functional driver. In case of the loopback functional driver, it binds two endpoints in the `bind` callback `loopback_bind`.

```
static int __init loopback_bind(struct usb_configuration *c, struct usb_
function *f)
{
        --cut--
        loop->in_ep = usb_ep_autoconfig(cdev->gadget, &fs_loop_source_desc);
        --cut--
        loop->out_ep = usb_ep_autoconfig(cdev->gadget, &fs_loop_sink_desc);
        return 0;
}
```

After successful configuration, the details of the configuration are passed on to the USB host during enumeration. When the host requires the loopback functionality, it acquires the interface with loopback functionality and calls the `setup` callback, which invokes `loopback_set_alt` and enables the loopback functionality using `enable_loopback`.

```
static int loopback_set_alt(struct usb_function *f, unsigned intf, unsigned
alt)
{
    --cut--
    return enable_loopback(cdev, loop);
}
```

Once the function is enabled, the functional aspect of the driver takes control over further transactions on noncontrol endpoints. The functional drivers must implement additional functions that handle the functional requirement, which is not USB specific and hence is beyond the scope of this book.

SUMMARY

The functional driver or the class driver is the soul of the Linux USB gadget framework, which decides the behavior of the USB device. The functional driver defines the necessary USB descriptors as defined by the USB specification and passes it to the host during the enumeration using the gadget driver framework. The functional driver handles certain enumeration requests and implements `struct usb_gadget_driver` callback over and above the functionality it supports. This section described the `struct usb_gadget_driver` implementation using the composite framework. You are encouraged to explore a standalone class driver implementation that directly interacts with the gadget framework to implement the device functionality.

The next chapter explores a new device framework: On-the-Go (OTG) devices and their Linux framework.

MORE READING

To understand the class driver, you need to understand the class specification defined by the USB device working group http://www.usb.org/developers/devclass_docs#approved. Other functional drivers are developed above the gadget framework, such as the file system implementation (`drivers/usb/gadget/inode.c`). Such implementation provides more insights of developing class drivers partly at kernel space and partly at user space. The composite framework also supplies utilities interfaces that allow you to enable and disable functional drivers. You can explore these at `drivers/usb/gadget/composite.c`.

PART III

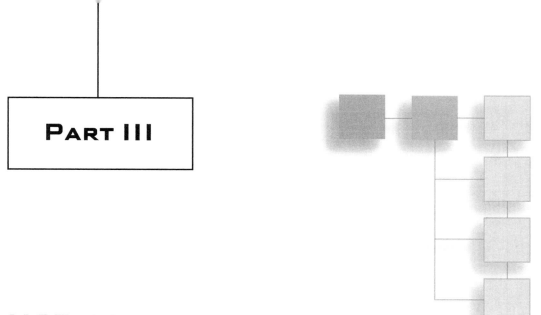

USB OTG

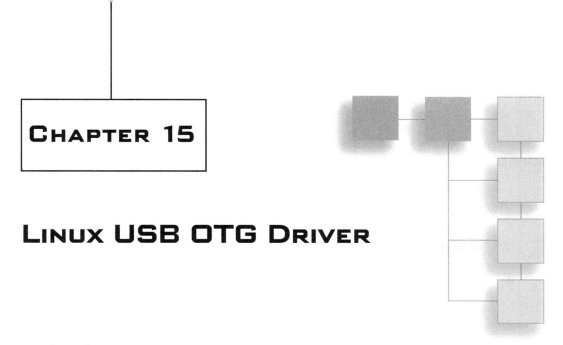

CHAPTER 15

LINUX USB OTG DRIVER

In This Chapter

- Bootstrap Essentials: OTG Driver
- OTG Driver Framework
- OTG Framework: Sample

The universal serial bus (USB) On-the-Go (OTG) specification, a supplement to the USB 2.0 specification that evolved in early 2000, was introduced to enable USB devices to support minimalist USB host capability that enables point-to-point communication. Such a setup allows embedded devices such as digital cameras, mobile phones, and printers to connect to each other directly, as illustrated in Figure 15.1.

An embedded USB device that switches roles, referred as *dual role device*, has features that include minimal USB host capability, Session Request Protocol (SRP), Host Negotiation Protocol (HNP), and 8mA on VBUS. You should read the OTG specification regarding these protocols and how the role switching takes place; the topic is beyond the scope of this chapter.

Linux has a simple infrastructure to support OTG devices. The OTG infrastructure is much closer to the hardware, similar to the peripheral device controller (PDC) driver, and the OTG framework is responsible for handling and responding to the OTG protocol negotiations such as SRP and HNP. At a

Applications:

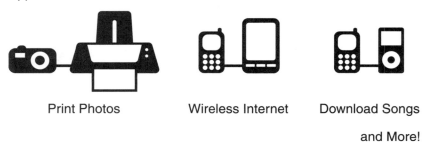

Print Photos   Wireless Internet   Download Songs

and More!

Figure 15.1
A typical OTG setup. (REF: http://www.usb.org/developers/onthego/)

broad level, the functionality of the OTG framework controls the USB transceiver hardware to meet the OTG requirement.

This chapter initially provides an essential bootstrap session for the Linux USB OTG infrastructure. Subsequently, it explores the OTG implementation on the Linux USB subsystem.

Bootstrap Essentials: OTG Driver

The data structures for the OTG framework are defined in `include/linux/usb/otg.h` of the Linux kernel, and the source files are maintained in the `drivers/usb/otg` folder. The OTG framework uses `struct otg_transceiver` as the main data structure to hold methods and information to manage OTG requirements.

```
struct otg_transceiver{
        struct device              *dev;
        const char                 *label;
        unsigned int               flags;
        u8                         default_a;
        enum usb_otg_state         state;
        struct usb_bus             *host;
        struct usb_gadget          *gadget;
        struct otg_io_access_ops        *io_ops;
        void __iomem                    *io_priv;
        /* for notification of usb_xceiv_events */
        struct blocking_notifier_head    notifier;
```

```
        /* to pass extra port status to the root hub */
        u16                     port_status;
        u16                     port_change;
        /* initialize/shutdown of the OTG controller */
        int     (*init)(struct otg_transceiver *otg);
        void    (*shutdown)(struct otg_transceiver *otg);
        /* bind/unbind the host controller */
        int     (*set_host)(struct otg_transceiver *otg,
                            struct usb_bus *host);
        /* bind/unbind the peripheral controller */
        int     (*set_peripheral)(struct otg_transceiver *otg,
                            struct usb_gadget *gadget);
        /* effective for B devices, ignored for A-peripheral */
        int     (*set_power)(struct otg_transceiver *otg,
                            unsigned mA);
        /* effective for A-peripheral, ignored for B devices */
        int     (*set_vbus)(struct otg_transceiver *otg,
                            bool enabled);
        /* for non-OTG B devices: set transceiver into suspend mode */
        int     (*set_suspend)(struct otg_transceiver *otg,
                            int suspend);
        /* for B devices only: start session with A-Host */
        int     (*start_srp)(struct otg_transceiver *otg);
        /* start or continue HNP role switch */
        int     (*start_hnp)(struct otg_transceiver *otg);
};
```

The `struct otg_transceiver` data structure provides callback methods to implement the framework that is necessary for the OTG transceiver. These methods help the Linux USB framework manage the OTG requirement. The following list details the methods of the OTG framework.

- `int     (*start_hnp)(struct otg_transceiver *otg);`

  This callback method starts the HNP session. The transceiver driver or hardware layer implements this callback. The interface function `int otg_start_hnp(struct otg_transceiver *otg)` invokes this callback.

- `int     (*set_host)(struct otg_transceiver *otg, struct usb_bus *host);`

This callback method receives the USB host data structure and saves it in the transceiver driver for subsequent usage. The interface function `int otg_set_host(struct otg_transceiver *otg, struct usb_bus *host)` sets this information.

- `int    (*set_peripheral)(struct otg_transceiver *otg, struct usb_gadget *gadget);`

This callback method receives the USB device data structure and saves it in the transceiver driver for subsequent usage. The interface function `int otg_set_peripheral(struct otg_transceiver *otg, struct usb_gadget *periph)` sets this information.

- `int    (*set_power)(struct otg_transceiver *otg, unsigned mA);`

This callback method sets the power in the VBUS during a default-B session. The interface function `int otg_set_power(struct otg_transceiver *otg, unsigned mA)` invokes this callback.

- `int    (*set_suspend)(struct otg_transceiver *otg, int suspend);`

This callback method suspends and resumes the transceiver. When the `suspend` parameter is set, the transceiver is to be suspended; when it is 0, the transceiver is to be resumed. The interface function `int otg_set_suspend(struct otg_transceiver *otg, int suspend)` invokes this callback.

- `int    (*start_srp)(struct otg_transceiver *otg);`

This callback method starts the SRP session, and the transceiver driver or hardware layer implements this callback. The interface function `int otg_start_srp(struct otg_transceiver *otg)` invokes this callback.

The OTG specification defines the state machine as part of the negotiation protocols, and the Linux USB framework defines part of an `enum usb_otg_state` in `include/linux/usb/otg.h`.

```
enum usb_otg_state {
        OTG_STATE_UNDEFINED = 0,
        /* single-role peripheral, and dual-role default-b */
        OTG_STATE_B_IDLE,
        OTG_STATE_B_SRP_INIT,
        OTG_STATE_B_PERIPHERAL,
```

```
        /* extra dual-role default-b states */
        OTG_STATE_B_WAIT_ACON,
        OTG_STATE_B_HOST,
        /* dual-role default-a */
        OTG_STATE_A_IDLE,
        OTG_STATE_A_WAIT_VRISE,
        OTG_STATE_A_WAIT_BCON,
        OTG_STATE_A_HOST,
        OTG_STATE_A_SUSPEND,
        OTG_STATE_A_PERIPHERAL,
        OTG_STATE_A_WAIT_VFALL,
        OTG_STATE_A_VBUS_ERR,
};
```

The next section explores how the Linux USB subsystem uses these OTG interfaces to enable the USB host framework to a USB gadget in an OTG setup or vice versa.

OTG Driver Framework

The OTG framework is not clearly defined like the gadget framework is; sometimes the OTG implementation is mixed with the other frameworks. The Linux USB subsystem source code of the OTG framework is maintained in the `/drivers/usb/otg/` folder. Some part of the `usbcore` module plays a key role (`drivers/usb/core/hub.c`).

Most of the OTG activities are based on the physical layer activity and the timing of the electrical signals. The role of the OTG software framework is minimal; it is responsible for setting up the signal and switching to different states defined by the OTG specification. Figure 15.2 illustrates a top-level breakdown of the OTG framework.

The OTG framework is divided into two major parts: callback methods and utility functions. The methods provided by `struct otg_tranceiver` are extended to the other Linux USB frameworks using wrapper functions. The OTG framework also helps save and retrieve the `struct otg_transceiver` object using utility functions. The other main part is interface methods of the transceiver to the platform.

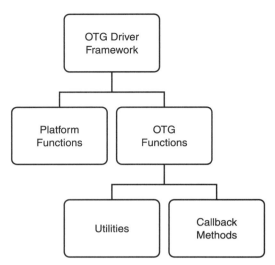

Figure 15.2
A simple top-level breakdown of the OTG framework.

The OTG driver flow consists of both the host and the device driver framework, taking its part to switch the role by using the OTG framework. Before you can understand what happens inside the driver framework, you need to understand the sequence of activities that occurs when the role switch takes place. Figure 15.3, extracted from the USB OTG specification, illustrates operations when two OTG devices having full OTG functionality are connected.

Figure 15.4 illustrates a simplified control flow of the OTG framework. Like any other driver, the OTG driver starts platform registration and is based on how the transceiver hardware is interfaced.

Like the PDC driver, the OTG driver is specific to the hardware and the platform for which the transceiver is developed. The OTG driver starts by registering itself successfully with the Linux platform, along with the platform callbacks such as the probe routine. The platform calls the registered probe routine when it detects the transceiver.

The probe routine maps the platform resource and creates the `struct otg_transceiver` object. The probe routine also sets the callbacks of `otg_transceiver`. You can save the object using the `otg_set_transceiver` utility

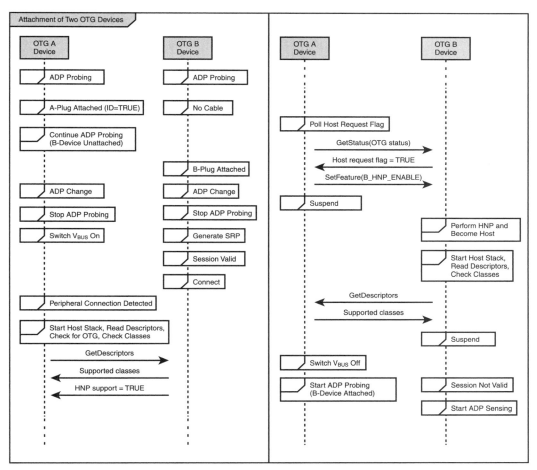

Figure 15.3
Sequence of operations between two OTG devices. (REF: A.2.1 Figure A-8 OTG specification)

function. (The saved object can be retrieved by other Linux USB frameworks using the `otg_get_transceiver` utility function.) Once the probe is successful, the OTG framework is functionally ready for the host and gadget framework to use it. The role switching and negotiations take place using control commands, as illustrated in Figure 15.3. The next section explores how to implement the OTG framework based on the OMAP USB OTG controller implementation, as this is referred to by the Linux USB documentation (http://www.linux-usb.org/gadget/h2-otg.html).

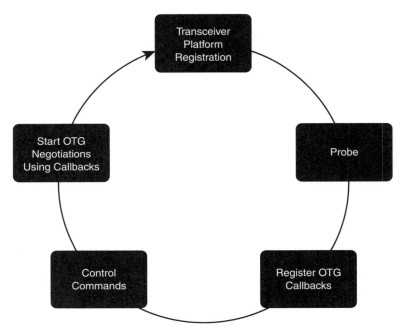

Figure 15.4
Linux USB OTG driver control flow.

OTG Framework: Sample

Recall from Chapter 2, "USB: An Overview," that USB controllers may be in different configurations. The transceiver portion is either built within the controller or interfaced with glue logic externally. Thus, an OTG framework driver depends greatly on the way the transceiver is interfaced with the digital controller. This section explores the OTG implementation of isp1301 available in drivers/usb/ otg/isp1301_omap, which is connected to the controller using an I2C interface.

The first step is to define the transceiver driver required by glue hardware with the kernel. Because the isp1301 OTG controller uses the I2C interface, declare a struct i2c_driver-based object, say isp1301_driver, and register it in the isp_init using i2c_add_driver.

```
static const struct i2c_device_id isp1301_id[] = {
        { "isp1301_omap", 0 },
        { }
};
```

```
MODULE_DEVICE_TABLE(i2c, isp1301_id);
static struct i2c_driver isp1301_driver = {
        .driver = {
                .name      = "isp1301_omap",
        },
        .probe             = isp1301_probe,
        .remove            = __exit_p(isp1301_remove),
        .id_table          = isp1301_id,
};
/*----------------------------------------------------------------*/
static int __init isp_init(void)
{
        return i2c_add_driver(&isp1301_driver);
}?
subsys_initcall(isp_init);
static void __exit isp_exit(void)
{
        if (the_transceiver)
                otg_set_transceiver(NULL);
        i2c_del_driver(&isp1301_driver);
}
module_exit(isp_exit);
```

The next step in the process is to implement the probe function of the transceiver driver. It is responsible for initializing the callbacks of the otg_transceiver object. The probe function also saves the otg_transceiver object for the gadget and host driver using the otg_set_transceiver utility function.

```
static int __init
isp1301_probe(struct i2c_client *i2c, const struct i2c_device_id *id)
{
        --cut--
        isp->otg.set_host = isp1301_set_host,
        isp->otg.set_peripheral = isp1301_set_peripheral,
        isp->otg.set_power = isp1301_set_power,
        isp->otg.start_srp = isp1301_start_srp,
        isp->otg.start_hnp = isp1301_start_hnp,
        enable_vbus_draw(isp, 0);
        power_down(isp);
        the_transceiver = isp;
        --cut--
```

```
        status = otg_set_transceiver(&isp->otg);
    --cut--

}
```

The `otg_transceiver` object is saved in `driver/usb/otg/otg.c`. When a driver requires the saved `otg_transceiver` object, the `otg_get_transceiver` utility function retrieves it. The next step is to implement the `transceiver` callbacks that are specific to the transceiver hardware. As a sample, the following provides a snapshot of SRP implementation. Notice from the following code the routine access hardware-specific registers of the platform that implement SRP functionality.

```
static int
isp1301_start_srp(struct otg_transceiver *dev)
{
        struct isp1301   *isp = container_of(dev, struct isp1301, otg);
        u32              otg_ctrl;

        if (!dev || isp != the_transceiver
                        || isp->otg.state != OTG_STATE_B_IDLE)
                return -ENODEV;

        otg_ctrl = omap_readl(OTG_CTRL);
        if (!(otg_ctrl & OTG_BSESSEND))
                return -EINVAL;

        otg_ctrl |= OTG_B_BUSREQ;
        otg_ctrl &= ~OTG_A_BUSREQ & OTG_CTRL_MASK;
        omap_writel(otg_ctrl, OTG_CTRL);
        isp->otg.state = OTG_STATE_B_SRP_INIT;

        pr_debug("otg: SRP, %s ... %06x\n", state_name(isp),
                        omap_readl(OTG_CTRL));
#ifdef  CONFIG_USB_OTG
        check_state(isp, __func__);
#endif
        return 0;
}
```

You can further explore the source along with the data sheet of isp1301 and the OMAP controller to better understand the implementation.

Once you've successfully implemented these callbacks, the OTG framework is ready for Linux USB frameworks such as hub and gadget to use them. You can enable the ISP1301 module through drivers/usb/otg/Kconfig. When you develop an OTG driver, update the Kconfig and the makefile in the drivers/usb/otg folder to enable the driver module as part kernel. The following snippet from drivers/usb/otg/Kconfig manages the isp1301 transceiver.

```
config ISP1301_OMAP
        tristate "Philips ISP1301 with OMAP OTG"
        depends on I2C && ARCH_OMAP_OTG
        select USB_OTG_UTILS
        help
```

SUMMARY

The OTG specification was introduced to enable USB devices to act as minimal USB hosts. The Linux USB subsystem's OTG framework was integrated to the kernel sometime in 2004. Some transceivers for controllers, such as OMAP, have adopted the OTG interfaces explained in this chapter, and others have implemented OTG functionality interleaving with host and gadget sources. This chapter explained the OTG implementation based on OMAP. You can accomplish future development in a similar way with clean interfaces for OTG requirements. Also, you may need to modify the Targeted Peripherals List in drivers/usb/core/otg_whitelist.h to ensure that the Linux USB framework allows the device you're interested in.

Forthcoming chapters of this book explore the way developers and other users can effectively use the Linux USB framework for development and debugging.

MORE READING

This chapter explored the basics of the Linux USB OTG framework that enable you to implement a simple OTG driver. You can check out the source files drivers/usb/otg/gpio_vbus.c and drivers/usb/otg/nop-usb-xceiv.c to enhance your understanding. The former source file is a simple General Purpose Input/Output (GPIO) VBUS sensing driver for the B peripheral. The reference from the Linux-USB Web site provides additional information on OTG; check out http://www.linux-usb.org/gadget/h2-otg.html.

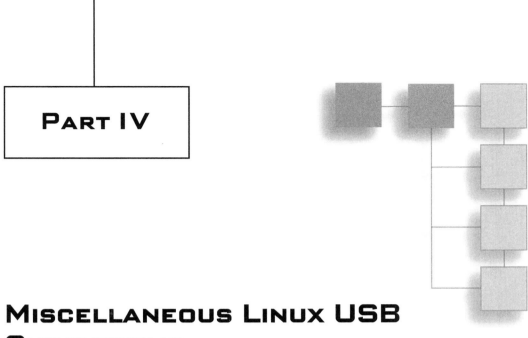

PART IV

MISCELLANEOUS LINUX USB SUBSYSTEMS

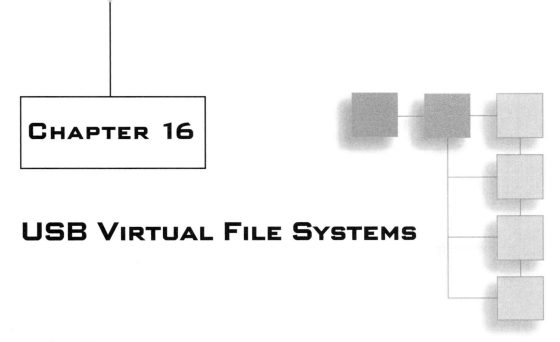

CHAPTER 16

USB VIRTUAL FILE SYSTEMS

In This Chapter

- USB Host Virtual File Systems
- USB Device Virtual File Systems

A Virtual File System (VFS) or virtual file system switch is an abstraction layer on top of the actual file system that specifies an interface between the kernel and the file system. Acting as a transparent layer file, it allows uniform access to client applications. A VFS does not need to know the format in which the file is stored. The format intricacies are handled by equivalent callback routines that are registered with VFS and return only the data required by the user application, thus providing necessary transparency to the user application.

Certain VFSs are categorized as special because they act as an interface to manipulate and control kernel data structures and devices connected to the kernel. Some special VFS files are mounted onto the /proc directory. These /proc files extend interfaces that provide access to physical devices connected to the system and provide options to control kernel data.

The Linux universal serial bus (USB) framework also has special VFS files that allow access to the kernel part USB framework and to the USB device at the user space. You know by now from the previous chapters that the Linux USB framework has host and gadget frameworks. Figure 16.1 illustrates the USB VFS files of the Linux USB framework. The Linux USB framework extends two VFS

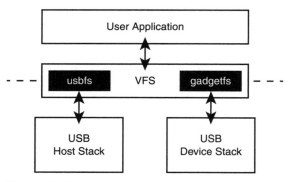

Figure 16.1
A simple representation of USB VFS files.

files: `usbfs`, which acts as an interface to the Linux USB host framework, and `gadgetfs`, which acts as an interface to the Linux USB gadget framework. Other files such as `devfs` and `sysfs` offer access to the kernel data structure and the USB device–specific information to user space. On Linux, these files are a means to export kernel data structures and their attributes to the user space.

This chapter discusses both the USB host and the device VFS files, which include how to set up the USB VFS, followed by their file format and functionalities. It also explores applications that use these VFS files. Later in this chapter, you will learn about the `devfs` and the `sysfs` files of the Linux USB framework and discover how the USB `devfs` and `sysfs` directories are organized.

OVERVIEW OF USBFS

From the previous chapters, you know that the USB host file system is part of the `usbcore` implementation. When the `usbcore` module is loaded into the kernel, the USB host VFS is initialized, and it is ready to be mounted in the user space. The `usbfs` file is generally mounted to the `/proc` directory. The following terminal activity illustrates the step to mount the `usbfs` virtual file:

`root@rajaram-laptop:/proc/bus/usb# mount -t usbfs none /proc/bus/usb`

Tip

> The VFS of `usbcore` was initially referred to as `usbdevfs` and later renamed to `usbfs` to avoid confusion with the `devfs` file system.

Using usbfs, a key VFS file of the Linux USB subsystem, usbcore exports USB device access to the user space. In the subsequent sections, you will learn about the usbfs file tree, which can help you understand how to develop a user space driver for USB on Linux. The following terminal activity displays the usbfs tree mounted on the /proc/bus/usb root directory.

```
root@rajaram-laptop:/proc/bus/usb# ls -alt
total 0
dr-xr-xr-x 2 root root 0 2010-06-08 18:48 007
dr-xr-xr-x 2 root root 0 2010-06-08 18:48 006
dr-xr-xr-x 2 root root 0 2010-06-08 18:48 005
dr-xr-xr-x 2 root root 0 2010-06-08 18:48 004
dr-xr-xr-x 2 root root 0 2010-06-08 18:48 003
dr-xr-xr-x 2 root root 0 2010-06-08 18:48 002
drwxr-xr-x 9 root root 0 2010-06-08 18:48 .
dr-xr-xr-x 2 root root 0 2010-06-08 18:48 001
dr-xr-xr-x 6 root root 0 2010-06-08 10:49 ..
-r--r--r-- 1 root root 0 2010-06-08 10:48 devices
```

The usbfs file creates two types of files. The first file is devices, which contains the information of all USB devices in text format. The second is a set of directories and files representing the USBs and devices connected to the system. The directory tree is of structure BBB/DDD, where BBB represents the USB number and DDD represents the USB device number. The following sections detail both of these files and look into USB applications using them.

usbfs: devices File

Sometimes during development as a system user, you may need to know the devices that are connected to a particular USB. Tools like the USBView provide this topological view of the USB device tree with a graphical interface. The tools retrieve this information from the devices file and present USB information to the user in an interactive way. The following section explains how information is represented in the devices file.

The devices file of usbfs contains USB- and device-related information in text format, as discussed earlier. This text information is arranged in a particular sequential order and includes details of the USB descriptors and related information. Each line in the file starts with a symbol (T, B, D, P, S, C, I, E)

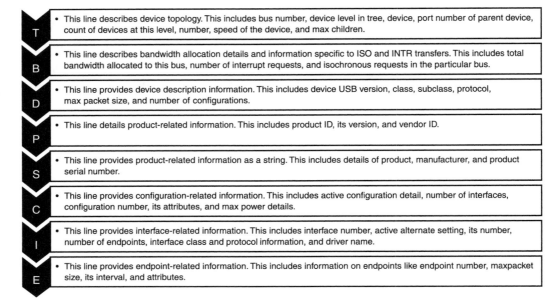

Figure 16.2
File format of the /proc/bus/usb/devices file.

indicating subsequent information in the line. Figure 16.2 illustrates the significance of these symbols.

Starting each line with a keyword or a symbol facilitates easy parsing of the file and helps extract information of interest. For example, to preview only USB details of the system, a grep of T: keys provides the desired result, shown here.

```
root@rajaram-laptop:/home/rajaram# cat /proc/bus/usb/devices | grep T:
T:  Bus=07 Lev=00 Prnt=00 Port=00 Cnt=00 Dev#=  1 Spd=480 MxCh= 6
T:  Bus=07 Lev=01 Prnt=01 Port=00 Cnt=01 Dev#=  2 Spd=480 MxCh= 0
T:  Bus=06 Lev=00 Prnt=00 Port=00 Cnt=00 Dev#=  1 Spd=480 MxCh= 4
T:  Bus=06 Lev=01 Prnt=01 Port=00 Cnt=01 Dev#=  2 Spd=480 MxCh= 0
T:  Bus=05 Lev=00 Prnt=00 Port=00 Cnt=00 Dev#=  1 Spd=12  MxCh= 2
T:  Bus=04 Lev=00 Prnt=00 Port=00 Cnt=00 Dev#=  1 Spd=12  MxCh= 2
T:  Bus=03 Lev=00 Prnt=00 Port=00 Cnt=00 Dev#=  1 Spd=12  MxCh= 2
T:  Bus=02 Lev=00 Prnt=00 Port=00 Cnt=00 Dev#=  1 Spd=12  MxCh= 2
T:  Bus=01 Lev=00 Prnt=00 Port=00 Cnt=00 Dev#=  1 Spd=12  MxCh= 2
```

A complete copy of the devices file is available on the CD-ROM as proc_ devices.txt. So that you can understand the format and how to use it, the following section extracts a portion of proc_devices.txt. In the example setup, a thumb drive is connected to bus number 07. You will now dissect the contents specific to the thumb drive from the devices file.

The first line of the text information starts with the keyword T. The text in this line indicates that the thumb drive is a high-speed device with device address 3. From the line, you can also understand that the device is connected to port 02 of bus number 07. All this information is in decimal format.

```
T:   Bus=07 Lev=01 Prnt=01 Port=02 Cnt=01 Dev#=   3 Spd=480 MxCh= 0
```

The second line that starts with the keyword D indicates that the line contains device descriptor information. The line indicates that the thumb drive is a USB 2.0 device with one configuration.

```
D:   Ver= 2.00 Cls=00(>ifc ) Sub=00 Prot=00 MxPS=64 #Cfgs=  1]
```

The subsequent line that starts with the keyword P contains product-specific information. The line provides the product and the vendor ID of the thumb drive.

```
P:   Vendor=1221 ProdID=3234 Rev= 0.00
```

The line that starts with the keyword S provides information as a string. This includes the manufacturer name, the product name, and the serial number of the device.

```
S:   Manufacturer=Udisk
S:   Product=Udisk 2.0
S:   SerialNumber=013CCFCFCFFAE59D
```

The next line that starts with the keyword C indicates device configuration–related information. The line indicates the thumb drive. The * indicates that the current configuration is the active one.

```
C:* #Ifs= 1 Cfg#= 1 Atr=80 MxPwr=10=0mA
```

The line that starts with the keyword I indicates interface-related information. The devices interface has two endpoints and is a storage device. Because it is a storage device, the usb-storage module is loaded as the driver for this interface.

```
I:* If#= 0 Alt= 0 #EPs= 2 Cls=08(stor.) Sub=06 Prot=50 Driver=usb-storage
```

The line that starts with the keyword E indicates endpoint-related information. Because it is a thumb drive, it has bulk IN and bulk OUT endpoints with a max packet size of 512 bytes. It is a bulk endpoint, so a time interval is associated with it.

```
E:  Ad=81(I) Atr=02(Bulk) MxPS= 512 Ivl=0ms
E:  Ad=01(O) Atr=02(Bulk) MxPS= 512 Ivl=0ms
```

The device information in the devices file is organized sequentially like a descriptor tree because most of its information is collected from the device's descriptors. The bus and device information is placed hierarchically.

Application Based on the devices File

To better present information in the devices file to the user, interactive applications are available on Linux. There is a graphical application (USBView) and a simple command-line script (usbtree) that present the information in a more readable format. You'll learn how to set up these tools in your system and how to use them in the following sections.

Graphical User Interface: USBView

USBView displays the devices file graphically and presents the USB device topology of the Linux system. You can install USBView on the system from http://www.kroah.com/linux-usb/ or use apt-get install usbview or similar package installer options.

After a successful installation, you can invoke USBView through the command line in super user mode or ensure that the user invoking the USBView has proper access levels. Also, for the tool to work properly, you must mount the usbfs file system in the standard path. If the path is different, configure the tool with the mount path, as illustrated in Figure 16.3.

Once the devices file path is configured, USBView provides the topological view of the USB devices in the system with device-related information.

Command Line: usbtree

Traditional Linux users prefer command-line tools to tools with a graphical interface. To list the USB device topology on the command line, you can use the usbtree script. You can download the script, written using PERL, from http://www.linux-usb.org/usbtree. For the script to work properly, ensure that the PERL package is properly installed in your system.

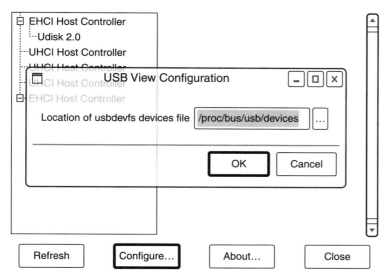

Figure 16.3
Configuring the /proc/bus/usb path in the USBView tool.

Once you have downloaded the script to your system, copy it to any system folder, such as /bin, so that you can invoke the script from any path. Also, ensure that the script has execution rights. In the example setup, a thumb drive is connected to the platform. To view the USB topologies, run the usbtree script in the terminal. The following terminal activity illustrates the output of usbtree script:

```
root@rajaram-laptop:/home/rajaram/Desktop# usbtree
/: Bus 09.Port 1: Dev 1, Class=root_hub, Drv=ohci_hcd/3p, 12M
/: Bus 08.Port 1: Dev 1, Class=root_hub, Drv=ehci_hcd/3p, 480M
/: Bus 07.Port 1: Dev 1, Class=root_hub, Drv=ehci_hcd/6p, 480M
    |_ Port 3: Dev 2, If 0, Prod=Udisk 2.0, Class=stor., Drv=usb-storage, 480M
/: Bus 06.Port 1: Dev 1, Class=root_hub, Drv=ehci_hcd/4p, 480M
    |_ Port 1: Dev 2, If 0, Prod=Acer Crystal Eye webcam, Class=video,
Drv=uvcvideo, 480M
    |_ Port 1: Dev 2, If 1, Prod=, Class=video, Drv=uvcvideo, 480M
/: Bus 05.Port 1: Dev 1, Class=root_hub, Drv=uhci_hcd/2p, 12M
/: Bus 04.Port 1: Dev 1, Class=root_hub, Drv=uhci_hcd/2p, 12M
/: Bus 03.Port 1: Dev 1, Class=root_hub, Drv=uhci_hcd/2p, 12M
/: Bus 02.Port 1: Dev 1, Class=root_hub, Drv=uhci_hcd/2p, 12M
/: Bus 01.Port 1: Dev 1, Class=root_hub, Drv=uhci_hcd/2p, 12M
```

From the output, you can infer that the thumb drive is assigned with device number 2 and is connected to port 3 of the USB with bus number 7. The output also shows you the drivers attached to the device. The script generates additional information, such as the product and vendor ID, when you invoke it with argument −1.

usbfs: BBB/DDD Files

The next files are the BBB/DDD files of the usbfs, which control and interact with a USB device. This directory tree is created based on the USB number (BBB) and the USB device number (DDD). Unlike the devices file, the BBB/DDD file is in binary format. The following terminal activity shows you how the BBB/DDD files are organized in the /proc/bus/usb directory.

```
root@rajaram-laptop:/proc/bus/usb# tree -A
.
+- 001
¦+-- 001
+-- 002
¦+-- 001

+-- 003
¦+-- 001
+-- 004
¦+-- 001
+-- 005
¦+-- 001
+-- 006
¦+-- 001
¦+-- 002
+-- 007
¦+-- 001
¦+-- 002
¦+-- 003
+-- devices
```

From the terminal log, you can infer that the thumb drive with device number 002 is listed below the directory under bus number 007. The contents of the file include device and configuration descriptors of the USB device. To interface with the device, open the device using the /proc/bus/usb/007/002 path. After a successful open call, you can read the file for the descriptors to ensure that you are connected to the right device and then bind to the interface to begin interacting with the device.

The user space driver generally employs these BBB/DDD files to control the USB devices. The drivers use input/output controls (IOCTLs) defined in /include/ linux/usbdevice_fs.h to control and interact with the USB devices. In the next chapter, you will study user space drivers in detail using these IOCTLs to drive the USB devices. The table that follows lists the IOCTLs and their functionalities supported by the usbfs file.

IOCTL	Description
USBDEVFS_CONTROL	IOCTL to send USB control messages. The user argument to call this IOCTL should be of type struct usbdevfs_ctrltransfer.
USBDEVFS_BULK	IOCTL to send USB bulk messages. The user argument to call this IOCTL should be of type struct usbdevfs_bulktransfer.
USBDEVFS_RESETEP	IOCTL to reset a particular endpoint. The user argument to call this IOCTL should be of type unsigned int indicating the endpoint.
USBDEVFS_SETINTERFACE	IOCTL to set a particular interface. The user argument to call this IOCTL should be of type struct usbdevfs_setinterface.
USBDEVFS_SETCONFIGURATION	IOCTL to set a particular configuration. The user argument to call this IOCTL should be of type unsigned int indicating the configuration number.
USBDEVFS_GETDRIVER	IOCTL to get a driver installed for a particular interface. The user argument to call this IOCTL should be of type struct usbdevfs_getdriver.
USBDEVFS_SUBMITURB	IOCTL to transfer USB Request Block (URB) messages. The user argument to call this IOCTL should be of type struct usbdevfs_urb.
USBDEVFS_DISCARDURB	IOCTL to kill a URB message. There is no argument for this IOCTL call.
USBDEVFS_REAPURB	IOCTL to reap a URB messages as a blocking call. The user argument is of a void data type.
USBDEVFS_REAPURBNDELAY	IOCTL to reap a URB messages as an unblocking call. The user argument is of a void data type.

Continued

IOCTL	Description
USBDEVFS_DISCSIGNAL	IOCTL to disconnect a device. The user argument to call this IOCTL should be of type `struct usbdevfs_disconnectsignal`.
USBDEVFS_CLAIMINTERFACE	IOCTL to claim a particular interface. The user argument to call this IOCTL should be of type `unsigned int` indicating the interface.
USBDEVFS_RELEASEINTERFACE	IOCTL to release a particular interface. The user argument to call this IOCTL should be of type `unsigned int` indicating the interface.
USBDEVFS_CONNECTINFO	IOCTL to get connection speed information. The user argument to call this IOCTL should be of type `struct usbdevfs_connect_info`.
USBDEVFS_IOCTL	A generic IOCTL to pass on IOCTLs. The user argument to call this IOCTL should be of type `struct usbdevfs_ioctl`.
USBDEVFS_HUB_PORTINFO	IOCTL to get USB hub information from the hub driver. The user argument to call this IOCTL should be of type `struct usbdevfs_hub_portinfo`.
USBDEVFS_RESET	IOCTL to reset a particular device. There is no argument for this IOCTL call.
USBDEVFS_CLEAR_HALT	IOCTL to clear a halt on a particular endpoint. The user argument to call this IOCTL should be of type `unsigned int`.
USBDEVFS_DISCONNECT	IOCTL to disconnect a particular device. There is no argument for this IOCTL call.
USBDEVFS_CONNECT	IOCTL to connect a particular device. There is no argument for this IOCTL call.
USBDEVFS_CLAIM_PORT	IOCTL to claim a particular port. The user argument to call this IOCTL should be of type `unsigned int` indicating the port.
USBDEVFS_RELEASE_PORT	IOCTL to release a particular port. The user argument to call this IOCTL should be of type `unsigned int` indicating the port.

OVERVIEW OF SYSFS

The sysfs tree contains all device-specific information connected in the system. Through the sysfs file system, the usbcore extends the USB device and USB interface–related information to the user space. The sysfs files for USB are mounted in the /sys/bus/usb directory. The contents of the USB sysfs directory are illustrated here.

```
rajaram@rajaram-laptop:/sys/bus/usb$ ls
devices  drivers  drivers_autoprobe  drivers_probe  uevent
```

The devices directory contains information on the USB devices connected to the system. The following terminal activity illustrates the /sys/bus/usb/devices directory.

```
rajaram@rajaram-laptop:/sys/bus/usb/devices$ ls
1-0:1.0  3-0:1.0  5-0:1.0  6-1      6-1:1.1  7-3      usb1  usb3  usb5  usb7
2-0:1.0  4-0:1.0  6-0:1.0  6-1:1.0  7-0:1.0  7-3:1.0  usb2  usb4  usb6
```

The usb* directories represent USB controllers connected to the system; the * indicates the bus number assigned to each controller. From the log, you can infer that the example setup has seven USB host controllers. The other entries in the directory with the format bus-port.port.port:config.interface represent the devices and their interfaces. For example, 7-3:1.0 represents a device connected to port 3, bus 7, configuration 1, interface 0. The other directories with format bus-0:1.0 represent the root hub's interface.

The device 7-3:1.0 connected to the system is a mass storage device. The following terminal activity illustrates the content of the 7-3:1.0 directory, which provides details of the connected device. Some information is read only, such as the bNumEndpoints and bInterfaceClass.

```
rajaram@rajaram-laptop:/sys/bus/usb/devices/7-3:1.0$ ls -alt
total 0
-r--r--r-- 1 root root 4096 2010-07-14 23:39 bAlternateSetting
-r--r--r-- 1root root 4096 2010-07-14 23:39 bNumEndpoints
lrwxrwxrwx 1 root root    0 2010-07-14 23:39 ep_01 -> ../../../../../../devices/
pci0000:00/0000:00:1d.7/usb7/7-3/7-3:1.0/usb_endpoint/usbdev7.2_ep01
lrwxrwxrwx 1 root root    0 2010-07-14 23:39 ep_81 -> ../../../../../../devices/
pci0000:00/0000:00:1d.7/usb7/7-3/7-3:1.0/usb_endpoint/usbdev7.2_ep81
-r--r--r-- 1 root root 4096 2010-07-14 23:39 modalias
drwxr-xr-x 2 root root    0 2010-07-14 23:39 power
-rw--r--r-- 1 root root 4096 2010-07-14 23:39 uevent
drwxr-xr-x 4 root root    0 2010-07-14 22:40 host4
drwxr-xr-x 5 root root    0 2010-07-14 22:40 .
lrwxrwxrwx 1 root root    0 2010-07-14 22:40 driver -> ../../../../../../bus/
usb/drivers/usb-storage
drwxr-xr-x 4 root root    0 2010-07-14 22:40 usb_endpoint
```

```
-r--r--r-- 1 root root 4096 2010-07-14 22:40 bInterfaceClass
-r--r--r-- 1 root root 4096 2010-07-14 22:40 bInterfaceNumber
-r--r--r-- 1 root root 4096 2010-07-14 22:40 bInterfaceProtocol
-r--r--r-- 1 root root 4096 2010-07-14 22:40 bInterfaceSubClass
lrwxrwxrwx 1 root root    0 2010-07-14 22:40 subsystem -> ../../../../../../
bus/usb
drwxr-xr-x 5 root root    0 2010-07-14 22:40 ..
```

The device directory contains subdirectories such as power and uevent. The power directory provides information related to USB device power management. The following terminal activity displays the contents of the power directory. The wakeup file listed in the log that follows provides information on the device's USB remote wakeup capability. The file is empty if the device doesn't support remote wakeup. When the device supports remote wakeup, the file contains either an enabled or disabled keyword. You can also write to the file to enable and disable the remote wakeup option.

```
rajaram@rajaram-laptop:/sys/bus/usb/devices/7-3:1.0/power$ ls -alt
total 0
-rw-r--r-- 1 root root 4096 2010-07-15 22:31 wakeup
drwxr-xr-x 2 root root    0 2010-07-15 22:31 .
drwxr-xr-x 5 root root    0 2010-07-15 22:30 ..
```

The uevent file is part of the hot plugging framework of the usbcore that supports USB hot plugging of USB devices. Most of the fields in the uevent file are self-explanatory. The information in the TYPE field contains the bDeviceClass /bDeviceSubClass /bDeviceProtocol, respectively. You can refer to the show_modalias function in </drivers/usb/core/sysfs.c> to understand the data along the MODALIAS field.

```
rajaram@rajaram-laptop:/sys/bus/usb/devices/7-3:1.0$ cat uevent
DEVTYPE=usb_interface
DRIVER=usb-storage
DEVICE=/proc/bus/usb/007/006
PRODUCT=781/5406/200
TYPE=0/0/0
INTERFACE=8/6/80
MODALIAS=usb:v0781p5406d0200dc00dsc00dp00ic08isc06ip50
```

The next folder in the /sys/bus/usb folder is drivers, which extends the struct usb_driver information. The following terminal activity lists the contents of the drivers folder.

```
root@rajaram-laptop:/sys/bus/usb/drivers# ls -alt
```

```
total 0
drwxr-xr-x 2 root root 0 2010-07-15 22:30 libusual
drwxr-xr-x 2 root root 0 2010-07-15 22:30 usb
drwxr-xr-x 2 root root 0 2010-07-15 22:30 usb-storage
drwxr-xr-x 2 root root 0 2010-07-15 22:26 ndiswrapper
drwxr-xr-x 2 root root 0 2010-07-15 22:26 uvcvideo
drwxr-xr-x 9 root root 0 2010-07-15 22:26 .
drwxr-xr-x 4 root root 0 2010-07-15 22:26 ..
drwxr-xr-x 2 root root 0 2010-07-15 22:26 hub
drwxr-xr-x 2 root root 0 2010-07-15 22:26 usbfs
```

In the example setup, a USB mass storage is connected to the system, which adds the usb-storage entries. The following terminal illustrates usb-storage directory contents. These files provide details on the driver and allow control over its loading. Later in the "Application of sysfs: /sys/bus/usb Files" section, you can read how to use these files to load and unload driver modules.

```
|-- usb-storage
|   |-- 2-3:1.0 -> ../../../../devices/pci0000:00/0000:00:1d.7/usb2/7-3/7-3: 1.0
|   |-- bind
|   |-- module -> ../../../../module/usb_storage
|   |-- new_id
|   |-- uevent
|   '-- unbind
```

The files drivers_probe and drivers_autoprobe include an option to configure automatic probing and loading of drivers by the USB driver. Chapter 6, "Device File System," goes into more detail about the data structures the USB subsystem exports in the sysfs.

Application of sysfs: /sys/bus/usb Files

The sysfs files contain information on the USB devices and interfaces at the user space exported by the usbcore module. You can read the sysfs files to learn about the device and write to the files to control the device and driver activity. The following section explains how you can manually bind and unbind a driver with a USB video drive. Such operations offer an alternative to the rmmod way of unloading driver for a particular device.

The following terminal activity lists information for a USB video device connected to the system. From the log, notice the device is bound with the uvcvideo kernel driver module.

```
rajaram@rajaram-laptop:/sys/bus/usb$ tree /sys/bus/usb/drivers/uvcvideo/
/sys/bus/usb/drivers/uvcvideo/
|-- 3-1:1.0 -> ../../../../devices/pci0000:00/0000:00:1a.7/usb3/3-1/3-1:1.0
|-- 3-1:1.1 -> ../../../../devices/pci0000:00/0000:00:1a.7/usb3/3-1/3-1:1.1
|-- bind
|-- module -> ../../../../module/uvcvideo
|-- new_id
|-- uevent
'-- unbind
```

The video device is connected to USB 3's port 1. The uvcvideo driver is bound to interface 0 and 1 of the USB video device. To unload the driver from interface 0, you need to run command echo n "3-1:1.0" to the unbind file, as shown in the following terminal log.

```
root@rajaram-laptop:/sys/bus/usb# echo -n "3-1:1.0" >
/sys/bus/usb/drivers/uvcvideo/unbind
```

While using the tree command in the uvcvideo directory, as illustrated next, notice that interface 0 is successfully unbound from the uvcdriver.

```
root@rajaram-laptop:/sys/bus/usb# tree /sys/bus/usb/drivers/uvcvideo/
/sys/bus/usb/drivers/uvcvideo/
|-- 3-1:1.1 -> ../../../../devices/pci0000:00/0000:00:1a.7/usb3/3-1/3-1:1.1
|-- bind
|-- module -> ../../../../module/uvcvideo
|-- new_id
|-- uevent
'-- unbind
```

To bind the uvcvideo driver with the interface, you can echo the interface to the bind file, as shown here.

```
root@rajaram-laptop:/sys/bus/usb# echo -n "3-1:1.0" >
/sys/bus/usb/drivers/uvcvideo/bind
```

You can confirm a successful binding of the interface to the driver using the tree command in the drivers directory.

```
root@rajaram-laptop:/sys/bus/usb# tree /sys/bus/usb/drivers/uvcvideo//sys/
bus/usb/drivers/uvcvideo/
```

```
|-- 3-1:1.0 -> ../../../../devices/pci0000:00/0000:00:1a.7/usb3/3-1/3-1:1.0
|-- 3-1:1.1 -> ../../../../devices/pci0000:00/0000:00:1a.7/usb3/3-1/3-1:1.1
|-- bind
|-- module -> ../../../../module/uvcvideo
|-- new_id
|-- uevent
'-- unbind
```

This is one simple application of the USB sysfs file among many. Recall from the earlier discussions that sysfs files allow power management of the device from the user space. The "More Reading" section provides details on how to use sysfs for power management.

OVERVIEW OF GADGETFS

The USB device controller driver framework, referred to as the gadget driver framework, extends control over the VFS from the user space. The gadget file system is not available by default; you must select it during kernel configuration. Figure 16.4 illustrates the kernel configuration option to enable gadgetfs.

Generally, gadgetfs is mounted to the /dev/gadget/ path. You can mount the gadgetfs file as shown here.

```
root@rajaram-laptop:/sys/bus/usb#mount -t gadgetfs path /dev/gadget
```

You can refer to /include/linux/usb/gadgetfs.h and drivers/usb/gadget/inode.c for the gadgetfs implementation. Chapter 13, "Gadget Driver," explains these files and details the gadgetfs implementation. The following section provides details on the gadget framework files.

Application of gadgetfs: /dev/gadget Files

The USB gadget framework provides file system–based user-mode APIs to control USB controller hardware. You use these APIs to implement class drivers or the functional driver in the user space. Recollect from Chapter 14, "Class Driver," that the class driver is responsible for providing the device descriptors and other descriptors. To support such needs of user space, the USB class driver gadgetfs must provide APIs for descriptor and endpoint management.

The gadget framework creates two types of files in the /dev/gadget directory to interface with the USB device. The file named /dev/gadget/$CHIP allows you to

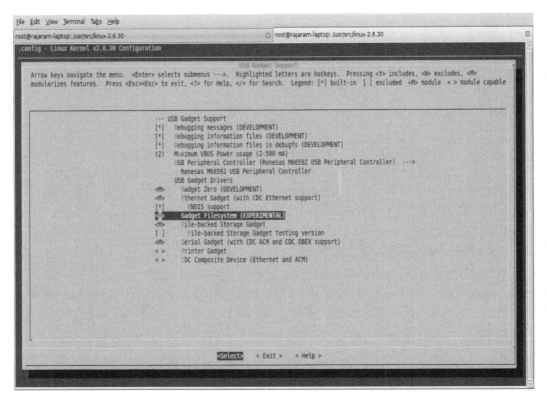

Figure 16.4
Kernel configuration option to enable gadgetfs.

configure the device through Endpoint Zero. The other set of files, named /dev/gadget/ep*, is created for each endpoint during the driver binding, which allows you to communicate respective endpoints.

The /dev/gadget/$CHIP file allows you to open Endpoint Zero and write descriptors to the gadget framework. This enables the kernel to bind to the USB controller and readies it for enumeration.

```
fd = open ("/dev/gadget/$CHIP", O_RDWR)
status = write (fd, descriptors, sizeof descriptors)
```

The device is active and ready for enumeration until you close the file descriptor. You can obtain the events in the next table when you poll the file and read the status of the gadget framework.

Event	Description
GADGETFS_CONNECT	This event is generated when the device setup is successful.
GADGETFS_DISCONNECT	This event indicates disconnection of the device from the gadget driver.
GADGETFS_SETUP	This event is generated when the gadget driver requests a device setup.
GADGETFS_SUSPEND	This event is generated when the gadget driver requests a device suspend.

Once the configuration of the device is successful, the /dev/gadget/ep* files are created to represent the endpoints. You can start using these files like any other file to read and write the gadget using read/write operations.

```
fd = open ("/dev/gadget/$ENDPOINT", O_RDWR)
status = write (fd, descriptors, sizeof descriptors)
```

The preceding operations illustrate steps to configure the endpoint by writing to the endpoint descriptors.

This endpoint file also supports IOCTLS to read the status of the endpoint and control the endpoint.

IOCTL	Description
GADGETFS_FIFO_STATUS	IOCTL to read the unclaimed bytes in the endpoint FIFO
GADGETFS_FIFO_FLUSH	IOCTL to flush out unclaimed data in the endpoint FIFO
GADGETFS_CLEAR_HALT	IOCTL to reset the endpoint and clear the halts

The user space application can use both synchronous and asynchronous input/output (I/O) read and write calls for the I/O operations. Using the asynchronous IO helps you eliminate I/O gaps and eases streaming.

Gadget Debug FS

The peripheral drivers in the gadget framework create debug files to dump debug information such as hardware details from the driver layer. The peripheral drivers use the procfs file system infrastructure to create these debug files. They are generally mounted to /proc/driver/udc for the user space applications to read. Few other drivers use the debugfs infrastructure to dump hardware debug information. The debugfs VFS is a lightweight VFS with no strict rules on how the data is shared; it enables easy removal when the kernel developers don't require it. These debug options are configurable through the kernel configuration, which allows developers to use these debug files only during development or debugging.

SUMMARY

Linux VFS has one of the key functionalities acting as the interface between the kernel and user space. The host side of the Linux USB framework exports different files to the sysfs and /proc file systems that enable you to control a USB device from the user space. Similarly, the Linux USB gadget framework extends gadgetfs as the programming interface. It also provides an option to configure debug file creation. These virtual files allow easy programming of the USB device from the user space and for system configurations like hot plugging. The user space drivers are simpler and faster to develop than the kernel drivers. The next chapter discusses USB user space drivers and illustrates how these VFS files are used to develop USB drivers (USBDs) from user space.

MORE READING

Refer to Documentation/usb/proc_usb_info.txt for more details on /proc/bus/usb files. You can also download source code from http://www.kroah.com/linux-usb/ to learn how to program using usbfs files. The next chapter offers additional tools that use these files to program USB devices. In addition, you can read drivers/usb/core/sysfs.c and drivers/usb/core/inode.c, explained in Chapter 6 to discover how the files are created and how they operate internally. Also, you can read the Linux kernel documentation Documentation/usb/power-management.txt to learn how to use the sysfs files to manage USB power management.

CHAPTER 17

USER SPACE USB DRIVERS

In This Chapter

- Overview: USB User Mode Drivers
- USB User Mode Driver Using libusb
- USB User Mode Driver Using UIO
- User Mode Driver Using gadgetfs

To develop a device driver in the kernel space, you need a thorough under-standing of the kernel infrastructures. These kernel drivers are complex and time consuming to develop, and they are applicable primarily for custom hardware. One of the common causes for more man-hours is that kernel drivers crash often and are difficult to debug.

Such issues do not arise in a user mode driver development because, in that setup, some functionality of the driver is implemented in the user space, whereas other functionality is implemented in the kernel space, thus reducing the complexity of the driver. These user mode drivers are faster and simpler, yet they efficiently meet most of the system requirements. You can use the user mode driver development as an effective alternative for developing drivers for protocols such as universal serial bus (USB).

On Linux, a user space application uses the Virtual File System (VFS) to read and control the kernel internals. Figure 17.1 illustrates possible options that

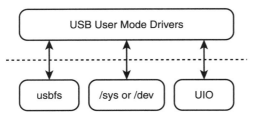

Figure 17.1
Different VFS programming options for USB user mode drivers.

programs can adopt to interact with a USB device from the user space. The usbfs, sys, and /dev files are part of the Linux-USB framework, where one part of the USB functionality lies inside the kernel drivers and a remaining part is controllable at the user level. The previous chapter detailed communication through normal file operations and through input/output controls (IOCTLs). This chapter starts with an overview of the Linux-USB host framework user space drivers and then covers how to develop USB user space drivers using usbfs and /sys files to interface with a USB device.

Linux also has certain generic frameworks to interact with devices from the user space, such as the user space IO (UIO), which provides a framework to write drivers in the user space. A minimal kernel driver using the UIO framework is developed to map the necessary hardware features to the user space. In the case of USB, you can adopt this generic method to develop a simpler validation system of USB controller hardware. Later, this chapter includes a quick bootstrap session on the UIO subsystem, explores how to program USB controller hardware based on the UIO subsystem, and writes a simple validation program using UIO for a USB device controller.

The chapter also covers the Linux-USB gadget framework user space programming using the gadgetfs file system to interface with a USB gadget framework.

OVERVIEW: USB USER MODE DRIVERS

Linux allows control of the physical devices from the user space through the VFS. The user space drivers are developed based on such virtual files. The Linux-USB framework provides virtual file usbfs to interact with the USB devices connected to the system. Also, remember with usbfs that the device driver is partly implemented in the kernel and partly at the user space.

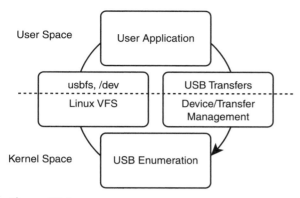

Figure 17.2
How activities are divided between user and kernel space.

Figure 17.2 illustrates a simplified control flow of programming a user space application.

You can infer from the figure that the Linux kernel USB framework driver takes care of the initial USB device enumeration. A successful enumeration of the device means it is available through the VFS. The VFS files are shown in user space to illustrate that the VFS files usbfs and /dev are mounted and accessed by user applications. Now from the user space you can program USB-specific transfers and other miscellaneous activity, such as reset. In other words, USB-specific device enumeration takes place at the kernel drivers, and device-specific functions are exported to the user space. Thus, the driver framework is generic for all USB devices.

USB User Mode Driver Using libusb

The libusb library is a generic USB host-side driver available on Linux. It uses VFS files of the USB framework, usbfs (USB device file system), and /dev or /sys to interact with a USB device. The libusb library acts as a wrapper between the USB file system and the functional driver applications. It provides application programming interfaces (APIs) to develop functional drivers. Figure 17.3 illustrates an architectural overview of how libusb, usbfs, and functional drivers interact with each other.

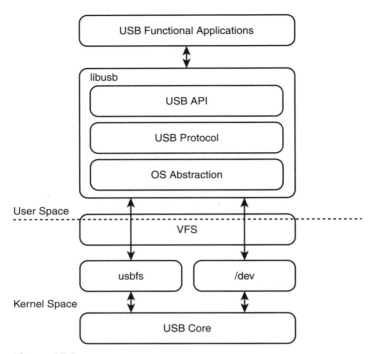

Figure 17.3
libusb blocks and libusb's interface with the Linux USB framework.

You can download the libusb source package from http://www.libusb.org/. The libusb library has two versions: libusb-1.0, and a legacy version named libusb-0.1. The following terminal activity illustrates a method to verify successful installation of libusb.

```
root@rajaram-linux-desktop:~#
root@rajaram-linux-desktop:~# libusb-config --version
0.1.12
root@rajaram-linux-desktop:~#
```

The http://www.libusb.org Web site has links to the source package and documentation of these versions of libusb. It also provides the list of APIs supported by these versions. The next section focuses on the legacy version and explores how applications are developed based on it.

Tip

The legacy version of libusb provides synchronous API interfaces, and libusb-1.0 provides synchronous APIs and asynchronous APIs to interact with a USB device.

Figure 17.3 captures the internal blocks of the libusb library and its interaction with the Linux USB framework.

The APIs of libusb can be categorized into four major functionalities: system (core) operations (Table 17.1), device operations (Table 17.2), transfer operations (Table 17.3), and miscellaneous operations (Table 17.4). These operations are implemented as part usb.c and part linux.c files in the libusb source package. You need to have an idea of APIs and their function of libusb before using them in an application. The following section provides a quick overview of these APIs.

Utilities Using libusb

The libusb library is a decade old, and by now many applications have integrated it as part of their package. This is because libusb provides an efficient method for USB application development. Two typical applications have adopted libusb: USB functional drivers and USB utilities. The first example to explore is libptp, a prominent user space functional driver developed to support Picture Transfer Protocol (PTP) devices such as digital cameras. The second example is a common utility used in most of the chapters: lsusb. This

Table 17.1 Core Operations

Operation	Description
usb_init	On libusb, usb_init does the necessary initialization of the libusb system. Any application that uses the libusb library must start this function before using other APIs. When called, the function checks the path of the USB virtual files and initializes the variable with the mount path of the virtual files.
usb_find_busses	After successful initialization of the virtual file path, the library must collect information on the USB busses available on the system. This API must be invoked after a successful usb_init call. This API finds and initializes internal data structures with USB bus details from the virtual files.
usb_find_devices	After successful execution of usb_find_busses, the library must collect the list of devices connected to these busses. This API finds and initializes internal data structures with the list of USB device details from the virtual files.
usb_get_busses	After successful execution of find routines, the library is ready with the list of busses and devices. The usb_get_busses API returns the USB bus list created by the earlier API calls.

Table 17.2 Device Operations

Operation	Description
usb_open	To interact with a device, you have to establish a proper channel. The usb_open API returns a handle to the device of interest. The function internally opens the device using the virtual file path.
usb_close	The usb_close API allows you to close a particular device using the handle returned by the open function.
usb_set_configuration	A USB device can have multiple functionalities, as indicated through the configuration descriptor. The application in the host can select a particular configuration using this API. Internally, it uses IOCTL_USB_SETCONFIG to communicate the application's requirement to the usbcore module of the Linux USB host framework.
usb_set_altinterface	USB devices support multiple interfaces in a single device. This API sets the active alternate setting of the current interface as per the function user space application's requirement. Internally, it uses IOCTL_USB_SETINTF to communicate the application's requirement to the usbcore module of the Linux USB host framework.
usb_resetep	Sometimes applications require reset of a particular endpoint for certain needs. usb_resetep allows reset of a particular endpoint for similar requirements. Internally, it uses IOCTL_USB_RESETEP to communicate the application's requirement to the usbcore module of the Linux USB host framework.
usb_clear_halt	When errors occur during transfer, endpoints are halted as per USB specification. An application may need to clear these halts. usb_clear_halt allows applications to clear halts that internally use IOCTL_USB_CLEAR_HALT to communicate the application's requirement to the usbcore module of the Linux USB host framework.
usb_reset	This API allows you to reset the device from the user space application. Internally, it uses IOCTL IOCTL_USB_RESET to communicate the application's requirement to the usbcore module of the Linux USB host framework.
usb_claim_interface	Applications must claim a particular interface before they can start a USB transfer operation. The usb_claim_interface claims an interface of a device for the application. Internally, it uses IOCTL_USB_CLAIMINTF to communicate the application's requirement to the usbcore module of the Linux USB host framework.
usb_release_interface	The usb_release_interface is to release a previously claimed interface after a successful transfer. Internally, it uses IOCTL_USB_RELEASEINTF to communicate the application's requirement to the usbcore module of the Linux USB host framework.

Table 17.3 Transfer Operations

Operation	Description
usb_control_msg	User space applications require a method to transfer standard control packets or vendor-specific packets. The usb_control_msg allows user applications to transfer control messages. Internally, it uses IOCTL_USB_SUBMITURB to pass on the control packet to the usbcore.
usb_get_string	Sometimes applications require details of the manufacturer and vendor as string descriptors. usb_get_string retrieves a string descriptor from the device. Internally, the API constructs the required control packet to retrieve this information.
usb_get_string_simple	Retrieves a string descriptor from a device using the first language.
usb_get_descriptor	Retrieves a descriptor from a device's default control pipe.
usb_get_descriptor_by_endpoint	Retrieves a descriptor from a device.
usb_bulk_write	User space applications require a method to perform a bulk OUT transfer. usb_bulk_write allows user applications to transfer bulk data to the device, which is an OUT transfer. Internally, it uses IOCTL_USB_SUBMITURB to pass on the bulk data to the usbcore.
usb_bulk_read	User space applications require a method to perform a bulk IN transfer. usb_bulk_read allows user applications to read bulk data from the device, which is an IN transfer. Internally, it uses IOCTL_USB_SUBMITURB to read the bulk data from the usbcore.
usb_interrupt_write	User space applications require a method to perform an interrupt OUT transfer. usb_interrupt_write allows user applications to transfer interrupt data to the device, which is an OUT transfer. Internally, it uses IOCTL_USB_SUBMITURB to pass on the interrupt data to the usbcore.
usb_interrupt_read	User space applications require a method to perform an interrupt IN transfer. usb_interrupt_read allows user applications to read interrupt data from the device, which is an IN transfer. Internally, it uses IOCTL_USB_SUBMITURB to read the interrupt data from the usbcore.

Table 17.4 Miscellaneous Operations

Operation	Description
usb_get_driver_np	Linux associates a driver for each interface of the USB device. This is informative at the user level to verify whether the proper driver is loaded for a particular interface. usb_get_driver_np returns the name of the driver associated with a particular interface. Internally, it uses IOCTL_USB_GETDRIVER to retrieve the application's requirement from the usbcore module of the Linux USB host framework.
usb_detach_kernel_driver_np	Sometimes a requirement arises to detach a kernel driver from the interface. Internally, it uses IOCTL_USB_DISCONNECT to pass on the application's requirement from the usbcore module of the Linux USB host framework.

utility is part of the usbutils package that was developed based on libusb. This section provides a brief overview of these applications and explores how to install and use them.

libptp

PTP is a standard developed by camera vendors to provide a way of interfacing an imaging device and a PC. PTP specification suggests USB as its transport layer, which most of the digital imaging devices such as cameras use. Thus, the libptp functional driver connects USB-based PTP devices with a PC. The libptp extends libusb interfaces to detect and interact with PTP devices. Linux-based applications such as gPhoto use libptp for image transfer. As a developer, you can also write test applications based on this library and test PTP devices. The development effort of test tools for devices decreases significantly when you use such predeveloped systems. You can download the source package from http://libptp.sourceforge.net/. You need to install libusb before you extract, build, and install the source in your machine.

usbutils

As seen earlier, lsusb is the most common command-line USB utility among USB developers. The tool reads device information, such as the descriptors, through libusb and displays it to the user in a more readable form. You can install lsusb from its source package downloadable from http://sourceforge.net/projects/linux-usb/, or you can use package installers as in Ubuntu apt-get install usbutils. You need to ensure that the system contains libusb for lsusb to work.

A Simple USB Test Application Using libusb

It's not always necessary to use libusb for standard applications such as lipptp or lsusb. Because libusb is a generic driver, it allows you to develop device drivers for custom devices. A custom device, for example, could be a standalone USB chip that has no device functionality available, doesn't fit into class drivers, and needs special drivers. Also, in a typical validation setup, USB transfer requirements could be different from the standard requests, perhaps to simulate and send a nonstandard size of bulk data to check whether the hardware can handle the transfer as per specification or to send invalid control data to check whether the software stack handles the situation properly. You can easily meet such needs of a validation system using libusb instead of developing device drivers, which are more complicated.

The following example illustrates how to write a driver that bulk reads and writes to a USB device. Any libusb program has to start with a call to initialization routines. The libusb library requires three such calls so that the libusb application is ready as a driver.

```
usb_init();
usb_find_busses();
usb_find_devices();
```

These steps allow the libusb to read the system configuration and update it with device information. Once these steps have been performed successfully, the program must identify the device using the Vendor ID and Product ID and take control of the device. The following code illustrates a possible method to get a USB device handle.

```
usb_dev_handle *open_usb_device(unsigned int MY_VID, unsigned int MY_PID)
{
    struct usb_bus *bus;
    struct usb_device *dev;

    for (bus = usb_get_busses(); bus; bus = bus->next)
    {
        for (dev = bus->devices; dev; dev = dev->next)
        {
            if (dev->descriptor.idVendor == MY_VID
                    && dev->descriptor.idProduct == MY_PID)
```

```
                        {
                            return usb_open(dev);
                        }
                }
        }
        return NULL;
}
```

Once the device handle is available, you can easily control the USB device to perform control and data transfers. The next step after opening the device successfully is setting the required configuration.

```
if(usb_set_configuration(device_handle, 1/*configuration number*/) < 0)
        {
            /*Handle error*/
        }
```

Once you've successfully set the configuration, claim the interface of the device for further data transfer.

```
if(usb_claim_interface(device_handle, 0/*interface number*/) < 0)
    {
        /*Handle error*/
    }
```

When the claim is successful, a program can start data transfer with the USB device through the claimed interface. The test application does a simple loop back using data through bulk endpoints.

```
if(usb_bulk_write(dev, EP_OUT, tmp, sizeof(tmp), 5000)
    != sizeof(tmp))
    {
        /*Handle error*/
    }

if(usb_bulk_read(dev, EP_IN, tmp, sizeof(tmp), 5000)
    != sizeof(tmp))
    {
        /*Handle error*/
    }
```

These data transfer APIs are synchronous calls; to avoid infinite blocking, they provide options to time out.

The legacy version of the libusb lacks certain functionality, such as asynchronous API calls and isochronous transfer API. The libusb-1.0 version overcomes these limitations and provides backward compatibility. Because most of the USB utilities and applications are developed based on the legacy APIs, the preceding sections covered the legacy APIs. The "More Reading" section includes details for exploring the newer libusb version.

USB User Mode Driver Using UIO

When USB devices are developed for products, you must develop drivers based on the Linux-USB framework. Development of such standard drivers can be time consuming and complex. User space programming using the VFS acts as an alternative to this constraint, but VFS is also part of the driver in the kernel layer. Moreover, VFS provides only limited access to the device through IOCTL interfaces.

Sometimes in a development environment, you require more control over the hardware. For example, a USB Internet Protocol (IP) test requirement may include validating low-level register states. To implement such requirements on a Linux environment, you end up developing custom kernel drivers or even modifying the USB core. Another interesting scenario arises when integrating proprietary stacks to a Linux environment. Although this is against Linux ideology, a business decision might lead to proprietary software modules.

The documentation on Linux says Linux UIO is not a candidate for USB devices, but it can fit as an ideal platform for USB development needs, as described earlier. This is because the UIO framework exports USB hardware completely to the user space and helps develop custom applications.

Bootstrap: Linux UIO

The initial version of the Linux UIO framework was introduced in kernel 2.6.22, and it is continuously being improved. Using the UIO framework, a developer can map and control a device's memory and interrupt through user space file operations. A simple kernel driver layer along with the UIO framework is required for mapping the hardware and interrupts completely to the user space. This complete hardware access at user space gives developers an easy way to develop a functional application without crashing the kernel. Note that, unlike other user space approaches, applications adopting UIO have fewer copy operations across memory space. Figure 17.4 illustrates a Peripheral Component Interconnect (PCI) driver using the UIO infrastructure.

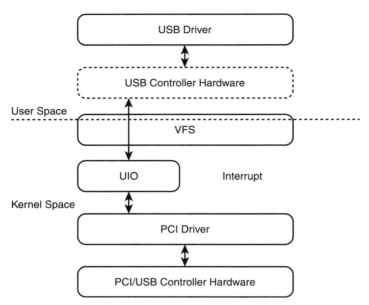

Figure 17.4
PCI-based UIO framework and user space application interaction.

Figure 17.5 illustrates how to enable the UIO framework as part of your kernel.

The linux/uio_driver.h and drivers/uio/uio.c files implement the Linux UIO subsystem. To enable device drivers to interact, the UIO subsystem exports the data structure struct uio_info and interface APIs uio_register_device, uio_unregister_device, and uio_event_notify.

struct uio_info is the key data structure of the UIO subsystem that collects all the necessary hardware details. The hardware information includes the memory address range, port details, and interrupts-related information of the device.

```
struct uio_info {
        struct uio_device       *uio_dev;
        const char              *name;
        const char              *version;
        struct uio_mem          mem[MAX_UIO_MAPS];
        struct uio_port         port[MAX_UIO_PORT_REGIONS];
        long                     irq;
        unsigned long           irq_flags;
        void                    *priv;
```

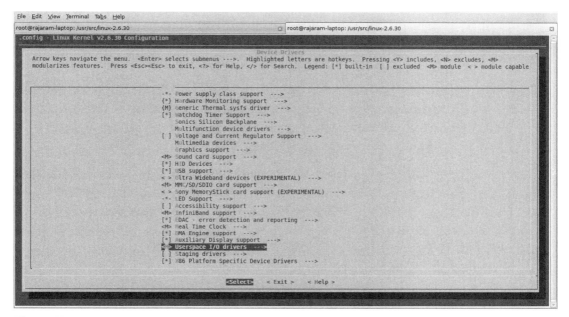

Figure 17.5
Kconfig option to enable the UIO module.

```
irqreturn_t (*handler)(int irq, struct uio_info *dev_info);
int (*mmap)(struct uio_info *info, struct vm_area_struct *vma);
int (*open)(struct uio_info *info, struct inode *inode);
int (*release)(struct uio_info *info, struct inode *inode);
int (*irqcontrol)(struct uio_info *info, s32 irq_on);
};
```

The data structure also extends function pointers for callback handler routines, which can facilitate mapping of hardware memory and control and handle interrupts. When you develop a UIO-based driver, initialize the struct uio_info object with your hardware details, and then register the object with the UIO subsystem.

The UIO subsystem exports three simple interface APIs to interact with other modules. The uio_register_device API allows the hardware driver module to register the uio_info object with the UIO subsystem. This registration is generally done in the driver probe routine. Once it's registered successfully, a new user space I/O device is created in the /dev/uio path.

```
int uio_register_device(struct device *parent, struct uio_info *info)
```

To remove a device from the UIO subsystem, use the `uio_unregister_device` API. You generally unregister from a module in the driver `exit` routine.

```
void uio_unregister_device(struct uio_info *info);
```

You can use the `uio_event_notify` API to be notified of interrupts received to the device. The user space application generally polls for such an event; once notified, it can read appropriate memory to infer more details.

```
void uio_event_notify(struct uio_info *info);
```

Successful registration of a device driver with the UIO subsystem creates `/dev` and `/sys` files as `/dev/uio*` and `/sys/class/uio*`, respectively, where `*` is a decimal number. The UIO subsystem provides the following file operations to access the `/dev` file from the user space.

```
static const struct file_operations uio_fops = {
        .owner          = THIS_MODULE,
        .open           = uio_open,
        .release        = uio_release,
        .read           = uio_read,
        .write          = uio_write,
        .mmap           = uio_mmap,
        .poll           = uio_poll,
        .fasync         = uio_fasync,
};
```

Now that you've had a quick overview of the UIO subsystem, it's time to write a UIO-based USB device controller driver.

UIO-Based USB Controller Driver

The PCI-based hardware development platform is a common method used to test and demonstrate USB controllers and USB software stacks. This example explores how to effectively use the UIO framework to develop a simple system to perform a register-level test of a PCI-based USB controller hardware from the user space. The driver has a thin kernel that maps all hardware to the user space using the UIO framework and functional firmware such as drivers in the user space.

The first step in the process is to develop the thin kernel driver for the USB controller hardware, in this case a PCI driver. You'll start the development with initialization of the `struct pci_device_id` object `usb_ex_pci_id`, as shown here.

```
static struct pci_device_id uio_usb_ex_pci_id[] = {
        { PCI_DEVICE(PCI_VENDOR_ID_XXXX, PCI_DEVICE_ID_XXXX), },
        { 0, }
};
```

In this case, the hardware is based on PCI, so the next step is to have a `struct pci_driver` object `uio_usb_ex_pci_driver`. Then register callback handlers for the `probe` and `remove` modules, as shown here.

```
static struct pci_driver uio_usb_ex_pci_driver = {
        .name = "uio_usb_example",
        .id_table = uio_usb_ex_pci_id,
        .probe = uio_usb_ex_pci_probe,
        .remove = uio_usb_ex_pci_remove,
};
```

Next, create the `init` and `exit` routines for the PCI driver. There is not much complexity in these routines other than providing hardware details to the PCI module.

```
static int __init uio_usb_ex_init_module(void)
{
        return pci_register_driver(&uio_usb_ex_pci_driver);
}
static void __exit uio_usb_ex_exit_module(void)
{
        pci_unregister_driver(&uio_usb_ex_pci_driver);
}
module_init(uio_usb_ex_init_module);
module_exit(uio_usb_ex_exit_module);
```

The next step in the process is to define the `probe` function of the PCI driver, which maps the memory region and installs the interrupt handlers to the `struct uio_info` data structure. In this driver, the IRQ handler's role is to clear the interrupt registers of the USB controller.

```
static int __devinit uio_usb_ex_pci_probe(struct pci_dev *dev,
const struct pci_device_id *id)
{
    struct uio_info *info;
```

```
    info = kzalloc(sizeof(struct uio_info), GFP_KERNEL);

    if (!info)
      return -ENOMEM;

    if (pci_enable_device(dev))
      goto error;

    if (pci_request_regions(dev, "uio_usb_example"))
      goto error_region;

        info->mem[0].addr = pci_resource_start(dev, 0);

        if (!info->mem[0].addr)
              goto error_map;

        info->mem[0].internal_addr = pci_ioremap_bar(dev, 0);

        if (!info->mem[0].internal_addr)
              goto error_map;

        info->mem[0].size = pci_resource_len(dev, 0);
        info->mem[0].memtype = UIO_MEM_PHYS;


    info->name = "uio_usb_example";
    info->version = "0.1";
    info->irq = dev->irq;
    info->irq_flags = IRQF_SHARED;
    info->handler = uio_usb_example_handler;
    info->i rqcontrol = uio_usb_example_irqcontrol;

    pci_set_drvdata(dev, info);

    if (uio_register_device(&dev->dev, info))
      goto error_register;

        --cut--

        --cut--


}
```

The complete source code of this driver is available on the book's CD as uio_usb_example.c. Now build the source to create a uio_usb_example.ko and insert it into the kernel. Before loading the kernel module, ensure the UIO framework is loaded to the kernel. The following terminal activity captures the commands to be executed.

```
root@rajaram-linux-desktop:~#
root@rajaram-linux-desktop:~# modprobe uio
root@rajaram-linux-desktop:~# insmod uio_usb_example.ko
root@rajaram-linux-desktop:~#
```

A successful registration of the USB PCI driver creates device files in the /dev/uio* and /sys/class/uio/ directories. You can also confirm successful registration by invoking the lsuio command. The lsuio utility can be downloaded from http://www.osadl.org/projects/downloads/UIO/user/lsuio-0.2.0.tar.gz. These files allow user space applications to access and collect information on the device.

The next step is to develop a user space driver to the USB controller using the UIO driver being developed. To access the USB hardware, open the device using the device name: /dev/uio0. The name uio0 could be different, based on how many UIO devices you have registered.

```
fd = open("/dev/uio0", O_RDWR|O_SYNC);
```

After successfully opening the device, it's time to map the memory collected during the probe routine to the user space.

```
iomem = mmap(0, size, PROT_READ|PROT_WRITE, MAP_SHARED,fd, addr);
```

A successful mmap routine brings in the complete hardware to the user space. The example program usb_uio_application.c on the CD is a simple application to read controller registers. You can use the UIO framework to develop a complete USB firmware driver; the complete hardware is available in the user space.

USER MODE DRIVER USING GADGETFS

The Linux USB gadget framework implements the device driver framework for USB controllers as three layers, the top one being the functional driver. Some of the functional layers are implemented as kernel drivers. The gadgetfs file system extends the gadget infrastructure to the user space to enable user mode gadget functional drivers. Chapter 16, "USB Virtual File Systems," had a detailed discussion on the various VFS files extended by the USB gadget framework to the user space. You can program the gadget in synchronous and asynchronous methods and transfer data. In the following sections, you study both these methods. A program is available on http://www.linux-usb.org/gadget/usb.c for both forms of transfers.

The first step in writing a user mode driver for the gadget framework is to define the descriptors of the device. The `descriptor` data structures are available as part of `linux/usb/ch9.h`. The `descriptor` objects are passed on to the host via the gadget framework during enumeration.

Once you've defined the descriptors, you can configure the endpoints per the requirements. You can also adopt the auto configure method in the example to configure the endpoints based on the requirements of the functional driver.

```
static int init_device (void)
{
        char            buf [4096], *cp = &buf [0];
        int             fd;
        int             status;
        --cut--

        status = autoconfig ();
```

After successfully building the configuration, you can write the descriptors to the gadget framework by opening the gadget with the chip name. This internally calls the `dev_config` function.

```
fd = open (DEVNAME, O_RDWR);
if (fd < 0) {
        perror (DEVNAME);
        return -errno;
}

*(__u32 *)cp = 0;          /* tag for this format */
cp += 4;

/* write full then high speed configs */
cp = build_config (cp, fs_eps);
if (HIGHSPEED)
        cp = build_config (cp, hs_eps);
```

```
/* and device descriptor at the end */
memcpy (cp, &device_desc, sizeof device_desc);
cp += sizeof device_desc;

status = write (fd, &buf [0], cp - &buf [0]);
```

Once the configuration is successful and a configuration is set, the endpoints are exposed as files for I/O communications.

The next step is to define functions that can handle control and data transfers. Ideally, you should have a separate handler for control transfer. The example creates three separate threads: control (ep0_thread), source thread (simple_source_thread, aio_in_thread), and sink thread (simple_sink_thread, aio_out_thread). The EP_IN_NAME and EP_OUT_NAME are the endpoint names configured for IN and OUT transfers, respectively.

```
static void *ep0_thread (void *param)
{
        int                     fd = *(int*) param;
        struct sigaction        action;
        time_t                  now, last;
        struct pollfd           ep0_poll;

        source = sink = ep0 = pthread_self ();
        pthread_cleanup_push (close_fd, param);

if (pthread_create (&source, 0,
              source_thread, (void *) EP_IN_NAME) != 0) {
        perror ("can't create source thread");
        goto cleanup;
}

if (pthread_create (&sink, 0,
              sink_thread, (void *) EP_OUT_NAME) != 0) {
        perror ("can't create sink thread");
        pthread_cancel (source);
        source = ep0;
        goto cleanup;
```

The ep0_thread waits on an infinite loop and handles control packets. It also handles connection and disconnection events. Both synchronous and asynchronous operations are available on Linux to perform I/O over the endpoints. The endpoint VFS files have to be open for this transfer. The example demonstrates both methods for I/O transfers.

In a normal synchronous transfer, the threads use normal read and write operations. These operations are blocking calls in which the function has to wait until the transfer is complete.

```
status = read (sink_fd, buf, sizeof buf);
status = write (source_fd, buf, len);
```

An asynchronous input/output (AIO) transfer is ideal for ISO transfers, which enable you to submit one or more I/O requests in a system call without waiting for completion.

```
io_prep_pwrite (iocb, source_fd,
    buf, fill_in_buf (buf, iosize),
    0);
io_set_callback (iocb, in_complete);
iocb->key = USB_DIR_IN;

status = io_submit (ctx, 1, &iocb);
if (status < 0) {
    perror (__FUNCTION__);
    break;
}
aio_in_pending++;
```

The AIO mode of transfer helps you develop an application to stream data over gadgetfs. You can refer to the "More Reading" section to learn more about how to program using the AIO infrastructure on Linux.

Summary

Developing drivers for the Linux kernel is more challenging and time consuming than developing drivers for user mode. User mode drivers satisfy the needs of protocols such as USB. On Linux, libraries such as libusb provide a generic driver infrastructure for USB devices that eliminates the need to develop device drivers in the kernel mode. Many USB applications on Linux have adopted libusb as their driver to reduce the developmental effort. Gadget functional drivers such as Media Transfer Protocol (MTP) also operate from user mode. The gadgetfs framework makes it easy to write applications and reduces developmental efforts.

You can adopt options such as the UIO for validation, which can provide a more stable, more flexible, and faster developmental setup than a kernel mode setup.

MORE READING

You can explore more about the internals of libusb by downloading the source from http://www.libusb.org/. There are two versions of libusb: the legacy version (http://libusb.sourceforge.net/doc/) and the libusb-1.0 version (http://libusb.sourceforge.net/api-1.0/). The newer version supports additional features such as isochronous transfer and asynchronous transfer. Over the years, many applications have adopted the legacy version. You can explore applications such as libptp (http://libptp.sourceforge.net/) and libmtp (http://libmtp.sourceforge.net/) to learn more about how functional drivers are developed based on libusb. The article found at http://blog.kernelkahani.com/?p=19 guides you to connect your MTP device on a Linux system. You can refer to http://www.linux-usb.org/gadget/ for a deeper understanding of gadgetfs. The site http://www.linux-usb.org/gadget/usb.c provides a simple application using gadgetfs.

You can further explore user space I/O from http://lwn.net/Articles/232575/ and http://www.osadl.org/UIO.uio0.0.html. The http://lse.sourceforge.net/io/aio.html link provides further insights on the AIO infrastructure.

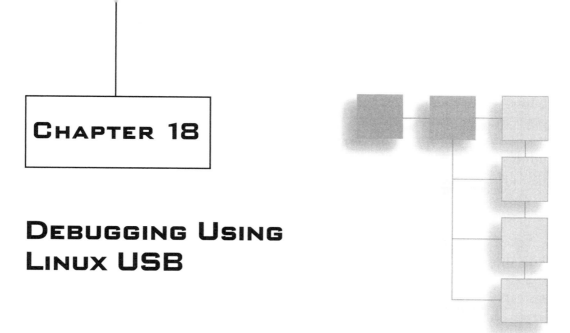

CHAPTER 18

DEBUGGING USING LINUX USB

In This Chapter

- USB Monitor: usbmon
- Debug Using usbfs_snoop
- Verbose Debugging for Host-Side USB

For a developer, developing a system is simple, but debugging the same system to find the root cause of the problem requires extra ingenuity. This ingenuity can come from tools that can collect information on the system's state at the time of the problem. The complexity increases when the system to be debugged is part of a kernel subsystem. You can use many approaches to debug a kernel subsystem. Printing debug information in American Standard Code for Information Interchange (ASCII) text form is a common method developers use to debug modules in the kernel space. However, printing this information has limitations in terms of buffer size available. Also, sometimes an increase in information nullifies the problem.

So what does a protocol system such as universal serial bus (USB) need? In a protocol system, packet transfer detail is the key to debugging. Thus, details of USB transactions between a device and a host help isolate and fix the cause of a problem. Printing of so much information in ASCII text is not advisable from a practical standpoint. Moreover, it is difficult to print complete transaction information from low-level layers in any closed operating system.

Linux is an ideal platform for such debugging because it provides complete access to the entire protocol layer. To debug a USB system, Linux uses the traditional ASCII text printing method, which provides limited user-readable information on USB transactions and a software-based USB packet capture tool called usbmon that can hook up USB packet transfers and share them to the user through the Linux debug file system.

This chapter explores the tools available on Linux that assist in debugging a USB subsystem. Initially, you learn how to configure USB packet capture usbmon on Linux, followed by a quick bootstrap session on the design of usbmon and how to use it. This chapter also looks at how to use usbfs_snoop, a lighter tool available on Linux that can capture USB transactions occurring between the user space drivers and usbcore module via the usbfs file system. Subsequently, you can see the kernel configuration option available to configure verbose debug information of the Linux-USB subsystem.

USB Monitor: usbmon

As discussed, debugging any system requires the proper tools and an approach that identifies the root cause of a problem. A common method of debugging a protocol system is to capture the packets it transmits. There are hardware sniffers and analyzers available for most protocols. They capture packets at the physical level and present the packet to the user in a human-readable form. For USB, companies such as LeCroy and Ellisys provide USB protocol analyzers that can capture USB transactions at the physical level and display the captured data in a human-readable form using graphical interfaces.

A typical USB analyzer setup capturing USB protocol transaction is illustrated in Figure 18.1.

Individual hackers and smaller teams generally cannot afford these hardware setups. An effective alternative to hardware sniffers is capturing packets using software at a higher layer than the physical layer. Referred to as *software packet sniffers* or *packet analyzers*, these act as effective alternatives to hardware tools. One such packet analyzer tool is the commonly used tcpdump, which enables debugging of networking protocols. A similar packet analyzer tool is available for USB on Linux to capture USB transfers between the USB host and the device. This section walks through implementation of a USB packet analyzer on Linux

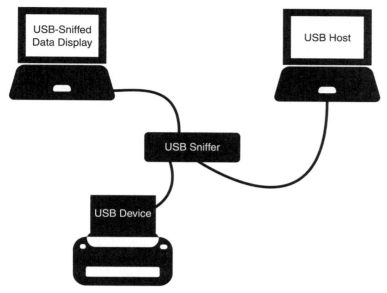

Figure 18.1
A typical USB analyzer setup.

and subsequently explores how to use it to capture USB packets for debugging any USB system.

USB monitor, or usbmon, is the Linux implementation of a USB packet analyzer. The usbmon module is a developer feature that is not generally available on a preinstalled Linux package. You need to rebuild the kernel after enabling the USB monitoring option in the kernel configuration.

Note

The usbmon module uses the debug file system (debugfs) feature. For usbmon to be functional, ensure that the debugfs feature is configured as part of the kernel.

Figure 18.2 illustrates the USB Monitor usbmon option in the Linux kernel configuration. It is available from Device Drivers, USB Support, USB Monitor.

For a platform developer, understanding how to use usbmon is the most interesting and useful part. However, to use usbmon effectively, it's necessary to understand its features and its capability.

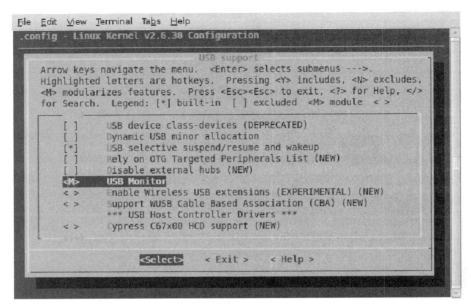

Figure 18.2
USB Monitor option in kernel configuration.

The `drivers/usb/mon/` directory of the kernel contains the `usbmon` implementation. The module implements a binary `mon_bin.c` and a text `mon_text.c` version of USB monitoring, interfaced through a main file `mon_main.c`. The main file also handles initialization and other interface functionalities with the `usbcore`. You can find the key data structures for this module in the header file `usb_mon.h`. In addition, `drivers/usb/core/hcd.h` contains a couple of interface declarations that facilitate interaction between the `usbcore` and the `usbmon`.

The `usbmon` module is a developer tool that captures USB Request Block (URB) activity between the peripheral drivers and the host controller drivers. This monitoring functionality consists of a kernel part that hooks the USB transfers and a user space part that provides access to the hooked information. From the earlier discussion, you know that the kernel portion of the `usbmon` has two implementations: a raw binary version and a text version. This chapter focuses only on the text version of the kernel implementation because it provides a good start to understanding USB monitoring and covers most of the debugging requirement. From now on, any reference to `usbmon` refers to the text version of the kernel implementation.

Bootstrap: USB Monitor

The usbmon operates like any other character device: it extends its resources (the hooked information) through file operations support. Therefore, the key data structures of the usbmon implementation are the file operation interfaces and the data structure to store hooked data. For a USB developer, it is unnecessary to look into the implementation details of this module, because there is no practical requirement to modify this code during development. To expand your understanding of this module and subsequently add features to the module, refer to the "More Reading" section at the end of this chapter, which points to additional documentation.

The drivers/usb/mon/mon_text.c file defines the data structure struct mon_event_text that maps the URB information when any one of the following events takes place in the host controller driver: a URB is submitted, a URB is completed, or an error occurs. After carefully mapping this URB event information to the struct mon_event_text, you can perform the read operation to access it. Understanding this data structure helps to analyze the information.

```
struct mon_event_text {
```

Multiple URB events typically occur before a read operation from the user space. The e_link variable maintains a list of such events for future reading.

```
struct list_head e_link;
```

The next member, type, indicates the type of URB operation that occurred. The three possible operations are submit, complete, or error, with values of S, C, or E, respectively.

```
int type;
```

Each event is provided with an ID and is stored in the member variable id. The ID in this case is the pointer address of the URB.

```
unsigned long id;
```

The next member variable in the data structure, tstamp, collects the time of URB activity.

```
unsigned int tstamp;
```

The busnum member variable indicates the USB bus in which the URB event took place. The Linux kernel assigns a unique number to each USB bus, starting from 1.

```
int busnum;
```

The `devnum` member variable indicates the device for which the URB event took place. The Linux kernel assigns a unique number to each USB device, starting from 1.

```
char devnum;
```

The `epnum` member variable indicates the endpoint to which the URB is processed. The endpoint value starts from 0.

```
char epnum;
```

The next variable, `is_in`, represents the direction of the URB event, with `true` indicating an IN USB transfer and `false` indicating an OUT USB transfer.

```
char is_in;
```

The next variable, `xfertype`, represents different transfer types available on USB. The variable can hold B, I, Z, or C, representing bulk, interrupt, isochronous, and control transfers, respectively.

```
char xfertype;
```

The next member, `length`, maps the length of data transferred in the URB. This could be the actual buffer length or the transferred length.

```
int length;
```

The next member, `status`, indicates the status of URB transfer. This field is valid only for nonisochronous URB transfers. The return status is based on the values defined in `include/linux/errno.h`.

```
int status;
```

The `interval` member variable indicates the transfer period for time-bounded transfers such as interrupt and isochronous transfers. The interval is based on the device configuration.

```
int interval;
```

The next member, `start_frame`, is specific to isochronous transfers and indicates the initial frame of the isochronous transfer.

```
int start_frame;
```

The member variable, `error_count`, is also specific to isochronous transfers and indicates the number of errors in the isochronous transfer.

```
int error_count;
```

The variable `setup_flag` indicates whether the data structure object is a setup packet and can hold the following values: 0 (Setup data captured), - (Unable to capture the Setup Packet), and Z (invalid).

```
char setup_flag;
```

The `data_flag` variable indicates whether the data structure object holds data as part of the event information. It can hold the following values: 0 (data available), ≤ (IN Completion), ≥ (OUT Submit), L (Length is 0), and Z (invalid).

```
char data_flag;
```

The next member, `numdesc`, maps `number_of_packets` from the URB structure that indicates the number of isochronous packets.

```
int numdesc;
```

Because this is a debug mechanism for the USB transfers, a complete hook of data from the URB is not required. Therefore, the text version of the `usbmon` maps part of the URB data. The following members capture/hold data based on the transfer type.

```
struct mon_iso_desc isodesc[ISODESC_MAX];
unsigned char setup[SETUP_MAX];
unsigned char data[DATA_MAX];
```

From the preceding macros, you can understand that the data field contains only part of the data. The binary version of `usbmon` provides complete information for the URB. However, this extra data is mostly class specific, and packet analyzers that are specific to those modules are more effective than `usbmon`. For example, there are class-specific packet monitors for classes such as mass storage, namely `scsimon`. Having seen a brief overview of the data structure that handles `usbmon`'s URB event, the subsequent section focuses on the sequence flow inside the `usbmon`, how it hooks information, and how it shares hooked information with the user space.

USB Monitor Internals

Like any other module, `usbmon` extends the Linux kernel details to the user space through a file system. Because the `usbmon` module is for debugging, it uses `debugfs` (instead of `usbfs`), a Virtual File System (VFS) added exclusively to assist export of debug data. You need to mount `debugfs` to view `usbmon` files in the user space. `/sys/kernel/debug` is the usual location if you are using Ubuntu.

Note

The debugfs VFS was introduced in kernel 2.6.10-rc3, with the intension of providing kernel developers a lightweight system with no strict rules on how the data is shared and enabling easy removal when not required.

Figure 18.3 illustrates an architectural view of how usbmon sits in the Linux USB subsystem. usbmon sits low down in the usbcore, a perfect place to hook the URB information.

You can infer from the figure that the usbmon module has two types of interfaces: one that interfaces with the usbcore closer to host controller driver, and the other that uses the debugfs infrastructure to interface with the user space applications. This section focuses more on how the usbmon module interfaces and less on its internal implementation, because the internals are less meaningful for a USB developer. However, you can continue to explore its implementation with the ideas given in the last sections of this chapter.

The data structure struct usb_mon_operations defined in /drivers/usb/core/ hcd.h provides the key callback interface methods. The usbmon registers its

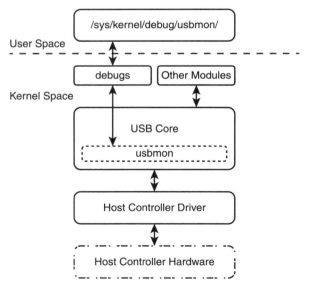

Figure 18.3
usbmon's design location in usbcore.

handlers for `usb_mon_operations` using the `usb_mon_register` interface function exported by the `usbcore`. This callback gives access to URB operations such as submit, complete, and submit error to the `usbmon` infrastructure.

```
struct usb_mon_operations {
        void (*urb_submit)(struct usb_bus *bus, struct urb *urb);
        void (*urb_submit_error)(struct usb_bus *bus, struct urb *urb, int err);
        void (*urb_complete)(struct usb_bus *bus, struct urb *urb, int status);
        /* void (*urb_unlink)(struct usb_bus *bus, struct urb *urb); */
};
```

Figure 18.4 illustrate the initialization action sequence of the `usbmon` module. During the initialization process, the `usbmon` registers two types of interface operations with the `usbcore` module. The first step during initialization operation is to register URB hook operations, and the next step is to register with the `usbcore` to get device notification on any addition of the new USB bus. While the former helps in hooking URB data, the latter enables creation of `usbmon` files in the user space using the `debugfs`. Once these handlers are registered, the `usbmon` is ready to tap the URB information, and the user can access URB information through the `usbmon` infrastructure.

The `usbcore`'s `drivers/usb/core/hcd.c` provides wrapper functions, namely `usbmon_urb_submit`, `usbmon_urb_complete`, and `usbmon_urb_submit_error`, which subsequently invoke the registered handlers to pass on the URB information. Figure 18.5 illustrates a sequence of function invocations that occur during URB submission and the location you can hook the URB information. The functional driver prepares the URB and submits it to the

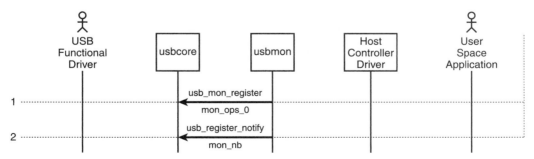

Figure 18.4
Initialization sequence of usbmon.

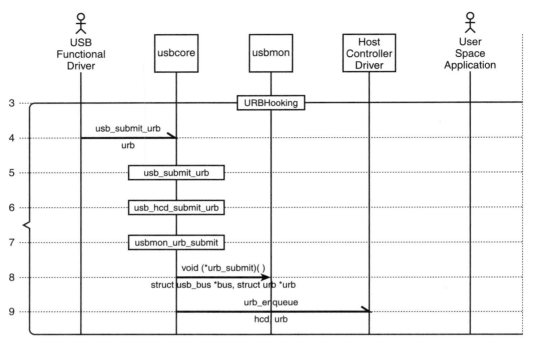

Figure 18.5
URB hooking sequence of usbmon.

usbcore using usb_submit_urb in urb.c. The URB is then passed down to the hcd.c of the usbcore after updating the URB structure with additional information. Now the URB is complete and ready for submission to the host controller driver using the usb_hcd_submit_urb function. Once the URB reaches the usb_hcd_submit_urb, the wrapper usbmon_urb_submit is invoked. If usbmon had registered its callback interfaces, the wrapper would invoke the callback with URB information.

The usbmon module creates files inline with the number of the USB bus available in the usbcore. The text mode creates two files with suffix u or t following the bus number. The file with a t suffix is a deprecated version, and the one with a u suffix contains more details, such as isochronous transactions. You need to mount the usbmon VFS to view these files, as explained in the next section, "How to Use usbmon."

`usbmon` extends three main file operations: open, read, and release to the user to get hold of the URB data that the kernel part captured.

Figure 18.6 illustrates a sequence of actions that occurs when the user space interacts with the `usbmon` module. From the figure, you can infer that when a user space application opens a `usbmon` file, perhaps `0u`, internally the open file operations that are registered (`mon_text_open`) are invoked. The open handler adds the text reader callbacks with `usbmon` using `mon_reader_add`. This starts the process of queuing subsequent URB activity in `struct mon_event_text` objects. A subsequent read operation from the user space application dequeues the URB activity and presents it to the user application. When the URB event list is empty, the user application process is added to a wait queue until the next URB transaction is made. So far, the preceding sections have focused on how `usbmon` interfaces with other modules. The subsequent section explores how to use `usbmon` to capture USB transactions.

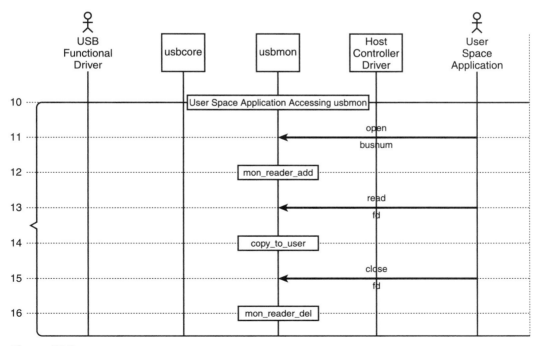

Figure 18.6
Interaction sequence between usbmon and the user space application.

How to Use usbmon

The `usbcore` module is responsible for setting up the USB debug framework's root directory during its initialization. It uses the `debugfs` infrastructure to initialize the framework for `usbmon`. The `usbmon` files are created relative to this root path. So when you mount `debugfs`, perhaps `in /sys/kernel/debug`, the `usbmon` files might be in the `/sys/kernel/debug/usbmon/` directory. Thus, for `usbmon` to function properly, the kernel needs to be built up with the `debugfs` module.

Thus, you need to mount the `debugfs` file system to view the `usbmon` files. Normally, it is mounted to `/sys/kernel/debug`. The following terminal activity shows how to mount the debug file system and its initial directory contents before you load the `usbmon` module.

```
root@rajaram-laptop:~# mount -t debugfs none_debugs /sys/kernel/debug
root@rajaram-laptop:~# cd /sys/kernel/debug/
root@rajaram-laptop:/sys/kernel/debug# ls
kprobes
root@rajaram-laptop:/sys/kernel/debug#.
```

After ensuring a successful mount of the debug file system, you are ready to insert the `usbmon` module into the kernel. After a successful modprobe of `usbmon`, the module creates `usbmon` files for each USB bus registered with the kernel. The following terminal activity shows you the contents of the `usbmon` directory after a successful insertion of the `usbmon` module.

```
root@rajaram-laptop:/sys/kernel/debug# modprobe usbmon
root@rajaram-laptop:/sys/kernel/debug# cd usbmon/
root@rajaram-laptop:/sys/kernel/debug/usbmon# ls
0s  1s  1u  2t  3s  3u  4t  5s  5u  6t  7s  7u
0u  1t  2s  2u  3t  4s  4u  5t  6s  6u  7t
root@rajaram-laptop:/sys/kernel/debug/usbmon#
```

In Linux, the USB number assignment starts at 1, and `usbmon` creates files with the bus number as a prefix to capture URB transactions on the particular USB bus. `usbmon` also creates a file with a 0 (0u) prefix to capture URB transactions of all busses. To capture the transactions of a connected device, you should know the bus the device is connected to. To determine the bus connection, you can either use `lsusb` or see a `devices` file exported by `usbfs`, generally in `/proc/bus / usb /devices`. In the sample setup, the device with ID `1221:3234` is the device of interest, and `lsusb` lists the device lists along with the bus number.

```
root@rajaram-laptop:~# lsusb
Bus 007 Device 003: ID 1221:3234
Bus 007 Device 001: ID 0000:0000
Bus 006 Device 002: ID 064e:a103
Bus 006 Device 001: ID 0000:0000
Bus 005 Device 001: ID 0000:0000
Bus 004 Device 001: ID 0000:0000
Bus 003 Device 001: ID 0000:0000
Bus 002 Device 001: ID 0000:0000
Bus 001 Device 001: ID 0000:0000
```

The device connected for this example is a mass storage device that is connected to the USB bus with bus number 7. To capture the URB transactions of the mass storage device, you can write a simple application that can read and display the information to you, or you can use the `cat` command on the file representing the device and pipe it to a log file. In the following terminal activity, the device of interest is connected to bus number 7 and piped to `usbmsclog.txt`.

```
root@rajaram-laptop:/sys/kernel/debug/usbmon#
root@rajaram-laptop:/sys/kernel/debug/usbmon# cat 7u >~/usbmsclog.txt
root@rajaram-laptop:/sys/kernel/debug/usbmon#
```

You can analyze offline at your own pace the URB information captured in `usbmsclog.txt`. The CD accompanying this book contains the complete log file. For ease of analysis, you see only part of the log file that captured transaction of the mass storage device. The snippet contains a couple of control and bulk transactions that occurred between the Linux host and USB mass storage device.

If you look at the log illustrated next, you can interpret the first line of the log file as a Control OUT transfer in bus 7 targeting endpoint address 0. The control transfer is a SET_ADDRESS request from the host with the USB device address of 5 to the device. The second line captures the SET_ADDRESS URB completion process indicated by C with successful completion status 0.

```
d2263a80 2613100221 S Co:7:000:0 s 00 05 0005 0000 0000 0
d2263a80 2613100276 C Co:7:000:0 0 0
d2263a80 2613121192 S Ci:7:005:0 s 80 06 0100 0000 0012 18 <
d2263a80 2613121399 C Ci:7:005:0 0 18 = 12010002 00000040 21123432 00000102 0301
```

```
cad4aa80 2613121452 S Ci:7:005:0 s 80 06 0200 0000 0009 9 <
cad4aa80 2613121662 C Ci:7:005:0 0 9 = 09022000 01010080 32
```

The log format matches the `struct usb_mon_event` data structure discussed in the previous section. The following section dissects the `usbmon` log in a more detailed manner.

Notice that the log starts with a URB address (d2263a80) followed by the URB submission time (2613100221). The time stamp logged along with the USB-related information helps in measuring the time taken to complete a URB transaction. Figure 18.7 provides a detailed breakdown of the `usbmon` log.

This section dissects a sample from the USB mass storage functional driver's URB transfer. The following terminal activity is a capture of command block wrapper (CBW) transfers from mass storage device 5 and bulk endpoint number 1. Figure 18.8 provide a detailed breakdown of the `usbmon` mass storage URB log.

```
d2263780 2618125421 S Bo:7:005:1 -115 31 = 55534243 01000000 24000000 80000612
00000024 00000000 00000000 000000
```

URB Address	Time Stamp	URB Event	Transfer & Direction	Bus Number	Device Number	Endpoint Number	URB Status	bRequest Type	bRequest	wValue	wIndex	wLength (Hex)	wLength (Decimal)
d2263a80	2613100221	S	Co	7	0	0	s	0	5	5	0	0	0

URB Address	Time Stamp	URB Event	Transfer & Direction	Bus Number	Device Number	Endpoint Number	URB Status	Length
d2263a80	2613100276	C	Co	7	0	0	0	0

URB Address	Time Stamp	URB Event	Transfer & Direction	Bus Number	Device Number	Endpoint Number	URB Status	bRequest Type	bRequest	wValue	wIndex	wLength (Hex)	wLength (Decimal)	Direction (IN)
d2263a80	2613121192	S	Ci	7	5	0	s	80	6	100	0	12	18	<

URB Address	Time Stamp	URB Event	Transfer & Direction	Bus Number	Device Number	Endpoint Number	URB Status	Length		bLength/ bDescriptorType/ bcdUSB	bDeviceSubClass/ bDeviceProtocol/ bMaxPacketSize (HEX)	Vendor ID /Product ID	bcdDevice/ iManufacturer iProduct	iSerialNumber /bNumConfiguration
d2263a80	2613121399	C	Ci	7	5	0	0	18	=	12010002	00000040	21123432	00000102	0301

Figure 18.7
The usbmon control data.

URB Address	Time Stamp	URB Event	Transfer & Direction	Bus Number	Device Number	Endpoint Number	URB Status	bLength		Mass Storage Information
d2263780	2618125421	S	Bo	7	5	1	-115	31	=	55534243 01000000 24000000 80000612 24000000 00000000 00000000 00000000

Figure 18.8
The usbmon bulk data.

You know by now that the usbmon provides comprehensive information about the URB states and the USB activity that occurred between the Linux host and the USB device. With this information, you can easily fix any USB-related issue in your platform.

DEBUG USING USBFS_SNOOP

The previous section discussed usbmon, a low-level tool that captures URB transactions in the URB flow to debug a USB system using Linux. Sometimes such detailed information is not required to debug a Linux USB subsystem. This paves the way to a simpler approach available on Linux that can snoop USB transactions. The usbfs_snoop is one such debug mechanism available as part of the usbcore that can snoop URB data at a higher level of the USB transaction and print it as part of the system log.

Figure 18.9 illustrates the usbfs_snoop placement in a Linux USB subsystem. As the name indicates, the usbfs_snoop feature snoops USB details from operations performed on the usbfs file system. It taps the URB passed by the user application to the usbcore through the usbfs file operations. Although the

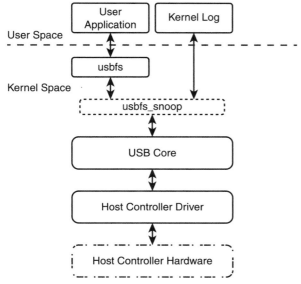

Figure 18.9
usbfs_snoop's design location in usbcore.

feature is part of usbcore, Figure 18.9 illustrates the feature outside the usbcore to better represent its role between usbfs and the usbcore.

In the usbcore, the /drivers/usb/core/devio.c file implements the usbfs file operations, an ideal location for usbfs_snoop to snoop URB operations and URB status information. The snoop_urb routine implemented in the devio.c handles this snoop activity.

```
static void snoop_urb(struct usb_device *udev,void __user *userurb, int pipe,
unsigned length,int timeout_or_status, enum snoop_when when)
```

The usbcore module defines the module parameter static int usbfs_snoop; in devio.c. This module parameter allows the user to configure and control the usbfs_snoop feature at runtime. To configure this usbfs_snoop parameter, the user should have the necessary privileges to update the parameter file.

```
static int usbfs_snoop;
module_param(usbfs_snoop, bool, S_IRUGO | S_IWUSR);
MODULE_PARM_DESC(usbfs_snoop, "true to log all usbfs traffic");
```

Generally, Linux exports its module parameters as a file, thus enabling the user to access them at the user space. This module parameter is declared as part of the usbcore module, and you can find the parameter in /sys/module/usbcore/parameters/. The following terminal activity illustrates module parameters of the usbcore module.

```
root@rajaram-laptop:~# ls -l /sys/module/usbcore/parameters/
total 0
-rw-r--r-- 1 root root 4096 2010-05-18 22:34 autosuspend
-r--r--r-- 1 root root 4096 2010-05-18 22:34 blinkenlights
-r--r--r-- 1 root root 4096 2010-05-18 22:34 nousb
-rw-r--r-- 1 root root 4096 2010-05-18 22:34 old_scheme_first
-rw-r--r-- 1 root root 4096 2010-05-18 22:34 usbfs_snoop
-rw-r--r-- 1 root root 4096 2010-05-18 22:34 use_both_schemes
root@rajaram-laptop:~#
```

In the earlier discussion, you saw the usbfs_snoop module parameter acting as a flag to control snoop of URB debug information. The snoop flag can hold the value true (Y) or false (N). The following terminal activity illustrates how to read the value of the module parameter usbfs_snoop and explains how to configure it. To know the current state of the snoop flag, you can run the cat command on the parameter file, as illustrated here. The output shows that when the usbcore is loaded, the usbfs_snoop parameter is set to false.

```
root@rajaram-laptop:~#
root@rajaram-laptop:~# cat /sys/module/usbcore/parameters/usbfs_snoop
N
root@rajaram-laptop:~#
```

To configure the snoop flag for capturing URB debug information, you can run echo 1 or Y to the usbfs_snoop parameter file, as illustrated next. This operation turns on the usbfs_snoop debugging.

```
root@rajaram-laptop:~# echo 1 > /sys/module/usbcore/parameters/usbfs_snoop
root@rajaram-laptop:~# cat /sys/module/usbcore/parameters/usbfs_snoop
Y
root@rajaram-laptop:~#
```

Once the flag is set, the URB information is snooped, and you are ready to collect the debug data as part of the kernel log message.

Note

The major difference between the usbmon and the usbfs_snoop is that the former captures URB information between the kernel functional drivers and the lower usbcore, and the latter captures the URB information between applications and the usbcore's file operations.

Another important point to remember is that you will not see usbfs_snoop debug data in the kernel log unless there is a USB transaction between a user application and the usbcore through the usbfs file system. For example, usbfs_snoop does not capture URB transactions during enumeration; instead, any user application using a file operation triggers a URB snoop operation.

To trigger snooping of URB using usbfs_snoop, you can perform a simple exercise, say lsusb -v, on the terminal. This user space application sends input/output control (IOCTL) and gathers information on the connected USB devices. After a successful lsusb -v, you can use a dmesg command to display debug messages snooped by usbfs_snoop. The following log illustrates the debug messages generated by usbfs_snoop because of a successful lsusb.

```
[ 3907.638710] usb 7-3: usbdev_ioctl: CONTROL
[ 3907.638723] usb 7-3: control read: bRequest=06 bRrequestType=80 wValue=0300
wIndex=0000 wLength=00ff
```

```
[ 3907.638946] usb 7-3: control read: data 04 03 09 04
[ 3907.638961] usb 7-3: usbdev_ioctl: CONTROL
[ 3907.638968] usb 7-3: control read: bRequest=06 bRrequestType=80 wValue=0301
wIndex=0409 wLength=00ff
[ 3907.639200] usb 7-3: control read: data 0c 03 55 00 64 00 69 00 73 00 6b 00 00 00 00
00 00 00
[ 3907.639229] usb 7-3: usbdev_ioctl: CONTROL
[ 3907.639235] usb 7-3: control read: bRequest=06 bRrequestType=80 wValue=0300
wIndex=0000 wLength=00ff
[ 3907.639445] usb 7-3: control read: data 04 03 09 04
```

In the preceding log, you can see IOCTL transactions when the lsusb utility is executed. The log contains details on the time of URB activity, bus and device number, and USB transfer information. The log is not as comprehensive as the usbmon, and debug data is captured at an initial stage of the URB creation.

Verbose Debugging for Host-Side USB

The verbose debugging method is not specific to the USB subsystem, but it's a more traditional approach that kernel developers use for debugging. In this method, the debug message is controlled by a DEBUG macro, and the modules print debug messages only in the debug mode. In release mode, this macro is disabled, so the debug messages are not printed. The USB subsystem verbose message is one such option available on Linux for debugging the USB subsystem. You can configure the verbose debug message through kernel configuration macros. Figure 18.10 illustrates how to enable the verbose debug option. The USB Verbose Debug Messages option mainly generates debug messages interleaved in the USB core and hub drivers' source of the Linux USB subsystem.

Sometimes it is necessary to generate debug information during the initial enumeration process by the usbcore to isolate problems, because neither usbmon nor usbfs_snoop covers this part. For example, the initial USB device setup is done via the hub layer of the usbcore, which needs some more informative debug messages to isolate low-level error. To get additional debug messages, enable CONFIG_USB_ANNOUNCE_NEW_DEVICES in the hub.c through the kernel configuration, as shown in Figure 18.10. This announces any new devices connected to the Linux USB subsystem. Sometimes such debug information helps you check whether the issue is in USB enumeration or lower in the usbcore.

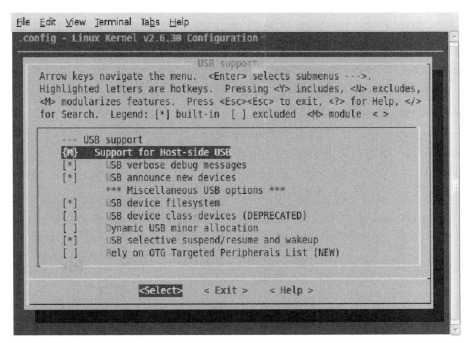

Figure 18.10
USB Verbose Debug and USB device announcement option.

The verbose output of debug information is available as part of `syslog` like any other log message.

SUMMARY

A key factor in successful software development is having proper internal debug mechanisms. The Linux USB subsystem provides solid debug methods and makes development using the Linux USB subsystem easy. The tools comprehensively cover different functionalities of the subsystem. This chapter explored these tools and discussed how to use them during development. You need to understand their design and apply them in proper places.

In the next chapter, you will learn various options available to test a USB system using the Linux USB framework.

More Reading

This chapter covered methods available on Linux to debug a USB system. These methods will serve the debugging needs of any USB developer. Linux documentation available at `/Documentation/usb/usbmon.txt` includes additional information about `usbmon`.

The `usbmon` developer's white paper is available at http://people.redhat.com/zaitcev/linux/OLS05_zaitcev.pdf. There you'll find more insights into the design and architecture.

As referred to in this chapter, `usbmon` implements a more comprehensive binary reader that provides access to complete URB information. To learn more about the binary version of `usbmon`, explore `drivers /usb/mon /mon_bin.c`.

A more detailed article titled "Snooping the USB Data Stream" is available on the Linux journal at http://www.linuxjournal.com/article/7582.

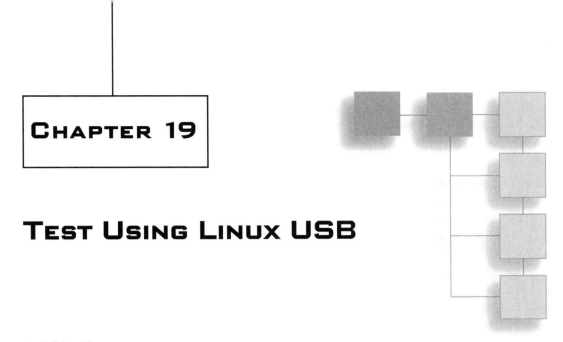

CHAPTER 19

TEST USING LINUX USB

In This Chapter

- Linux USB Unit Test Driver
- Linux USB Functional Test

Testing is an essential part of software development to ensure system quality and confirm whether a system meets its product requirements. Quality control and quality assurance are integral to the process and are achieved through proper testing. Testing a universal serial bus (USB) system involves various stages of evaluation and different characteristics of a USB device. Following are a few recommended tests that the USB-IF (Implementers Forum) recommends to a USB device vendor to develop a certified USB device.

- Full-speed electrical tests
- High-speed electrical tests
- Interoperability tests
- Functional tests

On Linux, the essential hardware and software environments to perform USB compliance testing are not available and can be performed only on Microsoft Windows operating systems. However, Linux provides tests as separate modules to validate Linux USB systems. This chapter initially explores the USB tests available on Linux to evaluate a USB host and a USB device. Subsequently, it explores how to use the Linux USB test module to evaluate a USB system.

Another important requirement involves testing a USB device as a system, discussed later. You'll also learn how to set up a Linux USB system for some of the key USB functionalities and perform basic function setup and testing.

LINUX USB UNIT TEST DRIVER

The Linux test module is part of the Linux USB subsystem's miscellaneous configuration that is implemented in `drivers/usb/misc/usbtest.c`. You can configure this module through the kernel menu configuration and generate `usbtest.ko`. You can control the test cases implemented in this module using user space applications. The tests include control transfer and data transfers such as bulk and isochronous (ISO). These tests exercise the host controller driver (HCD) and the gadget framework. Some of these tests must be run continuously to ensure that both the USB hardware and software are error free.

There are approximately 16 test scenarios. Table 19.1 explores the tests available as part of the `usbtest` module.

Table 19.1 Test Case Scenarios of usbtest Module

Test Scenario	Test Description
Test Case 1: Write data bytes N times	This test scenario writes data to a bulk endpoint of the device for N number of times, as specified by the user space application. Internally, the USB test driver calls the leaf function `simple_io` with the number of times data needs to be written and executed for the test scenario. The `simple_io` submits the URBs[1] using the `usb_submit_urb` formed by the `simple_alloc_urb` routine. This test scenario effectively tests the endpoints for contiguous write operations. The user space applications effectively design the data patterns.
Test Case 2: Read data bytes N times	This test scenario reads a bulk endpoint of the device for N number of times, as specified by the user space application. In this test scenario, the test driver calls `simple_io` to submit the URBs by `usb_submit_urb`. Such reads exercise your hardware endpoints. The user space software applications need to effectively pass on the loop count.
Test Case 3: Write data (varying length) bytes N times	This test scenario writes data of variable lengths to a bulk endpoint of the device for N number of times, as specified through the user space application. In this scenario, the test driver invokes `simple_io` but varies the data size. Such test cases can exercise the hardware with data of various sizes.

Table 19.1   (Continued)

Test Scenario	Test Description
Test Case 4: Read data (varying length) bytes N times	This test scenario reads data of variable lengths to a bulk endpoint of the device for N number of times, as specified through the user space application. In this scenario, the test driver invokes `simple_io` but varies the data size. Such test cases can exercise the hardware with data of various sizes.
Test Case 5: Write data bytes through `sglist` entries	This test scenario performs a write operation with I/O queuing on the bulk endpoint using a scatter gather framework. Internally, the test uses `alloc_sglist` to set up and `usb_sg_init`, `usb_sg_wait` to transfer the data. These `usb_sg_*` interface functions are available as part of `./usb/core/message.c`. These tests ensure a peak transfer rate, which is essential to exercise endpoints.
Test Case 6: Read data bytes through `sglist` entries	This test scenario performs a read operation on bulk endpoints using a scatter gather framework. Internally, the test uses `alloc_sglist` to set up and `usb_sg_init`, `usb_sg_wait` to transfer the data. These `usb_sg_*` interface functions are available as part of `./usb/core/message.c`. They ensure a peak transfer rate, which is essential to exercise endpoints.
Test Case 7: Write data (varying length) using `sglist` entries	This test scenario performs a write operation with I/O queuing on the bulk endpoint using the scatter gather framework by varying data size. These tests ensure a peak transfer rate, which is essential to exercise endpoints.
Test Case 8: Read data (varying length) using `sglist` entries	This test scenario performs a read operation with I/O queuing on the bulk endpoint using the scatter gather framework by varying data size. These tests ensure a peak transfer rate, which is essential to exercise endpoints.
Test Case 9: Perform Chapter 9 tests N times	This test scenario sends control messages to sanity test standard requests working with `usb_control_mesg` and other control message utility functions such as `usb_get_descriptor`. The test internally uses `ch9_postconfig` to run the predefined test N number of times, as specified by the user space application. This test is useful to verify basic operations often used in enumeration.
Test Case 10: Queue control calls N times	This test scenario queues multiple control messages and thereby tests control message queuing, protocol stalls, short reads, and fault handling. Internally, it uses `test_ctrl_queue` to form and queue control packets. The user application can decide the queue length and number of iterations. This is a stress test for control transfers; any USB device that runs on Linux should clear this test.
Test Case 11: Unlink read operation	This test scenario unlinks the URB read request submitted for N number of times, as specified by the user space application. Internally, the test invokes `usb_unlink_urb`, thereby cancelling submitted URBs. This scenario tests the host controller driver and the `usbcore` on the Linux host it runs.
Test Case 12: Unlink write operation	This test scenario unlinks the URB write request submitted for N number of times, as specified by the user space application. Internally, the test invokes `usb_unlink_urb`, thereby canceling submitted URBs. This scenario tests the host controller driver and the `usbcore` on the Linux host it runs.

(Continued)

Table 19.1 Test Case Scenarios of usbtest Module (*Continued*)

Test Scenario	Test Description
Test Case 13: Set and clear halt operations	This test scenario tests an endpoint's HALT feature of the host controller. Internally, the test uses usb_clear_halt and usb_control_msg to perform these tests. If your hardware doesn't support halting of endpoints, you can skip this test.
Test Case 14: Request vendor-specific control	This test scenario sends EP0 messages by varying the size of the control message by the values the user application indicates. Internally, the test uses usb_control_msg to perform these control requests. The control message uses the USB compliance's vendor-specific control request parameter, such as 0x5b,0x5c.
Test Case 15: Write ISO data bytes for N entries	This test scenario writes data to an ISO endpoint of the device for N times as specified by the user space application. Internally, the test queues ISO URBs using usb_submit_urb with various sizes. This test is useful for verifying ISO endpoint and ISO functionalities.
Test Case 16: Read ISO data bytes for N entries	This test scenario reads data to an ISO endpoint of the device for N times, as specified by the user space application. Internally, the test queues ISO URBs using usb_submit_urb with various sizes. This test is useful for verifying ISO endpoint and ISO functionalities.

[1]URBs = USB Request Blocks

The usbtest module work is part of the Linux USB framework's miscellaneous section that you can configure through the menuconfig option USB testing driver. The kernel module usbtest.ko is created after a successful build. The usbtest kernel driver detects and supports predefined USB devices that are part of struct usbtest_driver. The test driver also provides provision to indicate the device through module parameters. The module parameters vendor and product of the usbtest module allow you to indicate the vendor ID and product ID of the device. You should remove the standard driver of your device before installing the usbtest module. The following terminal activity illustrates how to load a generic USB device with the usbtest module. You should remember that you should have super user rights when you load the driver.

```
root@rajaram-laptop: # modprobe usbtest vendor=0xAAAA product=0xBBBB
```

Once the driver is loaded properly for the device, you are ready to perform the test scenarios detailed in Table 19.1 from the user space. Remember that your device firmware needs tweaks to support and respond to the test request. The Linux USB has two user space software files—testusb.c and test.sh—that can interface with usbtest driver and are available at http://www.linux-usb.org/usbtest/testusb.c and http://www.linux-usb.org/usbtest/test.sh.

You can download testusb.c and build and run the test application with the following command-line options.

```
root@rajaram-laptop: # testusb
must specify '-a' or '-D dev'
usage: testusb [-a] [-D dev] [-n] [-c iterations] [-s packetsize] [-g sglen]
root@rajaram-laptop: #
```

The next step in the process of testing a USB device after checking its basic protocol behavior is testing the functionality of a USB device. The next section focuses on setting up and testing some of the USB gadget functionalities.

LINUX USB FUNCTIONAL TEST

The previous section involving the usbtest module provides only a USB protocol level test framework, which tests the usbcore framework and the host controller driver in a USB host and the gadget layer in a USB device. The next stage of testing is verifying the Linux-USB as a complete system. The following section explores some key functionalities of the Linux platform, such as storage, serial transfer, networking, and input devices that adapt USB functionality. These functionalities are implemented based on the USB class specification defined by the USB-IF.

Storage USB Gadget

The USB-IF defines the Mass Storage Class Specification to support and implement USB-based storage devices. On Linux, the USB mass storage gadget functionality is implemented as File-backed Storage Gadget (FSG), and on the USB host, the storage functionality is supported by SCSI drivers, with the Linux-USB framework providing a USB glue layer. Figure 19.1 illustrates Linux USB storage modules in simple blocks.

In a typical mass storage device setup, a device's storage is exposed as logical unit numbers (LUNs) to the host. Internally, a LUN represents a block device or a file that the storage gadget driver wants to share. The drivers/usb/gadget/file_storage.c file implements the mass storage device functional driver g_file_storage.ko. To successfully associate LUNs and set other characteristics of

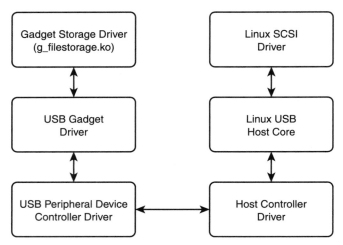

Figure 19.1
Linux USB storage modules in simple blocks.

the mass storage device, the functional driver module provides module parameters.

- **file.** To name the files or block devices that back storage.
- **ro.** To indicate whether the storage is read only. This holds a default value of `false`.
- **removable.** To indicate whether the storage is removable media. This holds a default value of `false`.
- **luns.** To indicate the supported LUNs.
- **nofua.** To indicate whether the storage supports force unit access (FUA). This holds a default value of `false`.
- **stall.** To indicate whether the storage driver can stall bulk endpoints.
- **cdrom.** To indicate whether the storage device is a CD-ROM that holds a default value of `false`.
- **transport.** To specify the transport protocol, namely CB (Control/Bulk), CBI (Control/Bulk/Interrupt), and BBB (Bulk Only). The default value is `BBB`.

- **protocol.** To specify the protocol name, namely RBC (Reduced Block Commands), 8020, ATAPI (AT Attachment Packet Interface), QIC, UFI (USB Floppy Interface), 8070, and SCSI (Small Computer System Interface). The default value is SCSI.

- **vendor.** To specify the USB vendor ID of the storage device. It holds a default value of 0x0525 (NetChip).

- **product.** To specify the USB vendor ID of the storage device. It holds a default value of 0xa4a5 (FSG).

- **release.** To specify the USB release number of the storage device that is stored in the bcdDevice field of the device descriptor.

- **serial.** To specify the serial number. It is a string of hex characters.

- **buflen.** To specify the buffer size used by the storage gadget driver. It holds a default size of 16384.

The following terminal activity illustrates how to load the file storage module successfully and set up a USB-based storage device.

```
root@rajaram-laptop: # modprobe g_file_storage file=/dev/sda1 stall=y
```

After successfully loading the module, connect the storage USB device to a USB host system, which supports the protocol specified to the storage driver module. On the host, you can view the LUNs as a storage drive. Now you can perform normal copying and formatting to test the device. The http://www.linux-usb.org/gadget/file_storage.html link provides additional information on managing the storage gadget driver.

Serial USB Gadget

The serial USB gadget exposes a tty-like serial interface for the host, and it uses a usb-serial driver to interact. The serial gadget driver also implements the USB IF-defined communication device class (CDC) requirements referred to as CDC Abstract Control Model (ACM). The host Linux requires the cdc-acm driver to support CDC ACM devices. drivers/usb/gadget/serial.c, drivers/usb/gadget/u_serial.c, drivers/usb/gadget/f_serial.c, and drivers/usb/gadget/f_acm.c implement the CDC requirements. Figure 19.2 illustrates Linux USB serial modules in simple blocks.

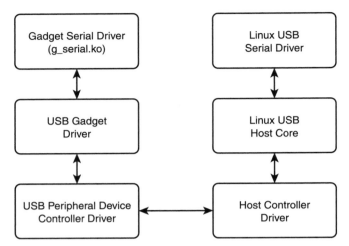

Figure 19.2
Linux USB serial modules in simple blocks.

The serial gadget module, g_serial, supports generic serial, CDC ACM, and Object Exchange (OBEX) functionalities. These functionalities are managed through the module parameter, as shown here.

- **use_acm.** This parameter informs the driver to support ACM when loading the g_serial driver. By default, the value of use_acm is set to true.

- **use_obex.** This parameter informs the driver to support OBEX when loading the g_serial driver. By default, the value of use_obex is set to false.

- **n_ports.** This parameter indicates the number of ports the driver creates. By default, the value of n_ports is 1.

The following terminal activity illustrates how to load the g_serial driver module to support the OBEX driver.

root@rajaram-laptop: # modprobe g_serial use_obex=y use_acm=n

The documentation available in the path Documentation/usb/gadget_serial.txt provides additional information to configure the USB serial gadget and functionally test the serial gadget.

USB Network Gadget

The USB-IF CDC specification also defines Ethernet emulation over USB through the Ethernet Control Model (ECM) class. This defines a communications class interface to configure and manage various Ethernet functions. On Linux, `drivers/usb/gadget/ether.c`, `drivers/usb/gadget/f_ecm.c`, and `drivers/usb/gadget/u_ether.c` files implement ECM gadget functionality and the host. Figure 19.3 illustrates the Linux USB Ethernet module in simple blocks.

The USB Ethernet module `g_ether` module supports ECM (Ethernet Control Model), EEM (Ethernet Emulation Model), and NDIS (Network Driver Interface Specification) functionalities. You can manage the `g_ether` module by module parameters listed next.

- **use_eem.** This informs the module whether it should support EEM. By default, the value is `false`.

- **host_addr.** This parameter sets the host Ethernet address.

- **dev_addr.** This parameter sets the device Ethernet address.

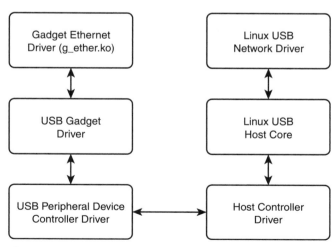

Figure 19.3
Linux USB Ethernet modules in simple blocks.

You can find additional information on how to configure and test Linux USB Ethernet in http://www.linux-usb.org/usbnet/ and http://www.linux-usb.org/gadget/.

HID (Human Interface Devices) USB Gadget

The USB-IF defines the requirements of USB HID devices and is available at http://www.usb.org/developers/hidpage/, which includes a mouse, keyboard, joystick, and more. On the latest Linux after 2.6.34, the HID gadget functional driver is implemented as part of http://lxr.free-electrons.com/source/drivers/usb/gadget/hid.c, and the host HID support is implemented through files in `drivers/hid/usbhid/`. Figure 19.4 illustrates Linux USB HID modules in simple blocks.

The HID devices are represented as `/dev/hidgX`, and you can read/write through that file. The Linux documentation in http://lxr.free-electrons.com/source/Documentation/usb/gadget_hid.txt includes a small interactive test program `hid_gadget_test` that allows you to test HID setup. You can also read http://lxr.free-electrons.com/source/Documentation/usb/hiddev.txt to learn more about using HID devices.

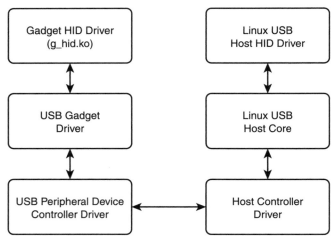

Figure 19.4
Linux USB HID modules in simple blocks.

Summary

The compliance testing of a USB device involves validating the device at the protocol and function levels. This chapter explored some of the keys for Linux USB–related tests available for developers.

Unlike other operating systems, using Linux to perform these USB tests gives developers an edge. Linux allows developers to pinpoint the exact module when a test fails. This is possible because the Linux kernel can be rebuilt with additional debug information to isolate the cause of the problem.

The Appendix provides a simple framework with scripting support that allows you to perform USB tests in a different way from user space.

More Reading

You can read more about how to perform other system-level tests such as soft connect and disconnect, suspend, Bluetooth, and audio from Linux USB documentation. The sites http://www.linux-usb.org/gadget/ and http://www.linux-usb.org/usbtest/ provide detailed coverage on the Linux USB tests and procedures. The site http://linux-usb-test.sourceforge.net/docs/interop-0.2/book1.html provides interoperability procedures available on Linux for USB devices. The source code of the `usbtest` available at `drivers/usb/misc/usbtest.c` enables you to properly adapt the test cases to your needs and add new scenarios.

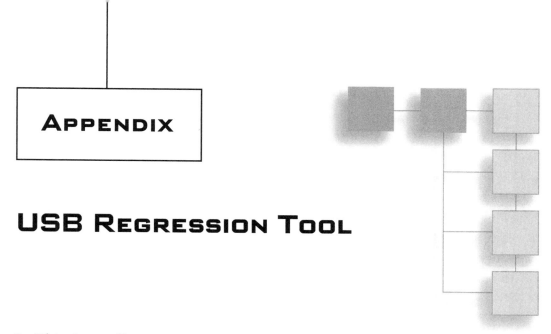

APPENDIX

USB Regression Tool

In This Appendix

- Overview of USB Regression Tool
- Script Definitions

In a development environment, developers write simple unit test code, compile it, and create an executable to set up a scenario. If the developer needs to change a certain parameter, he must recompile the test code to a new program, which takes time. In a system environment, when you connect a device under development to a universal serial bus (USB) host, you do not have much control on the host transfer. You cannot stop the host transaction and debug the device at a certain point in the middle of a transaction. In such cases, tools that enable a developer to write unit test scenarios and use them without needing to compile anything add value.

Defining scripting tools implements the test scenarios and generates reports more quickly. In a normal situation, the USB packet formation is with the kernel driver, and you can't do much to create an error. A scriptable tool makes it easy to develop errors because the complete control of the test is at the script level. The following section explores a simple scripting tool that allows you to send and receive USB data. Initially, the section provides a simple overview of the test tool. That's followed by the tool's usage and a brief overview of the script language.

OVERVIEW OF USB REGRESSION TOOL

The USB regression tool adds value to a developer and a tester by automating a few of their tasks. The USB regression tool integrates the most popular open source USB library, the `libusb`, with a powerful cross-platform `Qt` (cross-platform application and UI framework) environment. The tool uses the scripting support of the `Qt` environment, which is a JavaScript-like programming language. Figure A.1 provides a simple architectural block diagram of the tool.

To support USB transfers, additional script commands are added, which are explained in the next section. The USB regression tool also captures `usbmon` activity, along with the script execution, which allows you to easily analyze the activity between the devices. Because this tool accesses different system files, you need to run the tool in super user mode. You can also run this tool from an embedded host because Qt has cross-platform support.

The USB regression tool includes the provision to write scripts and view the activity when the script is executed. Figure A.2 captures an alpha version of the USB regression tool.

You can use the regression tool for four purposes.

- Notice the USB devices connected to the host, and note the vendor ID and product ID.

- Write a script per your requirements.

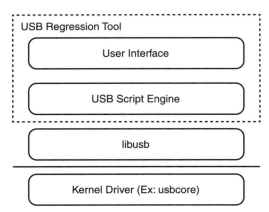

Figure A.1
The simple architecture of the USB regression tool.

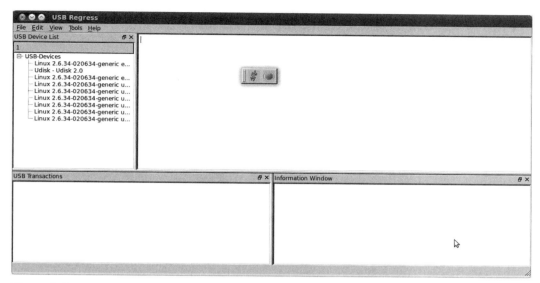

Figure A.2
A snapshot of the USB regression tool.

- Run the script using the Run option as part of the toolbar.
- View the results in the information and USB transaction widget, and save them as a report.

A detailed user manual on how to use the USB regression tool is available at http://www.kernelkahani.com/Tools.

SCRIPT DEFINITIONS

The script language is based on the ECMAScript standard, which allows you to write a JavaScript-like program. Over and above the functionalities supported by the scripting language, the tool provides functionalities to implement USB test scenarios. These extension functions are either generic USB functions or utility functions.

Generic USB Functions

The generic USB functions implement functions to control USB devices connected to the host and to perform data transfer.

- `int write_usb_bulk(int busid,int devid, int ep, char* data, int size, int timeout);`

This script function transfers bulk data to the USB device specified by the `busid` and `devid` parameters. You should call this function after successfully opening and claiming a device.

- `int read_usb_bulk(int busid,int devid, int ep, char* data, int size, int timeout);`

This script function receives bulk data to the USB device specified by the `busid` and `devid` parameters. You should call this function after successfully opening and claiming a device.

- `int write_usb_interrupt(int busid,int devid, int ep, char* data, int size, int timeout);`

This script function transfers interrupt data to the USB device specified by the `busid` and `devid` parameters. You should call this function after successfully opening and claiming a device.

- `int read_usb_interrupt(int busid,int devid, int ep, char* data, int size,int timeout);`

This script function receives interrupt data for the USB device specified by the `busid` and `devid` parameters. You should call this function after successfully opening and claiming a device.

- `int usb_control_message(int busid,int devid, int requesttype, int request, int value, int index, char* data, int size, int timeout);`

This script function transfers control messages to the USB device specified by the `busid` and `devid` parameters. You should call this function after successfully opening and claiming a device.

- `int claim_usb_interface(int busid,int devid, int interface);`

This function allows you to claim a particular interface of a USB device specified by the `busid` and the `devid`. You should call this function after successfully opening a device.

- `int release_usb_interface(int busid,int devid, int interface);`

  This function allows you to release a previously claimed interface of a USB device as specified by the `busid` and the `devid`. You should call this function after successfully opening a device.

- `int set_usb_configuration(int busid,int devid,int interface);`

  This function allows you to set a particular configuration for a USB device specified by the `busid` and the `devid`. You should call this function after successfully opening a device.

- `int open_device(int busid,int devid);`

  This function opens a USB device based on its `busid` and `devid` for the script engine's further communication.

- `int close_device(int busid,int devid);`

  This function closes a USB device based on the `busid` and `devid` that the script engine previously opened.

Utility Functions

The utility functions provide the necessary support to make the script suitable for a development environment.

- `void dump_log_message(char* text);`

  This function dumps the message specified in the `text` parameter to the information widget. This is useful for logging the script's activity.

- `void dump_hex_log_message(const char* text,int length);`

  This function dumps the message specified in the `text` parameter to the information widget as hexadecimal data. This is useful for logging the script's activity.

- `void dump_device_details();`

  This function dumps details of the USB device connected to the host in the information widget.

- `void script_sleep(int time);`

    This function stops the script execution for the `time` specified in the parameter. The waiting time is in milliseconds.

These functions are the basic infrastructure of the script framework. You can expand this infrastructure to support additional class drivers. Furthermore, you can contribute and download the tool from the GIT repository git://git .kernelkahani.com.

Summary

The alpha version of this test tool is available on the CD accompanying this book. You can find the source of this tool in the GIT repository git://git .kernelkahani.com and the subsequent upgrade in this location. You can also submit patches to the repository by referring to the TODO list, which provides possible enhancements.

INDEX

Like the Book?

Let us know on Facebook or Twitter!

facebook.com/courseptr

twitter.com/courseptr

License Agreement/Notice of Limited Warranty

By opening the sealed disc container in this book, you agree to the following terms and conditions. If, upon reading the following license agreement and notice of limited warranty, you cannot agree to the terms and conditions set forth, return the unused book with unopened disc to the place where you purchased it for a refund.

License

The enclosed software is copyrighted by the copyright holder(s) indicated on the software disc. You are licensed to copy the software onto a single computer for use by a single user and to a backup disc. You may not reproduce, make copies, or distribute copies or rent or lease the software in whole or in part, except with written permission of the copyright holder(s). You may transfer the enclosed disc only together with this license, and only if you destroy all other copies of the software and the transferee agrees to the terms of the license. You may not decompile, reverse assemble, or reverse engineer the software.

Notice of Limited Warranty

The enclosed disc is warranted by Course Technology to be free of physical defects in materials and workmanship for a period of sixty (60) days from end user's purchase of the book/disc combination. During the sixty-day term of the limited warranty, Course Technology will provide a replacement disc upon the return of a defective disc.

Limited Liability

THE SOLE REMEDY FOR BREACH OF THIS LIMITED WARRANTY SHALL CONSIST ENTIRELY OF REPLACEMENT OF THE DEFECTIVE DISC. IN NO EVENT SHALL COURSE TECHNOLOGY OR THE AUTHOR BE LIABLE FOR ANY OTHER DAMAGES, INCLUDING LOSS OR CORRUPTION OF DATA, CHANGES IN THE FUNCTIONAL CHARACTERISTICS OF THE HARDWARE OR OPERATING SYSTEM, DELETERIOUS INTERACTION WITH OTHER SOFTWARE, OR ANY OTHER SPECIAL, INCIDENTAL, OR CONSEQUENTIAL DAMAGES THAT MAY ARISE, EVEN IF COURSE TECHNOLOGY AND/OR THE AUTHOR HAS PREVIOUSLY BEEN NOTIFIED THAT THE POSSIBILITY OF SUCH DAMAGES EXISTS.

Disclaimer of Warranties

COURSE TECHNOLOGY AND THE AUTHOR SPECIFICALLY DISCLAIM ANY AND ALL OTHER WARRANTIES, EITHER EXPRESS OR IMPLIED, INCLUDING WARRANTIES OF MERCHANTABILITY, SUITABILITY TO A PARTICULAR TASK OR PURPOSE, OR FREEDOM FROM ERRORS. SOME STATES DO NOT ALLOW FOR EXCLUSION OF IMPLIED WARRANTIES OR LIMITATION OF INCIDENTAL OR CONSEQUENTIAL DAMAGES, SO THESE LIMITATIONS MIGHT NOT APPLY TO YOU.

Other

This Agreement is governed by the laws of the State of Massachusetts without regard to choice of law principles. The United Convention of Contracts for the International Sale of Goods is specifically disclaimed. This Agreement constitutes the entire agreement between you and Course Technology regarding use of the software.